Know Your Fabrics

STANDARD DECORATIVE TEXTILES
AND THEIR USES

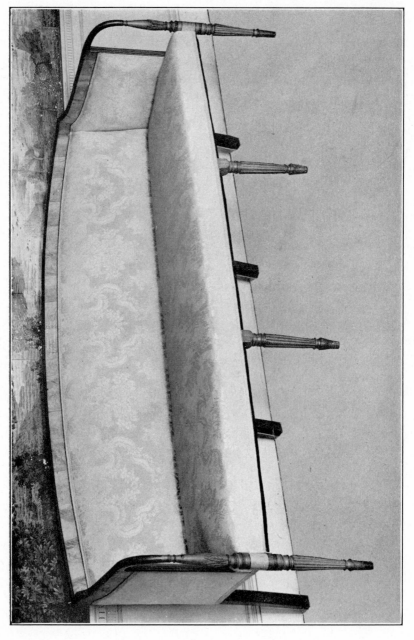

Light-weight damask of appropriate scale on beautiful old Sheraton sofa.

COURTESY MUSEUM OF FINE ARTS, BOSTON

Know Your Fabrics

STANDARD DECORATIVE TEXTILES AND THEIR USES

LUCY D. TAYLOR

Lecturer, New York School of Interior Design

John Wiley & Sons, Inc.
NEW YORK

Chapman & Hall, Ltd.
LONDON

To my students
in appreciation of their eager interest
and its inspiration

Contents

Section 3. Choosing Coverings for Chairs of Today

SECTION ONE

*Standard Fabrics
and Their Uses
as Based on Structure*

Introduction

BEGINNERS IN DECORATIVE WORK ARE BEWILDERED BY THE MANY KINDS OF fabrics. The need is urgent for them to acquaint themselves as quickly as possible with the major types. They also need to learn what the possibilities of fabrics are in terms of practical use. This type of information precedes intelligent use of the fabrics from the standpoint of design. It involves learning to recognize the standard types by their structure and then learning to apply this knowledge reasonably so as to avoid forcing the fabrics beyond their natural ranges of expression or expecting service in terms of wear impossible for either the substance or the weave to render.

No attempt has been made in this section of the book to go beyond these elemental considerations. Attention is concentrated wholly on recognition of the different fabrics by their weaves and on their uses solely as types of cloth. The design, or "putting-together" story, belongs in another type of book dealing with room composition.

Only standard types of fabrics have been included. They do not change rapidly from season to season as do novelties. If the basic fabrics are understood, novelties can usually be identified, structurally, even though they vary a great deal from the old standards. Most of them have special trade names and for their brief lives are known solely by them. Many are exceedingly attractive, and they should by no means be slighted by the student after a foundation for recognition has been acquired.

Students are advised to gather clippings from every possible source, segregate those that are clearly standard in type, and study them carefully. No one ever learns to recognize fabric structure by listening to lectures or by reading books, though both these means are of inestimable value at the start. The information thus acquired should be supplemented by close observation of the actual cloth with the aid of pin and thread counter or pick glass. The counter is a small magnifying glass made for this particular purpose, and, under ordinary conditions, it is not expensive. If one cannot be obtained, any kind of reading glass will help. The fabric clipping should be placed under the glass and probed until it is seen clearly how the threads are put together. This structural information will form a reasonably sound basis upon which to build future decorative work.

1

Thin Materials

UNDER THIS HEADING ARE PLACED THE MATERIALS COMMONLY REFERRED
to as glass-curtain materials. They have, in many instances, other
uses, though they are made especially for the glass-curtain purpose.
Many of them are delightful when well designed and well draped as
dressing table covers. Some make good bedspreads; a few can be
used to advantage as lamp shades. These additional possibilities for
use will be mentioned in the descriptive text for each material.

GLASS CURTAINS

WHAT ARE GLASS CURTAINS?

Glass curtains are the thin, transparent or translucent curtains
that hang next to the glass of the window. Their position defines
the degree of importance they hold in the decoration of the room
as a whole. Properly considered, they are always subordinate to the
overdraperies and, in effect, always should look as though they were
in back of them, toward the window, leaving the overdrapery as the
dominating portion of the decoration.

WHAT ARE THEIR DECORATIVE PURPOSES?

These thin, translucent materials do several decorative jobs for
us besides the very practical one of affording protection from prying
eyes.

(1) They modify and soften the light in the room. In most
rooms, the windows are staring holes of bright light in darker, opaque
walls. The light streaming through them is harshly accentuated by
this contrast. If the contrast is softened, eye comfort becomes marked.

(2) The strong light from windows without glass curtains makes
the furniture shapes sharp silhouettes, standing isolated from each

5

other. As soon as the glass curtains are put up, these rigid contours lose their gaunt isolation. The room flows together because of the modifying lights and shadows. It no longer looks like a furniture shop.

In new buildings where light is gently diffused through glass walls or where the light that windows admit and the shapes of the areas formed have become part of a well-modulated and well-balanced design, a different condition obtains. Glass curtains for the purposes outlined above may not be necessary. The light, although there is a great deal of it, has already been softened by the way in which its flow throughout the room has been regulated and by the decrease of the sharp contrasts with the shapes of dark wall areas.

(3) Glass is hard, cold, brittle. All around the room are forms covered with soft fabrics. Soft fabrics, more often than not, are on the floor and at the windows as overdraperies. The hardness of the glass is unpleasant in contrast, particularly when the window panes are large. The soft, thin, shadowy folds of glass curtains can temper this hardness and give a quality similar to that of the other furnishings, thus pulling the room together. Overdraperies are insufficient. The light passes by the edges of their opaque masses. The thin, transparent glass curtains make a pleasant transition between solidity on the one hand and the openness of the glass on the other. They also carry on the quality of softness of texture, thus reducing the harsh, abrupt contrast from overdrapery to glass.

Some people object to glass curtains because they wish to see out of the window more easily or because they feel shut in by them. But these curtains can always be draped so that the view may be enjoyed freely and the maximum amount of light let into the room. They are seldom omitted in a well-decorated room.

The use of a marked color in the curtain nearest the glass—which shows from the outside of the house—may be inadvisable. In large apartments, this is not a problem as the individual windows are lost in their multiplication over the whole façade. In private houses, however, all the windows, or at least a major portion of them on one or two sides, are glimpsed at once. If you are conscious of bright-pink *organdy* at the windows in the room upstairs at the right of the entrance door, and of bright-yellow at the corresponding windows on the other side of the door, the effect is very unpleasant. Inside the room, the effect may be perfect; outside, it is bad. The outside could easily have been unified and regulated by using another thin material on the glass side of the organdy drapery. One of the *nets* or a sheer *marquisette* would have served the purpose well. Sometimes it works well to use net at all the downstairs windows for the glass curtains and marquisette at the upper ones. Then the inside draperies can be whatever fits the individual room and your personal taste. Both the net and the marquisette may be so sheer as to be scarcely noticeable; thus the inside drapery, the organdy, seems to be the real curtain of the room.

STRUCTURE OF GLASS-CURTAIN MATERIALS

The majority of glass-curtain materials are in so-called *plain weave*.

WHAT IS MEANT BY PLAIN WEAVE?

All cloth is woven with at least two sets of threads—those that are strung in vertical position, the up-and-down of the cloth, and those that are woven into these from left to right, horizontally. The up-and-down threads are the warp. Those going from left to right, that is, from selvage to selvage, are the weft. The loom is strung or set up with the warp threads. The warps are raised and lowered to admit the easy passage of the shuttle, in whatever order is desired, by means of the heddle. The order in which this is done follows three major types, known as the three *fundamental weaves*. They are the *plain,* the *twill,* and the *satin weaves.*

PLAIN WEAVE

When the weft threads go over and under the warp in regular alternation, as over one, under one, etc., we have the ordinary weave technically known as the plain weave. (Plate 6*a*.) This weave produces very varied results: by means of adjustment of the distances between the warps, by means of the spaces between the wefts, by means of the relative sizes of warp and weft, by the manner in which the threads are spun—loosely or tightly twisted—and by the way in which the colors are handled. Thus materials as widely variant as scrim and taffeta, voile and repp, gingham and gauze all come under this major classification, plain weave.

In the majority of glass-curtain materials, the warp threads are widely spaced. So also are the weft threads. This accounts for the open weave effect of scrim, voile, etc. The various drapery nets do not come under this classification. They are laces, orginally hand-made, nowadays made by machine. This fact does not make them one of the machine *woven* fabrics, owing to the difference in handling. The threads are twisted, not woven together.

In plain weave fabrics, especially in novelty effects, the warp and the weft are often grouped in varying spaces although the alternating sameness of count is maintained. Sometimes, as in the ordinary basket weave, the threads are doubled, two warp, two weft threads, under and over in regular alternation. However, regardless of the variations, the weave of any fabric that has a regular alternation of under and over in continued sequence and of equal count comes under this first classification, plain weave.

SOME COMMONLY USED GLASS-CURTAIN MATERIALS

SCRIM—WHAT IS IT?

Scrim is one of the simplest glass-curtain materials in common use. It is made of loosely twisted cotton threads in simple plain weave. The threads are spaced fairly wide apart. The loose twist of the thread itself gives the cloth a rather fuzzy effect, especially noticeable in the examples with the smaller spaces between the threads.

WHAT ARE THE DECORATIVE USES OF SCRIM?

The material hangs in soft folds but always shows some of this fuzziness as the light comes through it at the window. Thus it is never smooth and dressy. With a taffeta for overdrapery, for example, it looks rough and unfinished. However, with some of the less formal linens that are rather bold and vigorous in decorative quality, and with many of the rougher-textured cotton novelties, or even with rough-textured silks, it can be used to advantage. It lacks clean-cut definition to fit the fine drawing and carefully modulated color in the handsome chintzes and linens, the fine weaving and beautiful surfaces of silks and velvets. But with overdrapery that is good, though neither delicate nor richly fine, it often is wholly satisfactory and can be used in place of some of the more expensive materials, thus keeping down the costs.

HOW DOES IT HANG BEST?

Scrim does not lend itself to tie-back curtains; it is best hung in straight folds, shirred on the rod or French-headed; the latter is best when it is used under really good decorative conditions. The pleating of the French heading at the top forces the material into more regular, better-shaped folds than when it is merely shirred on the rod.

IN WHAT COLORS DOES IT COME?

It comes usually in the ordinary range of white, cream, and ecru.

It may seem a matter of small moment whether white, cream, or ecru should be used in a glass curtain. But, when one realizes that a glass curtain should always seem to stay back of the overdrapery, hugging the window, never calling undue attention to itself either at the expense of the overdrapery or the rest of the room decoration, it is not difficult to understand that the color of the glass curtain is as important as its texture. White may stand out too prominently, or ecru may look dirty compared with the color of the chintz draperies. Ecru as a color may be clear and clean, or it may be a darker, rather drab sort of tone. Its type, when it is used, must be carefully tuned to the overdraperies (1) to be harmonious and (2) to keep its place and not intrude upon the attention at the expense either of the wall or the overdrapery.

VOILE—WHAT IS IT?

Like scrim, *voile* is an open weave, thin material in plain weave. It differs from scrim, however, in that in its better qualities it is made of smaller, finely twisted threads which give it a much more finished appearance. In the poorer qualities, it tends to be sleazy, thus decreasing its decorative character because of its lack of clean-cut quality. In the better grades it is usable under excellent decorative conditions.

Although voile is made of a variety of materials, the term is usually applied only to fabrics made of cotton, mercerized cotton, and some of the synthetic fibers. The others are best known under their specific trade names.

WHAT ARE THE DECORATIVE USES OF VOILE?

As the weave of voile is a little closer than that of scrim, it gives more protection at windows where neighboring houses or apartments are close. This is particularly true of the plain cotton voiles which ordinarily are a little thicker and a little more closely woven than the mercerized ones. They provide excellent daytime protection when hung in straight folds across the window.

This characteristic quality of closeness of weave with resulting thickness definitely affects both the amount and the color of the light in a room. The cotton voiles come in a great variety of colors from light to dark. In all the more positive tones, such as the yellows, peaches, greens, blues, and lavenders, they can make or mar the color of the room according to the light that sifts through them. In some cases, these positive tones may be a marked asset; in other cases, they may be a definite drawback. In a room that tends to be dull with cold light, a yellow voile curtain can be a godsend. On the other hand, if it is used with an overdrapery that is weak and delicate in tone, it may be so overpowering in effect that the whole balance of the color scheme of the room is upset. Or again, in a sunny room where the light flows evenly throughout the space, the yellow may be much too insistent even though it is perfectly tuned to the overdraperies. In another sunny room where the windows are in one end and the opposite wall is so far away that that end of the room always remains shadowy, yellow voile curtains may be the saving note that spreads the sun effect, if they are properly framed by the right overdraperies.

Some colors, such as orchid, lilac, blue, and green, can have a very dulling effect upon a room. This same fact may be a great asset if the light is too intense for the use to which the room is to be put.

It is wise to hold the material up to the light to see just how it will look when it is hanging at the window with light coming through it. Most curtains will be toned down a good deal in comparison with their appearance with the light on them. This simple trial may save many a mistake and alter radically an original choice that did not take into consideration the actual conditions to be met.

Mercerized voiles being for the most part thinner and in more open weave do not affect the light as markedly as do the plain cotton ones.

The wide range of texture in voiles, from plain cotton to synthetic fiber material, makes possible innumerable combinations with over-drapery materials. As a general guide, the following suggestion may be of assistance. Both chintzes and linens, whether considered as overdrapery material or upholstery coverings, depend for their texture effect upon the character of the design and its coloring rather than on the fact that one is cotton and the other is linen. A bold linen, with vigorous, careful drawing that has a good deal of modeling, gives an impression of richness and depth. It can be used safely and to advantage with other materials that give similar richness of effect—silks, velvets, etc. The same applies to chintz of bold and vigorous scale and character. If the drawing and coloring of the chintz are less bold, giving less effect of depth but still finely modulated and full of interesting variety, the lighter silks and satins will be in order, such as the taffetas and more delicate damasks. If the drawing were less well handled, the whole effect flatter with less variety and contrast, then the native thinness of the cotton base would be more apparent and that particular chintz would be less happily combined with the lustrous materials. This would be the time to make sure that the cotton glass curtains were not so closely woven as to overbalance the effect of the chintz overdraperies. Nor would one use the mercerized type. It probably would appear slick and shiny by contrast. With a chintz of stronger drawing it might be excellent. Few voiles look well with the linens, as most of the latter are too bold and their little roughness adds to the depth and boldness. The voiles are too flat for them except for a few of the best of the mercerized ones or those of the synthetic fibers. Once the idea of the effect of texture against texture as influenced by pattern and color, as well as the native aspect of the cloth itself, is assimilated, successful combination becomes largely a matter of common sense.

IN WHAT COLORS DOES VOILE COME?

As already indicated, voile comes in a wide range of colors particularly among the lighter tones. White, cream, ecru, beige, sand, flesh, apricot, peach, green, blue, orchid, maize, gold, champagne, pink, and henna are common.

HOW MAY VOILE CURTAINS BEST BE HUNG?

Voile looks best when hung in straight folds either shirred on the rod or French-headed. It does not lend itself to tiebacks as it is too soft and tends to appear mussy.

NINON—WHAT IS IT?

Ninon is a cellulose acetate rayon—a synthetic yarn product of smooth, flat, silk-like aspect. It has a pleasant sheen, much finer in quality than the older-type rayon voiles. Plain weave is the regular form. There are some novelties which are variations of the plain weave.

WHAT ARE THE DECORATIVE USES OF NINON?

It is an excellent glass-curtain material for windows where fineness and silkiness of aspect are required. To a large extent it has taken the place of silk gauze. It has also replaced the finer marquisettes and some of the nets on medium-type jobs. For the finest decorative work, however, there are times when the sheen of ninon does not equal the characterful aspect given by the silk of a fine silk gauze. There is a smoothness about it that is almost too sleek at times and this detracts from its decorative value. With some of the finest satins, taffetas, damasks, and brocades, where there is subtle and interesting variation in weave, pattern, or both, the glass curtains need to have similar subtlety and variation. Ninon is uniformly smooth and flat, mechanically perfect. But its very mechanical perfection is a limitation when it is combined with fabrics that have the interest of more variation, whether produced by hand or by machine. Nevertheless, under a wide range of ordinary conditions it has proved to be a most valuable addition to the list of decorative materials of excellent quality.

In general, ninon is best with the lighter decorative effects. With boldly patterned linens or with rough textures its smoothness gives too much contrast. With a great many fine chintzes of high grade and decorative quality and with many modern materials, both silk and cotton, that are markedly textured without being coarse and rough, it is very nice. It is excellent also with the less luxurious taffetas, satins, and damasks. It is so attractive that nice discrimination is required to avoid misusing it and stretching it beyond its native limits of decorative quality and character, so that, when the room is finally assembled, the glass curtains will look right.

HOW SHOULD IT HANG?

It is best hung straight, shirred on the rod or French-headed. The latter is preferable if the draperies are being pleated and the effect demands that all the folds fall in regular fashion. Ninon does not lend itself so well to tiebacks, as it is rather too soft.

IN WHAT COLORS DOES IT COME?

It comes in a great variety of colors of excellent quality. Maize, peach, beige, copper, Nile, argent, ivory, shrimp, champagne, ecru, and white are some of the most-used tones.

Ninon also comes in pattern—a tiny self-colored stripe, scarcely visible yet very smart; a satin stripe, broader and bolder; and in figures blocked out in shadowy fashion so that they are inconspicuous for the most part, yet very effective where the furnishing will admit of this activity in the glass curtain.

Ninon is one of the thin materials that can be used as the only curtain if either the budget precludes the use of overdraperies or the room layout makes it wise to avoid featuring the windows with the lines of overdraperies. When it is used in this way, a very modest trim may serve to give the curtain a little more feeling of substance and finish. A French heading is advisable also, to keep the folds clean and regular.

ORGANDY—WHAT IS IT?

Organdy is a crisp, thin muslin, of plain weave, which is somewhat stiff so that the material has a certain amount of substance or body. The best qualities are sheer and have a permanent finish. These can be laundered safely with full assurance that the crispness will be retained. It is always well to make sure that the material is of the "permanent-finish" grade if the work in hand requires it. A question at the right time can save a great deal of trouble later.

WHAT ARE THE DECORATIVE USES OF ORGANDY?

Organdy drapes well—in interesting folds that are crisp and stay in place well. It is one of the few thin materials that can be used satisfactorily to hang over the wood trim of the window when a glass curtain is used without overdrapery. This is due to its stiffness, which makes it round out and away from the background, thus covering the woodwork color completely. The stiffness of its folds also gives a certain finish to the window that the other thinner softer materials cannot supply when used in this fashion. For the same reasons organdy may be carried to the floor successfully as a long curtain. The majority of the glass-curtain materials are best when stopped a bit above the sill. They should never be allowed to cross the wall and woodwork when the color of either will show through. The walls, the furniture, the upholstery, all call for a finish to the window drapery to complete their effect. Among the less expensive materials, organdy, with its stiffness, supplies an answer. There are deep luminous shadows in those rounding folds which give both character and body.

When organdy is used as the overdrapery or as the finish for the window, the effect is much nicer if a softer thinner material is used between it and the glass. The stiffness of the organdy against the hard glass is eliminated, and a much pleasanter effect is obtained. One of the nets is often employed for this purpose.

Organdy can also be used for glass curtains with overdrapery of another material. However, care must be exercised to make sure that its stiffness is not so overpowering as to take the attention away from the overdraperies. Those crisp and somewhat stiff folds do not always blend well with the folds of the chosen overdrapery. However, skillfully used, especially in white with nicely pleated or fluted edges, it can give a snappy freshness of effect which may be exactly what the coloring, texture, and drawing of the overdrapery need.

Sometimes two sets of organdy curtains are used together, one acting as the glass curtain, the other as the overdrapery. In such cases, the most effective results are obtained when the inner curtain (glass) is of much lighter color than the outer one (overdrapery). The contrast in color value makes the transition from outside curtain to inside curtain evident where there is no change in texture to emphasize it.

Organdy is especially nice to use in bedrooms where there is a chintz paper that has small accents of bright color. A solid material at the window may appear too solid for the quick, light motion of the staccato color accents on the wall. An organdy with the light playing through its crisp folds gives some of the same kind of feeling, is far from solid, and can be delightful.

It is possible and occasionally desirable to use organdy for dressing tables or bedspreads. It is better for the tables than for the bedspreads, as it has the drawback of folds that are apt to be too large to fall in sufficiently regular shapes to look especially well in the small areas of the dressing table. As a bedspread, the major difficulty is that the material is easily mussed as it is taken off and put back. Once organdy is mussed or creased, it has lost its greatest charm—crispness. It can be used effectively for ruffles on a four-poster, although some of the softer materials such as dimity are better. Occasionally lamp shades of bedroom or boudoir type can be made of organdy to advantage. Organdy can also be used effectively sometimes for pillow coverings on a chaise longue. Neither of these last-named uses is really native to the character of the cloth itself.

HOW SHOULD ORGANDY BE HUNG?

Organdy curtains are best ruffled, fluted, or pleated and tied back. They seldom look well in straight folds with plain edges at windows of the ordinary size and type. Sometimes, at a small window, as in powder or bathroom, they may be attractive hung straight with a tiny pleated or fluted edge. In larger areas the stiffness of the material does not lend itself to straight folds; they are apt to get out of hand and look scrawly. Organdy, properly draped so as to use its native quality, never bounces in untamed folds. When used long, as over-draperies to the floor, the curtain must be very carefully handled to avoid this bouncy effect. The curtain that is draped high, held back by rosette or collar, and then falls in jabot fashion below the tieback is one of the attractive treatments for this particular material.

IN WHAT COLORS DOES ORGANDY COME?

Organdy comes in a wide range of colors from white to the very dark tones, such as dark green and dark brown.

Some machine-embroidered organdies, both self-toned and in color, are very attractive, and some of these, as well as some of the so-called shadow organdies in which a pattern is stopped out with chemicals, can be used either draped or hung straight. The pattern changes the conditions because of the variations of surface that are introduced.

SWISS MUSLIN—WHAT IS IT?

Swiss muslin in the better grades is a fine, sheer cotton material. In the cheaper grades, it is apt to be sleazy. It comes both plain and with dots. The latter is the type most used in decorative work. The dots are sometimes the same color as the ground, sometimes in contrast to it.

WHAT ARE THE DECORATIVE USES OF SWISS MUSLIN?

Because of its slight stiffness, Swiss muslin, like organdy, lends itself to be used as the sole curtain at windows without overdraperies. The roundness of the folds and their slight opacity contribute largely to this special use of the material. It is too light and fluffy to be used under formal conditions. It is more satisfactory in simple rooms because of its cottage aspect. When slip covers appear on the formal furniture in the summer, both Swiss muslin and organdy become drapery possibilities, but with the winter aspect of formal furniture they are inadequate.

Swiss muslin is very easy to use satisfactorily, although one warning relative to the size of the dots is worth mentioning. The dots make light and shadow and in so doing set up a definite feeling of motion. If that motion is very quick, as is the case when the dots are very small, you may wonder why your curtains do not seem to have the style effect that you expected. The answer may be that the motion is too fast for your furniture, and so the curtains appear trivial. If a larger dot is used, the curtains will probably take their proper place in the room and the desired freshness, crispness, and style will appear. On the other hand, scale and motion can be over-bold. A few of the Swiss muslins have very bold dots. With lightly scaled furniture, the contrast with the muslins may be so bold that your attention is drawn irresistibly to the window. If the windows are overdone, the room lacks ease. It is a simple matter of common sense to adjust this scale.

The Swiss muslin with contrasting colored dots is a special favorite for kitchens, breakfast nooks, and bathrooms, as well as some bedrooms. The colors most commonly used are red, green, yellow, blue, and black. In this group, the red holds up best against the light when there is no cross light from other windows to shine on the material and bring the color out. The green and sometimes the blue have a tendency to lose their color as they are silhouetted against the light and thus may be quite disappointing. The yellow has a tendency to float ineffectually. The black often is very snappy and attractive when the dots are not too prominent. As already said, it is well always to hold all glass-curtain material up to the light to see how it looks with the light coming *through* it before deciding upon it. The light causes many changes, and the method suggested is the only safe way to form a judgment, until you have handled so many pieces of these thin materials and seen them in place at the windows under such a variety of conditions that you can be sure of the effect at the window.

A few of the colored Swiss muslins have self-toned dots. They are often dainty and effective in bedrooms where a little more dressy effect is desired than the plain white can give and organdy is too stiff. And often it is wise to combine them with another, thinner curtain between them and the glass as was suggested for organdy when an especially nice effect is desired.

HOW SHOULD SWISS MUSLIN HANG?

Swiss is best used as a tieback curtain. The folds are apt to be unmanageable when hung straight, and draping brings out all the best features of the peculiar stiffness and crispness of the material. This characteristic stiffness is one reason why in groups of windows in simple houses where there is a wide central window with two quite narrow ones at each side, Swiss muslin is an unsatisfactory material to use. The curtains for the two narrow side windows should hang straight, regardless of whether the central window is treated with curtains hanging straight or tied back. If those at the narrow windows are tied back, the effect is rather oddly one-legged and distinctly uncomfortable, because the resulting lines direct the attention immediately to the woodwork between the windows instead of making the curtains themselves the focus of attention. In cases where this general type of curtain is desired and the Swiss will be unsatisfactory it is customary to substitute either net or marquisette, both of which can be used either as tiebacks or as straight curtains.

Swiss ordinarily is used with a ruffle. Its stiffness seems to call for some such treatment at the edge. Cotton ball fringe also makes a good finish.

IN WHAT COLORS DOES IT COME?

Swiss comes in plain white, white with self-colored dots, white with colored dots, and in various light tones, pink, blue, peach, and yellow with self-colored or white dots.

Swiss muslin in both the plain and dotted types is one of the curtains materials that can be used attractively for the draping of dressing tables. It falls in easier, softer, and more regular folds than organdy, and, as the finish is not so high, it adapts itself easily to the small areas of the dressing table. Some of the delicate colors with self-toned dots are very nice for this purpose and work up into dainty effects. Swiss also makes good summer bedspreads and does not muss quite so badly as organdy. In the plain white-dotted type it is useful for ruffles on four-post beds. All the types can be used to make very pretty lamp shades for bedrooms and boudoirs.

Swiss launders well but does not have a long life as curtains. Sunlight shining through glass burns it out. However, it is so inexpensive that most people do not object to replacement after a few years.

MARQUISETTE—WHAT IS IT?

Properly, *marquisette* does not belong under the plain weaves, although some people prefer to consider it a variation of them. It is a leno weave, i.e., the warp threads usually run in pairs, are twisted around the wefts where the warp and weft intersect. This weave gives the cloth a firmness that the thin materials with sparsely spaced warp and weft merely crossing each other do not have. Marquisette comes both plain and with dots and, except for its wiriness and openness of weave, looks very much like the dotted varieties of the smoother, more closely woven Swiss.

WHAT ARE THE DECORATIVE USES OF MARQUISETTE?

Marquisette has become one of the most commonly used glass-curtain materials because of its durability, its neat appearance, and the wide range from fine to coarse weave which makes it very adaptable to many kinds of rooms and types of furniture. It comes in large, medium, and small weaves with several sizes in each category. The variety of weave makes it very flexible for use with overdraperies of

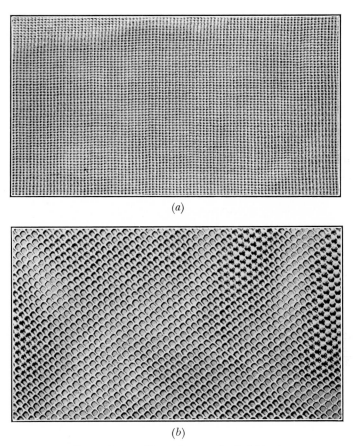

(a)

(b)

Plate 1. *a. Marquisette.   b. Bobbinet.*

various types from fine to bold character. The coarser weaves work well with the heavier chintzes, some of the lighter linens, and some of the silks that are of not too luxurious softness and lustrous sheen. The slight wiriness of the marquisette, due to that twist of the warp threads, with resulting harshness that is seen even in the fine, sheer types, is a definite drawback with the softer, more lustrous silks. The contrast of texture with the smooth and lush silk is too strong.

Because of its durability and adaptability marquisette of the dotted type has replaced, in large measure, dotted Swiss, although decoratively as a substitute it lacks the clean-cut crispness of Swiss for some types of work. Plain marquisette has a place in the decorative field, however, that nothing else fills. The dotted type is good but not so effective as Swiss, decoratively speaking.

Some marked exceptions to this statement may be noted. For example, used as glass curtains under living-room conditions, marquisette may be far superior to Swiss because it is so much thinner and more open, thus calling less attention to itself. The choice will depend finally upon the character of the overdraperies or the arrangement of the windows or the effect of the furniture and its coverings. No general statement can cover all the conditions. If Swiss seems to cloud the window under the given overdraperies, it may be well to turn to marquisette. If, on the other hand, marquisette in a given room looks too wiry and skimpy with the overdraperies, Swiss should be tried. Marquisette works admirably in rooms where there are two narrow windows at the sides of a large central one. As already pointed out, Swiss should be tied back, and at a narrow side window of this type, a tieback is never satisfactory. The attention is forced directly to the bare section of the woodwork between the windows instead of to the curtains themselves. Yet Swiss is often mistakenly selected for this arrangement of windows.

Marquisette is not good as the sole curtain for any window. It never makes the finish that Swiss and organdy give with their stiffness and crispness. One of the dotted varieties of marquisette used in this way is much better than the plain type, but alone it is never excellent decoration. The folds do not hold their own against wood trim and wall color. The material is too open to say, "This is the end of the window. I am the frame for it." With overdraperies, however, marquisette far surpasses both organdy and Swiss for general use and has a wide range of possibilities.

HOW DOES MARQUISETTE HANG BEST?

Marquisette hangs nicely in straight folds, shirred on the rod. The folds are so good that it seldom is French-pleated. It can also be used as tiebacks if preferred. This arrangement is the customary treatment for the dotted varieties.

IN WHAT COLORS DOES IT COME?

The plain marquisette that is used on most decorative jobs comes in white, cream, and ecru of various shades. The dotted marquisettes come mostly in white—with both white and colored dots—and in pale tones such as cream, yellow, blue, pink, and peach. Those in pale colors usually have self-toned dots although a few have white.

Marquisette in all varieties lends itself nicely to the draping of dressing tables where a light effect is desired. It hangs in good folds and ruffles nicely; both are necessary features of any material that is to be draped, not shaped, as for a dressing table. Marquisette also makes excellent lamp shades of the lighter variety. For bedspreads it is not good; it is too soft, although it is possible to use it over a firmer colored material. Other materials can give a better effect with much less work and expense. Its wiriness makes it definitely objectionable for pillows.

Care should be taken in buying marquisette to get the type that is guaranteed not to shrink. Properly selected, and properly handled, marquisette is one of the most useful of the glass-curtain materials.

Marquisette is also made in the synthetic fibers. It lacks, however, the character of the cotton ones. The effect is too slick for the native wiriness that is produced by the weave. Curtains made from it have a tendency to be rather slinky in the folds.

DIMITY—WHAT IS IT?

Dimity is a fine, sheer cotton with a tiny cord making a pattern, either in stripes or plaid. The threads are finer and closer together than in the materials already discussed. The weave is plain.

WHAT ARE THE DECORATIVE USES OF DIMITY?

Dimity is not used as curtain material, although it can give a pretty and crisp effect when the conditions are similar to those under which Swiss is more often employed. The striped varieties are better for this purpose than the little plaids as they hang and drape better. The plaids are apt to look fussy.

Dimity seldom appears in the decorative market in any range of patterns and sometimes cannot be found there at all. It is usually available among the dress goods, and some of these patterns can be used satisfactorily for decorative purposes. The cheaper varieties have the bad fault of splitting on the cord.

HOW DOES IT HANG BEST?

Dimity hangs in crisp, clean folds and may be used either straight or tied back, depending largely upon the character of the individual pattern and how it affects the way the cloth hangs naturally. The best test is to hold a piece in the hand and let the folds fall as they will. The choice also depends in some measure upon how the pattern looks best decoratively. The more pronounced the movement of the pattern, the less likely is it to look well tied back. It is for this reason that the little plaids seldom look well tied back, but hung straight with either a small crisp ruffle or ball fringe they can be very nice.

Dimity is one of the standard materials for ruffles on four-post beds. It also makes attractive, simple dressing tables and summer spreads.

IN WHAT COLORS DOES IT COME?

The dimity that is ordinarily used in decorating is all white. It does, however, come in light colors and is sometimes printed with a pattern.

THE LACES

Among the commonly used materials for glass curtains are certain laces. Originally handmade, all the standard types described below now are made by machine in weights and meshes suitable for this particular purpose. As they are not woven fabrics, they do not come under the classification of any of the fundamental weaves. The threads are twisted together in somewhat the same way as the laces made by hand with needles or bobbins. Special machines—not weaving looms—are required. The following laces are included here because of their widespread use as glass curtains for fine work in decoration.

BOBBINET—WHAT IS IT?

Bobbinet is a plain lace with hexagonal meshes. As the size of mesh varies from very sheer to quite coarse, it is very adaptable. See Plate 1*b*. The coarser varieties are sometimes called cable net.

WHAT ARE ITS DECORATIVE USES?

The shapes of the meshes—they look round when seen from even a moderate distance—soften the effect of the material as the light comes through it, giving it a quality of fineness far superior to the wiriness of marquisette, the slickness of ninon, or the thicker smoothness of voile. Bobbinet adds an interest that rather defies description. It is soft, yet it has character and style. That is the reason why it is used for so much fine work in places where delicacy and graciousness are required.

Bobbinets with the finer meshes are used with the softer and more lustrous silks, the most delicately drawn of the chintzes, and the nicest of the damasks and brocades. Bobbinet with the larger meshes, though still a fine material, may be heavy enough to serve well with some of the more heavily textured silks like the antique satins and with the more boldly colored and drawn chintzes, as well as with some of the lighter and less-bold linens. In the sheer varieties, care has to be exercised to use the material sufficiently full so that the glass curtains with the light coming through them will not be lost because of the extreme delicacy of the shadow lines of the folds and the thinness of the threads of the lace. The folds may be so faintly penciled against the light as to be almost nonexistent to the eye. If the curtain is made fuller, this difficulty is obviated and the result is delicately gracious. The same condition is in evidence when this material is used on French doors. The alternative to greater fullness than usual is to use a coarser mesh and heavier thread. As there is such an abundance of choices among the bobbinets, this alternative may prove to be the best answer. Care should be exercised, however, to make sure that the effect is not too heavy nor too coarse for the overdraperies or the general room character, thus making the curtains intrusive. If a more sheer bobbinet is right for the windows in the room, a slightly heavier one may be used on the door, if desired, provided that the contrast is not too great. The fact must not be overlooked that bobbinet shrinks when washed and is another reason for additional fullness.

HOW DOES THIS MATERIAL HANG BEST?

Bobbinet may be used to hang in straight folds or it may be tied back. If straight, it is usually not ruffled. If tied back, it should be ruffled. The thinner and the more delicate it is, the less likely is it to look well hanging straight. Ruffles and tiebacks with their curving folds are needed to give body. With the folds carefully draped in pleasing lines, not merely crowded back into the collar, it gives a thin but exquisite effect.

Sometimes excess zeal dictates that ruffles shall be five to six or more inches deep. Even if they are effective when new, which is debatable, they soon begin to droop and in a few weeks are apt to look merely dowdy and drabbled. One should study the particular piece of bobbinet that has been chosen for the job and then determine how much depth of ruffle that size of thread and mesh will take and hold reasonably. It is easy to be deceived by the newness of the material which makes it seem stiffer than it really is or will be later. Too short a ruffle, likewise, is inadvisable in bobbinet. It looks fussy, and the inherent style of the material is lost. There should be sufficient depth to let the material fold easily and naturally. In general it is well to think of the ruffle as being three to four inches deep—then increase or decrease it according to the actual piece of net being used and to suit the room effect. Then the result will not only be good when new but will be likely to stay so. It may be well to let it droop a little under some conditions but not to allow it to flop. If it is too short, it is merely a crumbly mess.

IN WHAT COLORS DOES IT COME?

Curtain bobbinets are usually in white, cream, and ecru. Sometimes they appear in the market in the lighter pastel tones, but the standard colors are those named.

Bobbinet makes delightful dressing tables. It can be used sometimes for spreads, but it must be handled very skillfully. It is easily adapted to lamp shades of the light, dressy, novelty types for bedrooms and boudoirs and also for pillows over a lining.

POINT D'ESPRIT—WHAT IS IT?

Point d'esprit is a variation of bobbinet with tiny dots scattered over it. Like bobbinet, the meshes vary greatly in size as do also the dots. See Plate 2a.

WHAT ARE ITS DECORATIVE USES?

The dots give point d'esprit a little more body than bobbinet, thus making it more substantial against the light. Because of this fact, it can often be used where bobbinet is too fine and sheer. Both types

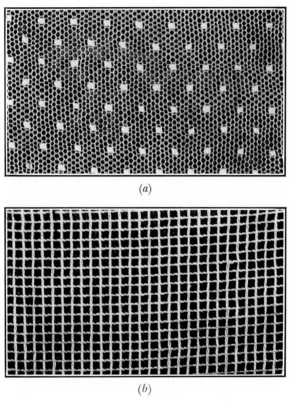

(a)

(b)

PLATE 2.   *a. Point d'esprit.*   *b. Filet.*

are excellent with the lighter French and English furniture forms, and assist materially in keeping the delicate quality that characterizes the furniture. Both materials can be used to advantage over Venetian blinds, when the latter seem necessary for practical purposes, but the rigidity and the harshness of light and shadow on them are out of keeping with the furniture. Under these conditions the point d'esprit will usually look best hung straight with a traverse, French-headed, like a casement curtain, and the bobbinet will be best ruffled and tied back.

HOW CAN THE MATERIAL BEST BE HUNG?

Point d'esprit may be hung either straight or tied back under ordinary conditions, the choice depending on whether the straight lines or the draping will look better with the rest of the room decoration. It is much better than bobbinet when hung straight because of its greater body, due largely to the dots and the slightly heavier threads.

IN WHAT COLORS DOES IT COME?

Most of the point d'esprit used in the good decorative work is white or pale cream. It does, however, come in some of the pale tones like pink and peach.

Point d'esprit makes good dressing tables and the lighter types of boudoir lamp shades. It does not lend itself particularly well to bedspreads.

FILET NET—WHAT IS IT?

Filet is lace with a square mesh knotted at intersecting corners. The size of mesh varies from small to very coarse. See Plate 2*b*.

WHAT ARE ITS DECORATIVE USES?

Filet never can be used with as great freedom as bobbinet or point d'esprit. The square corners of the mesh, with their knots, make a very pronounced and slightly heavy effect, even in the varieties of the smaller meshes. Filet lacks the subtlety of the other two laces. With the heavier overdraperies—the bolder linens in the earlier design types (Jacobean, Spanish, and Italian), the brocatelles and heavier damasks, and some of the rough-textured cottons and silks—it is excellent. It is much used in rooms that are furnished with the heavier furniture of oak and walnut, where strong accents are easily absorbed.

Cheap imitations of filet, under the names of various novelties, are often very bad. The threads are so conspicuous that the effect is clumsy and awkward. Big holes stand out at the window because of the size of the meshes, their squareness, and the prominent threads that far too often are brightly colored. Sometimes such a novelty is the sole curtain with very unpleasant effect. The material is not sufficiently substantial to act in place of overdrapery; the holes are too conspicuous. As an inner or glass curtain, it usually calls far too much attention to itself at the expense of the overdrapery to be considered good decorating.

A good filet is always more prominent than a bobbinet or point d'esprit, but it can be depended upon to hold only its due amount of attention when used with overdrapery of the right texture, drawing, and color.

IN WHAT COLORS DOES FILET COME?

The filet that is used in fine decorative work usually comes only in white, cream, and ecru. The novelties come in many different colors.

Filet is best as curtains although it is possible to use it over another material for both beds and dressing tables, as it lets a great deal of color through. It is also used for lamp shades.

2

The Materials That May Be Used for Either Glass Curtains or Casements

IN THE PRECEDING CHAPTER WE DISCUSSED THE VERY THIN MATERIALS. In this chapter we shall consider the thin materials that can be used as glass curtains and in many cases also as casements. They are translucent rather than transparent, thus having sufficient body to make an adequate frame for the window. Sufficient light filters through them so that there is no harshness of effect as when overdraperies are used without glass curtains softening the edges and making easy transition from their solidity and opacity to the light.

SILK GAUZE—WHAT IS IT?

Silk gauze in decorating parlance is a thin, translucent silk of plain weave. Usually there is a slight irregularity in the threads which gives a pleasing quality to the curtains without making them rough. They are never slick.

WHAT ARE ITS DECORATIVE USES?

For many years gauze was the outstanding glass-curtain material for fine work where the nets were not used. The texture is interesting; it has in itself real decorative quality; it hangs in good folds, neither too regular nor too slick. It also affords excellent protection from overly curious neighbors and passersby. Sometimes in big houses with important windows set well back in thick walls, it is used in conjunction with one of the nets, the net being hung next to the window, the gauze next, and then the overdrapery. This is to give greater body to suit the scale of the room and to make a more complete transition from the heavy overdraperies to the deep window.

When it is used on the budget basis as the only curtain, care must be exercised to get the color that will (1) hold its own with the light coming through it; (2) not be in too great contrast with the wall so that it either looks too light and flimsy or too dark, as it easily can against a very light wall. Ordinarily it is wise to keep the value of the gauze, that is, its degree of lightness, about the same as that of the wall, trusting to the color (hue) accent to make the emphasis necessary for the gauze to serve well as a frame for the window. It is usually more attractive to have the gauze a little lighter than the wall than to have it darker. The movement from the darker wall through the somewhat lighter tone of the curtain to the full light of the window is easier to look at than the effect when the translucent curtain is darker than the wall. The translucence in darker values may produce an odd and indefinite effect. This darker curtain can be used but a great deal more skill and experience are required to achieve the right result.

Sometimes there are windows in the far corners of a room jammed against a side wall. In rooms where the furnishings are relatively simple, one of these translucent materials that do double duty may be more satisfactory than to use overdraperies. If the thin material is kept about the same value as the wall, the out-of-balance aspect of the windows can be greatly minimized in the room, whereas long or short opaque overdraperies might accentuate the effect. If the room were large and the furniture quite heavy and formal, this type of curtain would probably be entirely inadequate. However, under these conditions probably there would be other windows that would bear the main part of the window-decoration story so that the poorly placed one would not be noticeable if all the windows were treated simply without excess draping.

Gauze is effective also in small rooms where the windows occupy an undue amount of space so that any featuring of them would make them overpowering. Again, care must be exercised to make sure that the value contrast of the curtains against the wall is not so great that it has the effect of thrusting the curtains too far forward. Often color (hue) contrast without value contrast solves this problem, as, for example, a soft green wall with gauze curtains in a soft bronzy peach tone. A lighter peach without the bronze quality might be too light, too thin in aspect and thus too conspicuous for the size of the room.

This gauze may be used also under small room conditions in double thickness, one set of curtains over another, where softness of light and mild variety in color are desired, the light from the outside being very strong. One set of curtains may give neither quite enough body—or color—nor filter the light sufficiently. If the two sets are of neighboring tones, one a little bluer, the other greener, for example, the resulting effect can be very pleasant. It has to be done by a very skillful decorator who will not make the mistake of trying to get contrast with this very soft, slightly shimmering material. She would merely modulate the color and the light.

Gauze is also used on French doors. Even though the windows in the same room have only simple curtains and the glass curtains are one of the cotton materials, gauze may be correct on the doors. The repetition of the glass-curtain material on the doors often makes them stand out too much for their function and place in the room design. A gauze, toned so as to make as little contrast as possible against the wood trim, can keep the door properly subdued. The amount of accent can be regulated easily by adjustment of the value and color (hue) contrast.

Sometimes there are small windows skyed over bookcases in narrow wall spaces at the end of a room. Or there may be small windows at each side of a fireplace in narrow spaces, as often happens in dining rooms in small houses. All of these present a similar problem. They bear no relation, decoratively, to the rest of the window design in the room but make unpleasant holes of light constantly drawing attention to themselves. One of the gauzes, shirred on a rod at top and bottom of the window, with small heading, and kept the value of the wall and quite near the wall in color, too, can almost reduce these troublesome windows to a condition of peace and quiet, so that they do not upset all the rest of the room design.

HOW CAN GAUZE BEST BE HUNG?

Gauze hangs best in straight folds, shirred on the rod or French-headed. French-heading is the better treatment in most cases, as it regulates the fall of the folds and makes them neater and trimmer. The slight unevenness that gives the material character needs a little regulation to get the best results.

When used on French doors, it is stretched between two rods, top and bottom of the glass. On the small windows spoken of in the preceding section, this double rod treatment may not look well if the windows are quite long. It is wiser then to let the lower edge go free as the stretched curtain may draw attention to itself by its very tightness and trimness. This is particularly true when the windows are in the narrow spaces by a fireplace. Sometimes there are three or four of these small windows over a long bookcase on a long side wall. They may form one unit; they may be separate. If they form one unit, they are likely to look best with the double rods; if they are isolated, they are likely to look best if the lower edge is loose. This is because of their size contrast with the length of the bookcase; the loose edge makes it less noticeable. In all these cases, the material should be kept at sill length—never below. Let the wood of the window be the frame against the wall.

IN WHAT COLORS DOES GAUZE COME?

Gauze comes in a great variety of colors from white to reds, greens, blues, etc., both light and dark. There is also a wide range of colors within each major color group especially among the lighter tones. In fine work it is well worth while to be very painstaking about the exact tone that fits the overdrapery. A yellow, a champagne, or a peach, may be too clear, or it may be too cloudy. It may be too light or too far toward the yellow or the orange. With fine overdraperies, the difference may be just enough to throw the whole effect out of balance, making the glass curtain conspicuous just because it is not perfectly tuned to the overdrapery.

Gauze is essentially a curtain material. It can be used for dressing tables, but there are so many other, better fabrics that it seems futile to try this one which does not lend itself naturally to that use. It can be used as lamp shades, but, again, there are many other, better materials for this purpose.

CHINA SILK—WHAT IS IT?

China silk is a flat, smooth silk of plain weave. It is smoothly woven of even-sized threads and is somewhat thicker than gauze. It is mildly translucent. It is not always available in the market.

WHAT ARE ITS DECORATIVE USES?

China silk lets in less light than gauze and is a little less character-ful. It can be used as a casement curtain or like gauze as a double-duty curtain—without a glass curtain. As a double-duty curtain, it makes a firmer finish than the gauze as it has more body.

HOW DOES IT HANG BEST?

China silk should always be hung in straight folds. The neatness o trimness of its folds is one of its outstanding qualities in decora-tive effects. It can either be shirred on the rod or French-headed, preferably French-headed, as it makes a more finished job. A small, soft trim may be added to advantage if desired.

IN WHAT COLORS DOES IT COME?

China silk comes in a fine range of colors from dark to light.

HABUTAI SILK—WHAT IS IT?

Habutai silk is another thin silk of plain weave. Ordinarily it comes in three weights—very thin, medium, and one that is heavier, although still a little lighter than China silk. Habutai does not have the smoothness that is characteristic of China silk. If you hold a piece of each in your hands, you will find that the China silk will fall into better folds than the habutai, because the threads are more even and regular.

WHAT ARE ITS DECORATIVE USES?

The two thinner types are used mostly for lamp-shade linings. The heavier one is seldom used for curtains because the folds do not hang especially well. However, if nothing else is available, it is a possibility.

HOW DOES IT HANG BEST?

The folds need the regulation given by French heading as the material is too light to fall into folds without assistance. It should always be hung straight.

IN WHAT COLORS DOES IT COME?

Habutai silk comes in a wide range of colors from dark to light in all three weights.

SHIKII SILK—WHAT IS IT?

Shikii is both the trade name of a particular type of thin silk and the name used to designate a special aspect of plain weave. In relation to weave it connotes the variation of texture in materials caused by unevenly spun threads, usually weft threads. The unevenness is so marked that there are large nodules scattered over the whole surface of the cloth. In the dress-goods field shantung and pongee illustrate this process. In the decorating field, the method is used in the thin silk already mentioned and is also employed in most types of cloth to give added texture effect—taffetas, satins, damasks, brocatelles, brocades, and also in cut velvets where the background of the cloth shows. At the moment, however, we are considering only the first use of the word—the thin silk that is known specifically in the trade as Shikii.

WHAT ARE ITS DECORATIVE USES?

Of all the plain thin silks, with the exception of gauze, it is by far the best looking and the most useful for the double-duty curtains. Patterned thin silk, such as some of the thin, sheer damasks, belong in a different category.

Shikii is too substantial for glass curtains under ordinary room conditions at windows of usual size, and it is not so satisfactory for casement curtains over which overdraperies will hang as some of the cloths made for that specific purpose. But for the double-duty curtains, it is excellent. It has sufficient body, hangs in characterful folds, takes the light well, and, with an adequate but not overdone trim, can be used in a wide variety of rooms from simple cottage to more elaborate effects. As casement curtains, its folds may prove to be a little too characterful. The conditions governing the specific problem control the choice of fabric. If Shikii looks too thick or its folds look too active—if they call too much attention to themselves—it is not a good selection for that place. On the other hand, these same qualities may be an asset because of special conditions.

HOW DOES IT HANG BEST?

Shikii should not be ruffled; it should not be tied back. Its slightly textured surface looks best in straight folds. It is effective either shirred on the rod or French-headed.

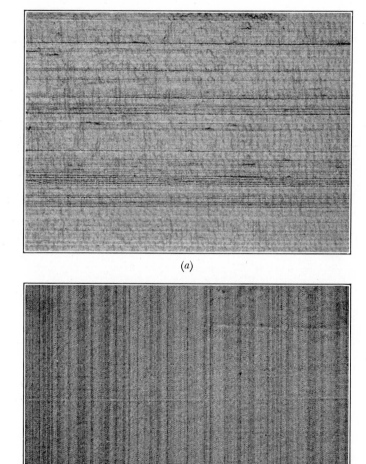

(a)

(b)

PLATE 3.   *a. Antique taffeta showing shikii effect in plain weave.   b. Silk taffeta showing strié effect.*

IN WHAT COLORS DOES IT COME?

It comes in exceedingly attractive colors in a wide range of tone from light to dark.

PONGEE—WHAT IS IT?

Pongee may be either the Chinese wild-silk product or the imitation made in this country from various materials—cotton, spun silk, or synthetic fibers combined with cotton.

WHAT ARE ITS DECORATIVE USES?

Dress pongee, as well as the Chinese type, shrinks badly, unevenly, and is thus not a product to be used to any extent in decorating—especially as curtains. There is a domestic brand made for decorative work that is not quite so interesting merely as cloth but it has the virtue of holding its shape and not shrinking. It is excellent where a fairly heavy casement or a material heavier than gauze is needed for French doors. With a good trim it may serve also for those double-duty curtains.

HOW DOES IT HANG BEST?

It is most satisfactory when French-headed, although it can be used shirred on the rod.

IN WHAT COLORS DOES IT COME?

Decorator's pongee usually comes only in the tan tones that simulate the natural color of the Chinese product.

CASEMENT CLOTHS

CASEMENT CLOTH—WHAT IS IT?

Casement cloth is made of almost every conceivable combination of fibers—for the most part in plain weave or in very simple modifications. Some modifications show small solid figures or have a small figure within an area of open weave. The type with the open weave is often very useful where the casement cloth is the only curtain and the wholly plain or solid-figure type appears too thick and heavy.

WHAT ARE ITS DECORATIVE USES?

Casement curtains are used in place of the ordinary draw shades, especially on large-scale windows with leaded glass. They should be thick enough to afford complete protection. Actually, they are not adequate for night protection; shadows are clearly outlined on them. This can be avoided only either by using a second set of curtains or by lining the casement cloth. Lining usually destroys the natural hang of the folds, making them thick and clumsy; therefore it is better to use the two sets of curtains. Under these conditions, there are two rods, one for the lining set of curtains and one for the casement set. During the day the lining set can be kept drawn back so that it is not seen or both sets can be drawn back together. The lining set is usually made of sateen. If casement curtains are used with overdraperies that can be pulled across the windows at night, the second lining set is, of course, unnecessary.

In small houses with small windows, casement curtains are apt to look too heavy, too thick and solid. The very quality that makes them appropriate for the large, heavy windows found in so many of the half-timbered houses of English style becomes a liability instead of an asset in a smaller house with smaller windows. However, some times they are invaluable—most often when there are no overdraperies. As double-duty curtains casement cloths are often used in offices and institutions.

Casement cloth is also a favorite material for French doors, shirred on rods at the top and the bottom of the glass of the door. If complete protection is needed at night, the treatment already suggested for the window curtains is necessary—the double curtain.

Each type of casement cloth has its place decoratively, according to the degree of solidity or openness that the particular window and room seem to need. Some hang in neat trim folds; some hang in bolder, well-shaped folds; and some hang in bulging ugly ones. Some shrink quickly to a dowdy, drab effect after a little time. Others hold their own for a long time, wash or clean well, and wear well. It requires good judgment to select the correct type from the practical standpoint. It is wise to handle the piece of material and see just how the folds do fall. One should observe also how much light comes through the material and determine whether the material will swathe or shroud the window too completely or have just the right solidity for that room and window. One should be as careful about the color, texture, and pattern of casement cloth as though choosing a linen or a chintz.

HOW DO THEY HANG BEST?

The standard treatment for casement curtains is to French-head them and use a traverse so that they can be drawn easily across the window to do the work of the window shades which have been eliminated. On French doors, they are shirred on rods at the top and the bottom of the glass. If they are lined, the second or lining curtain is placed on a rod directly in back of the casement curtain rod—neither above nor below it.

IN WHAT COLORS DO THESE CASEMENT CLOTHS COME?

The majority are in light tones of cream, tan, ecru, or white. There are always a few in colors, such as yellow, green, etc.

Casement cloth can also be used, often to advantage, in small windows where it may be stretched on rods at the top and the bottom. In such cases, it is used in a color and a weave to make it as inconspicuous as possible against the wall. Its purpose is more apt to be disguise than decoration.

One should always remember that, in handling materials, it is necessary to learn to read their decorative character. Merely knowing the weave, the name of the material type, and the stuff of which it is made, although essential, is a small part of the work. A good dressmaker or a good tailor studies cloth for its inherent character and thus gets to know its possibilities, that is, how it can best be cut and draped. They both discard the materials that do not show the desirable qualities of adaptability and clean-cut expression. They never try to make one piece of cloth struggle to do something that another will do easily and well. Each type of material has its natural advantages. So too good decorators work with their materials. The market, under normal conditions, is filled with various types, some of which are assets, decoratively, and some, liabilities, though merely as material they may be very attractive to look at. How will they drape? Will they cut to advantage for the places for which they are being considered? Will they look well in folds or only when they are seen with the pattern spread out? Are thin folds or heavy folds needed in a given room and which will the material give? It seems as if one could continue indefinitely. One can never be too sensitive to these inherent possibilities of a piece of cloth.

3

Some of the Lighter-Weight Fabrics That Have Many Uses

PLAIN WEAVE

GINGHAM, CHAMBRAY, INDIAN HEAD—WHAT ARE THEY?

There are a few more simple fabrics of plain weave that serve as double-duty curtains where there is no overdrapery. Perhaps the best-known are the *ginghams, chambrays,* and *Indian head.* All of them are made of cotton. The first two need no special description; everyone knows them. Chambray is really a plain gingham, often with a white weft thread which gives a quality of lightness to the cloth. Indian head is the trade name of a colored cotton cloth which has a very nice finish.

WHAT ARE THEIR DECORATIVE USES?

All these materials may be used either with or without a glass curtain. If the problem is one of small windows over a kitchen sink, no glass curtain is used ordinarily with one of these materials. Ruffled and tied back, if the space is large enough so that they will not appear fussy, they can be very effective. If the space is too small for the tie-back, the double-sash curtains, commonly known as double Dutch, may be used. Sometimes curtains with merely a neatly turned hem and hanging straight are all that the space will allow. These materials are effective in similar fashion for dinettes, breakfast nooks and rooms, playrooms, and simple bedrooms.

When the solid colors are used for bedrooms, bathrooms, and even living rooms in cottage-style houses, an inconspicuous glass curtain and a trimmed edge on the gingham, chambray, or Indian head can give a finish that will avoid "cuteness" and make the curtains interesting and more dignified. Under these latter conditions they may be lined if desired; especially in the medium and darker tones of both the chambray and Indian head, they can be very good looking as well as inexpensive.

HOW SHOULD THEY BE HUNG?

Gingham and chambray lend themselves either to straight folds or to tiebacks. They ruffle well, but the ruffles should be short in order to be smart. The Indian head is more satisfactory when hung straight, preferably French-headed, although this heading is not absolutely essential.

All these materials are usable and attractive for many purposes other than curtains. Bedspreads—not necessarily in cottage-type rooms—can be very nice in some of the chambray or the Indian head colors. All make satisfactory slip covers. And all work well under widely varying conditions for dressing tables. All can be used for lamp shades of the simpler sort suitable for bedroom or cottage effects.

TAFFETA—WHAT IS IT?

Taffeta is usually thought of as a crisp and rather stiff silk material. However, taffetas are also made of cotton, synthetic fibers, linen, and even wool mixed with one of these. In taffeta, the weft threads are a little larger than the warp threads, with the result that the warps pile up on the wefts in a slightly ribbed effect. Where the difference is very slight, the material feels almost as flat and smooth as a China silk, though a little thicker, stiffer, and more crisp. When there is a great difference in the sizes of the threads, the material feels and looks like a light-weight *faille* with marked horizontal ribs. The majority of the taffetas are between these two extremes.

Taffeta is plain weave. The ribbiness is caused only by the difference in the sizes of the threads.

Old-time silk taffeta is a thing of the past. It was strong and lustrous, and some varieties were so stiff that they could almost stand alone. Some were so soft, on the other hand, that they could be hung in the smallest of exquisite folds. Many of the cheaper ones were saturated with a preparation of tin to make them seem to have the substance, weight, and much-desired rustle of the better qualities. The tin broke the silk threads and rotted in sunlight, with the result that the material cracked deplorably.

The present-day silk taffetas are neither so heavy nor so fine as the best earlier ones, largely because of price fluctuations. Many are silk mixed with cotton or synthetic fibers; some are synthetic fibers alone. These newer types have proved serviceable, and in the better grades they are good looking and much less costly.

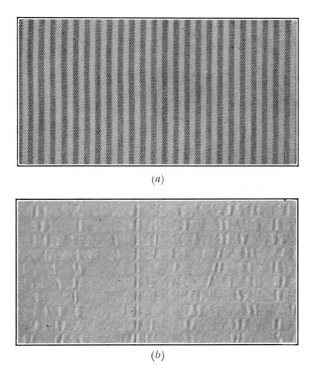

(a)

(b)

PLATE 4. *a. Cotton taffeta, mercerized, showing regular stripe. b. Crackle taffeta.*

Among the silk taffetas, made either entirely of real silk or partly of synthetic fibers, there are several standard types: plain taffeta, in which the warp and weft threads are identical in color; changeable taffeta, in which the warp is one color and the weft another; crackle taffeta, often changeable also, in which some of the threads are strung on the loom more tightly than others so that there is a slight crinkly effect; antique taffeta, in which the weft threads are unevenly spun as in shikii (not really antique but deriving its name from the supposedly old appearance given by the roughness of the threads); strié and jaspé taffetas, in which the warp threads, of one color or of different colors, make rather indefinite, vertical stripes. See Plate 3*b*.

In strié, the same color that makes these random stripes continues vertically in uniform tone. In jaspé, the color of the stripes is spotty on the up and down of the cloth so that the stripes are indistinct. It is almost a pepper-and-salt effect. See Plate 8. It is produced either by printing the colors on the thread so that they appear on the surface of the cloth at varying intervals, or by the fact that the thread is made up not of one color but of several strands of varying tones. Strié, at present, is much more common than jaspé. In both, the change of color produces the effect of an irregularly placed stripe from left to right.

WHAT ARE THE DECORATIVE USES OF THE SILK TAFFETAS?

All-silk taffetas make beautiful curtains because of the crispness and interest of the folds. However, curtains of this material do not wear particularly well, as sunlight through glass burns out the threads. One may be tempted to line taffeta curtains in order to increase their longevity. To get the best effect, however, they should never be lined. The inherent crispness of the material made by the quick changes from sharp highlights to equally sharp shadows is destroyed when the curtains are padded; they hang then in unnatural thickened folds. The material looks tortured. Another material should be selected, unless one is willing to take the chance of replacing the curtains every five or six years. Most people who love the characteristic taffeta effect face this possibility cheerfully. Crackle and antique taffetas can often be used in rooms that are not quite so dressy as those in which the plain and changeable taffetas are normally used. The elimination of a part of the luster in the crackle type because of the slight crinkle and in the antique type because of the texture roughness and its resulting light and shade results in a good deal of difference in the effect when these materials are used for curtains. This reduced luster makes it possible also to use them for bedspreads and dressing tables in places where the more lustrous taffetas would be too striking or too dressy and formal. As lamp-shade material, antique taffeta is particularly useful in rooms that have fairly heavy furniture. Antique taffeta is also very useful for pillows on sofas under conditions where the full luster and sheen of regular taffeta would make the pillow too prominent. It provides a finishing touch without appearing to bounce off the sofa.

Silk-and-wool taffetas are not common; in fact there are times when they are not in the market. They, too, lack the dressiness of the regular form of the silk taffeta, but they have the virtue of wearing better. Often, too, in rooms where there are a great many windows with many lines of curtains, it is desirable to have a thin material that will not overdo the windows and make them conspicuous. Silk-and-wool taffeta is excellent for just such a place. If it is not obtainable, one of the antique taffetas may be an excellent substitute.

Strié and jaspé taffetas usually have a very fine, rather lightly delicate effect, which makes them especially suitable with the lighter furnishings of the late eighteenth century—French, English, and American. As curtains, if the stripes are very small, the effect can become monotonous when the material is used on many windows or in rooms where the windows are too large for the scale and motion of the little stripe. Properly scaled, however, they can give exquisite and dainty effect. They often make most interesting lamp shades, particularly if the shade is pleated.

Some of the regular stripes (not strié) and a few of the plaids in taffeta are made in a heavy grade for upholstery. During the eighteenth century, both in England and in France, many of them were used. They are very effective, and, when the cloth is woven for this particular purpose, it wears well. A few of the finer French taffetas of this type appear on our market in normal times. Curtain taffeta was never meant for seating material and on chairs or sofas should not be used if one expects the upholstery to last long.

The Celanese taffetas (the trade name for an acetate rayon product) are much less expensive than the real silk ones. They come in good colors which, however, lack the subtlety of color of the best all-silk taffeta. They drape well and consequently are very effective when properly used. They should be regarded as having their own special merits rather than as substitutes for the older types of silk taffetas. The draped effect is not exactly like that of silk taffeta. The folds are smooth and regular. They do not have the quick changes of direction which give the characteristic crispness and jauntiness to the silk product. When the Celanese is tied or looped back, especially if the tie is high as for a jabot-type curtain, it does not fall in the same sort of folds as the all-silk: the folds are more regular and smoother. The fullness at the top has a tendency to flatten as the smooth material gradually slips a little at the collar and its weight pulls it downward. If proper allowance is made for this tendency and the decorator or client understands how to pull the folds up and reshape them, it is not a matter of great importance. But, because of this extreme smoothness, the material does require different handling from other taffetas in regard to trim and draping. One has to plan on smoothness and a soft, almost liquid quality, as the very essence of the design of curtains that are being made of Celanese. One must forget the crispness and sharpness of the other taffeta and refuse to substitute one for the other. They are inherently different.

HOW DO THE TAFFETAS HANG BEST?

Taffetas adapt themselves readily to almost every type of draping. They look well hanging in straight folds under some conditions; they look well draped and tied back under most conditions. Probably, however, their particular qualities are best displayed when they are draped. They can be used for long curtains or, upon occasion, for short ones, if not too lustrous.

Taffetas also lend themselves admirably to many other uses—bedspreads, dressing tables, pillows, and lamp shades. But not all types of taffeta are equally valuable for each purpose. For example, Celanese is best suited to curtains, dressing tables, and, less often, pillows. It does not work as well for upholstery and should not be used for that purpose. Also, as its surface lacks the variety and interest that come from the constant changes of light in the older types of taffeta, it may not fit given conditions for a bedspread or a dressing table. However, that slickness or smoothness, framed by the right trim, may be exactly what is needed for a particular room or window. Each taffeta has its own range of expression and within that range can be effective and useful.

REPP—WHAT IS IT?

Repp is a variation of plain weave made by using heavy threads in the weft. These are so much heavier than the warp threads that they produce a definitely marked series of horizontal ridges extending across the cloth from selvage to selvage. In the decorative field, the term repp is nowadays applied, for the most part, to cotton materials of this type. Some are light in character and are used for curtains; more of them are heavy and suitable only for upholstery. The majority of the heavier repps are mercerized, and often the weave is varied a little to make a marked texture pattern. There are occasionally silk repps but they are not common.

WHAT ARE THE DECORATIVE USES OF REPP?

As already noted, cotton repps are used for curtains or upholstery, according to their weight and texture. As curtains they are ordinarily chosen for reasons of economy or to serve under temporary conditions. They are apt to fade badly and for this reason should not be selected if long wear is a requisite. However, where a nice effect for temporary purposes is required at low cost, they can be satisfactory if used skillfully. They hang in good folds and can be draped in dignified style. Some of these lighter repps of curtain type are woven with the slightly rough shikii effect. They appear in the market under various special trade names. When not overdone, this effect adds greatly to the decorative interest. Some of them can be used successfully in simple rooms for both dressing tables and bedspreads.

The upholstery repps have the same tendency to fade, but less direct exposure to sunlight due to their position in the room does not test their color so severely. Nevertheless it is always wise to question the salesman regarding the type of complaints that have been received before choosing any specific colors. Generalities are useless in this case.

HOW DOES REPP HANG BEST WHEN USED AS CURTAINS OR FOR DRESSING TABLES?

Repp curtains look best when hung full length to the floor. Repp may be draped back or hung straight, but it should be French-headed in either case. It is too thick for wholly satisfactory use in high draping as in the jabot type of curtain. It is rather dignified and should be so treated.

When used for dressing tables, it is best to turn the material sideways so that the ribs run up and down. Otherwise the folds are likely to be too large and prominent. This probably will necessitate piecing which, if well done, will not show but be lost in the folds.

This treatment is also best when the material is used for bedspreads with a deep ruffle or flounce falling over the sides of the bed.

FAILLE—WHAT IS IT?

Faille, like repp, is characterized by marked horizontal ribbing. According to present-day usage the word faille is applied only to a

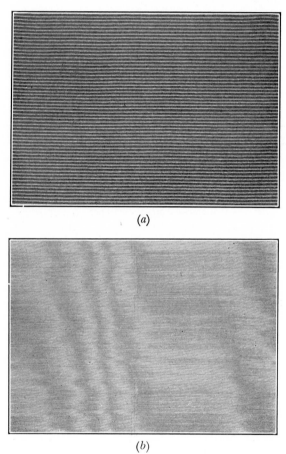

(a)

(b)

PLATE 5.   *a. Faille.   b. Moiré.*

silk material made of either natural or synthetic threads.   In real silk, or silk and cotton, it varies from a rather fine, very soft and flexible material to one that is quite stiff with bolder ribbing.   The majority of the synthetic fiber-yarn failles are the stiffer type.

WHAT ARE THE DECORATIVE USES OF FAILLE?

Faille is used for both curtains and upholstery. For curtains, the horizontal ribs give body and weight to the silk, which make the material hang in good folds, provided that the curtain design is kept simple. Except in the lighter, soft types, it does not lend itself easily to draped effects. The heavier stiff types, with their bold horizontal ribbing, do not fall into easy and graceful folds as they should. They are apt to look clumsy and bunchy. On the other hand, the lighter failles, with a lighter rib that merely supplies interesting variation of texture and body without stiffening the cloth across the grain, are perfect for swag draperies and valances. They serve a wide range of purposes, depending on the ribbing and the character of the material—more or less luster—more or less stiff or soft.

For upholstery, faille is especially good on chairs of the early nineteenth century (English and French), particularly if they are in bedrooms, boudoirs, or drawing rooms in which clothing contacts are not likely to leave their marks. If the upholstery has constant contact with out-of-door clothing, the little ribs of faille quickly soil where the material is stretched over the front edge of chair or sofa. This portion of the chair can be kept clean by constant attention, but constant attention also means constant friction and wear, with the result that the cloth is likely to give way or change color much too soon at those spots. Where indoor clothes are worn, this tendency is no drawback and faille can be beautiful and satisfactory covering for the Directoire, Empire, or English Regency chair or sofa, for example. Its slightly textured but still dressy aspect fits these mannered curves especially well.

The failles that are made from synthetic fibers vary in decorative interest. Some of them are boldly ribbed. As coverings for the traditional furniture forms, they are coarse and heavy. But, from the texture standpoint, as contrast to the bold, plain surfaces of modern furniture, they may be most effective.

The bolder types do not work well as curtains. Most of the smaller-ribbed ones are excellent under conditions already noted. The test always is, "How will the folds hang and drape?"

The same considerations control the uses of faille for bedspreads, dressing tables, and pillows. The heavy ones are seldom usable for either dressing tables or pillows. The lighter ones are often very effective.

HOW DOES FAILLE HANG BEST FOR CURTAINS?

The best treatment of faille for curtains depends again on the size of the ribbing. The coarser, heavy types do not lend themselves well to being draped or tied back nor do they look particularly well in swag valances. The lighter ones are good either hung straight or draped.

MOIRÉ—WHAT IS IT?

Moiré has a faille background with a waving, irregular pattern produced merely by pressing down portions of the ribbing. This process makes the watered pattern that is its dominant characteristic. The result is obtained by running the cloth between heated rollers which have raised portions. The pressure exerted by these portions pushes the ribs down and makes the pattern. See Plate 5*b*.

WHAT ARE THE DECORATIVE USES OF MOIRÉ?

Moiré is used like faille although, because of the extra sheen due to the changing lights on the water markings, it often gives a more dressy appearance than do many of the failles, especially when it is hung in folds as for curtains or dressing tables.

Like faille, it is usable on both traditional and modern furniture, according to the character of its ribbing and marking. Some of the moirés have a fine and varied marking that denotes lightness and delicacy. They are excellent with late eighteenth-century English and French furniture. Others are bolder, have less interesting or characterful motion. They are more obvious and commonplace and belong on furniture that is correspondingly less fine and varied. At the other extreme are the boldly marked types that belong with the equally bold modern designs with their plain surfaces.

HOW DOES MOIRÉ HANG BEST FOR CURTAINS?

The ribbing controls the draping qualities of moiré as it does those of faille. The conditions are the same for the two fabrics in this respect.

Moiré, unless it is composed of cellulose acetate rayon fiber, should always be dry cleaned as the markings, that are the pattern, come out if the material is steamed or wet.

This completes the group of major standard items of the plain weave type. The innumerable novelties, as already noted, change too rapidly to be commented on in a textbook. If the basic types are clearly understood, the novelties can usually be classified without much difficulty.

Twill Weave

The second fundamental weave is the *twill*. Its dominant characteristic is the diagonal aspect of the weave as we look at the front

(a)   (b)

Plate 6. *a. Diagram of plain weave. b. Diagram of twill weave.*

surface of the cloth. In twill, there is always a grouping of the threads—unlike the regular alternation of plain weave. This grouping may be, for example, two under and three over, or vice versa. Various counts are used for various purposes. However, the groups are closely related in number. For that reason, twill is sometimes called a "short-series weave," i.e., the groups of threads do not run to the five or seven that are commonly used in satin weave. In twill, if the weft thread goes over two warps, then under three, there will be more warp threads on the surface than wefts. Furthermore, as each of the weft threads is one step beyond the preceding row where it comes to the surface—the other thread being engaged as before—this arrangement, repeated row after row, has the effect of making a diagonal. See Plate 6*b*. The warps, in the meantime, each time are one step farther down, thus forming the remainder of the diagonal effect. In a very steep diagonal, the count may have much more contrast, approximating the satin counts. This explanation is crude, but it is hoped that it may lead to closer observation, as the cloth is studied under the thread counter, aided and abetted by a pin. The count I have cited is only one example, a simple one. Often the count is staggered to produce interesting effects. This is particularly true of men's suitings. Common illustrations of twill in dress goods are serge and gabardine. Because of the hard twist of the thread and the height of the little diagonal ridges, both these materials have a marked tendency to wear shiny. They are very firm, however, and endure a great deal of wear.

In the decorative market, twill has come into its own with the advent of modern and the search for materials that show interesting texture without definite pattern. The plain surfaces of most modern furniture do not harmonize with the great variations of contour, scale, and color that occur in the traditional designs. Hence strong emphasis has been placed upon textured effects for upholstery fabrics. What has been accomplished is surprising. The necessity of keeping costs down during the depression years resulted in many unusual uses of materials—cottons, for example, were brought out in new guises and with new appeal. The twill weave proved to be an able ally in developing many of these new texture effects. Before the depression, it was quite difficult to find twill in a decorative fabric except in conjunction with other weaves, such as the standard type of brocatelle. Nowadays twill is found in many kinds of fabrics made from fibers ranging from silk to synthetic fibers. See Plate 7*a*.

As these materials have no standard names, like taffeta, faille, etc., it is impossible to list them. They are known from season to season by the trade names that the dealers give them. Some appear in silk, some in cotton and rayon. There are many combinations. Some are firm, excellent for upholstery. Others are soft and fall in beautiful folds for curtains. Some have boldly marked diagonals which have to be used with much discretion in order to hold the diagonal movement within the confines of the furniture. Others are small, neat, and tidy; these are usable many times when the older-type furniture is being high-styled for modernized rooms. There is wide variey.

Satin Weave

The third fundamental weave is the *satin* weave. It should be distinctly understood that when I say satin I am referring now to a method of putting threads together, not merely to one type of silk cloth. Satin—like taffeta—may be made of cotton, silk, or any other fiber. All types of fibers are used for satin weave. It is another series weave like the twill, only this time the series consists of one thread to a long group of threads. Plate 7*b*. The weft thread goes over one warp and under five or seven, for example. Both are common counts. It can be seen readily that this count results in many warp threads on the surface, with the weft threads showing little, if at all. If the weft happens to be much smaller than the warp, as is usually the case, it will be scarcely discernible on the surface of the cloth. It is there, however, and holds the web of the cloth together. The characteristic sheen of satin, especially in silk fabrics, is explained by this particular construction. The silk is naturally lustrous. When the threads lie close together in uninterrupted lengths the light flows over them and reflects in soft, edgeless sheen. This effect is in sharp contrast to that of taffeta, where the constant changes of the thread surface, as the warp and weft go over and under in short alternation, catch the light at the high spots, and make uniform tiny shadows at the low ones and thus produce the quick crispness of taffeta.

Satins may be *warp satins* or *weft satins* according to whether the majority of the threads on the surface are warp or weft threads. The one described above is a warp satin because it shows five or seven warp threads to one weft on the surface. If the *weft* thread went over five or seven warp threads, then under one, and so on, the result would be a weft satin, because there would be mostly weft threads on the surface of the cloth.

There are three standard types of satin in common use in the decorative field; first, the regular smooth, shiny-surfaced material with which everyone is familiar under the name of satin; second, a variation of the first which has a small and inconspicuous jaspé effect; third, the so-called antique type which is made with loosely twisted threads that are much larger than those used in the other two types.

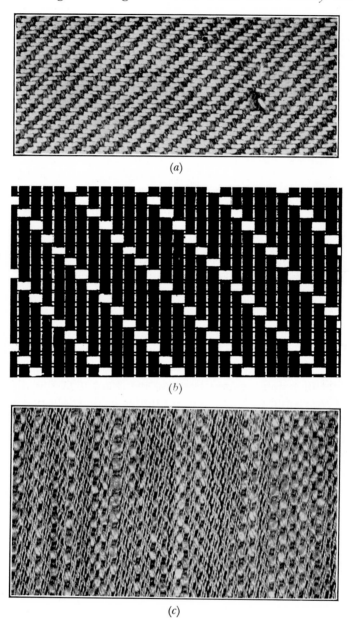

(a)

(b)

(c)

PLATE 7.   *a. Twill showing one simple type of the weave.   b. Satin diagram show-ing one simple type of the weave.   c. Antique satin showing strié effect and use of threads of different sizes.*

ORDINARY SMOOTH SATIN

SATIN—WHAT IS IT?

Satin (the cloth) is a smooth, lustrous fabric made by means of the satin weave as already described.

WHAT ARE THE DECORATIVE USES OF SATIN?

This ordinary smooth satin has many uses. It comes in a variety of weights, some of which are particularly well adapted for curtains, others for upholstery. The satin for curtains hangs in soft folds which hold their shape well. The upholstery satins are made either with heavier thread or are made of silk mixed with cotton or linen to give strength. Some of the thinner, softer versions of upholstery satins also drape well as curtains. For the most part, however, they are too stiff. The folds stand out in edgy fashion, and the luscious softness of the material is lost.

Satin in silk is always a dressy fabric, whether used for curtains, upholstery, bedspreads, dressing tables, or pillows. It reflects a good deal of light, a fact that has to be taken into consideration with regard to the positions of the pieces of furniture on which it is used. The color, when the piece of material is held in the hand, may seem perfect. When it is put in the place that it is to occupy in the room, the fabric may catch so much light that it makes the chair or bed so outstanding as to upset the whole color composition. On the other hand, with too little light on bed, chair, or curtains satin may be the answer to the problem of insistent under-emphasis. It may reflect enough of what light there is to bring the object up in value sufficiently for it to take its proper place in the scheme.

As part of the texture composition of a room, satin, when properly used, affords many interesting opportunities for accent. For example, if the room seems to lack the finishing notes that give it vitality, the effect may be improved a good deal by using satin covers on one or two side chairs, or by introducing satin with the scheme on some of the pillows. If satin accents are overdone, of course, they will merely bounce around as isolated spots.

HOW DOES SATIN HANG BEST WHEN USED AS CURTAINS?

Satin can be used in almost any type of draping. It hangs well in straight folds; it drapes well, it lies in beautiful clusters of folds when pulled out on the floor in very long curtains. It can be used for plain, shaped valances, properly trimmed. It is admirable for draped valances with various types of swags.

JASPÉ SATIN

Jaspé satin is a fine lustrous material with little indefinite stripes. Until the rather recent advent of the so-called antique satin, this jaspé

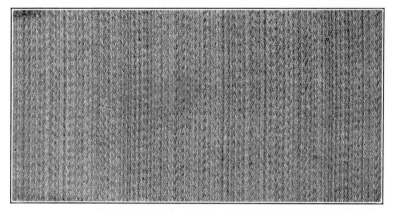

PLATE 8. *Satin showing jaspé effect.*

satin was known as antique satin, and occasionally it is so-called now— a confusing fact. The slight jaspé effect reduces somewhat the sheen of the silk and makes it a little less dressy than many of the ordinary smooth satins.

WHAT ARE ITS DECORATIVE USES?

In the darker colors, such as red, blue-green, and brown, jaspé has been used a great deal for curtains in rooms where the furniture is nice but neither delicate nor dressy. The little jaspé effect has the decorative virtue of breaking up a color that might otherwise appear too solid, making the curtains too important. This material has also been used a great deal for seat covers for side chairs in positions where it has been desirable to keep them simple, but not too solid or too flat.

HOW DOES JASPÉ SATIN HANG BEST AS CURTAINS?

Jaspé satin hangs best in straight folds as curtains. It is usually a little too thick to drape well in tiebacks.

ANTIQUE SATIN

ANTIQUE SATIN—WHAT IS IT?

Antique satin is made of heavier, more loosely twisted threads than either of the other two types. Some of it is made of threads that are not smoothly spun; thus a nubbly effect, somewhat like the shikii effect, is obtained.

WHAT ARE ITS DECORATIVE USES?

Antique satin is one of the materials that may be used equally well with traditional or with modern furniture. For the most part, the rougher types are used with modern, although in some kinds of modern rooms the smoother ones may be acceptable.

Antique satin comes in such a variety of weights and thread counts that it is sometimes difficult to classify or even to recognize. Some types are meant to be used only as curtain material. They are the thinner ones, which are sometimes even a bit sleazy. Others are stiff and sturdy and are meant to be used as upholstery.

One should never judge the possible durability of one of these antique satins by picking at the threads on the surface. Picking is not the way by which the material is worn out unless a cat is allowed to exercise her claws on it. It is better to pull the material from side to side with one hand while the other hand holds it firmly. If both hands pull it, see-saw fashion, it may wiggle badly. Most materials would do so. A fabric that will stand this pulling test will also stand a great deal of the squirming and rubbing to which it is subjected when on a chair or a sofa. The less firm antique satins are likely to be excellent for curtains, hung in soft folds. See Plate 7c.

HOW DOES ANTIQUE SATIN HANG BEST AS CURTAINS?

Antique satin looks best when hung in straight folds, not draped back. It is usually fairly heavy, and the straight folds seem to express its quiet dignity better than draping. On the other hand, there are occasions when straight folds would not be the best choice for a particular group of windows, though antique satin might seem to be the best texture to use because of the remainder of the room scheme. In that case, one of the lighter antique satins, even a sleazy one, may be draped. The stiffer, heavier ones never look right when they are draped.

Antique satin lends itself admirably also for use as bedspreads, especially in rooms where the furniture is rather heavy or bold in contour. It can also, under a few similar conditions, be used satisfactorily for draping dressing tables. It is too heavy for most rooms. For pillows it is often excellent.

SATEEN

SATEEN—WHAT IS IT?

Sateen is another satin weave material. It usually is made of cotton—mercerized in the better grades. Sometimes it is a warp satin weave, sometimes a weft satin weave.

WHAT ARE ITS DECORATIVE USES?

Sateen is used mostly for lining curtains. Occasionally, for budgetary reasons, it is used for slip covers while the furniture is awaiting a permanent cover. It also can be trimmed and made into effective curtains in simple furnishing effects, especially in the lighter colors. Under similar conditions, it can be used for both dressing tables and bedspreads. It drapes nicely.

ARMURE

ARMURE—WHAT IS IT?

At first glance an old-time *armure* may appear to be a damask of small pattern. (See Plate 9.) Closer examination, however, will reveal the fact that, where the pattern appears, the warp and the weft are not interwoven. The warp threads have been allowed to float on the front surface of the cloth; the weft threads are doing the same on the back.   Plate 10.   A pin can be inserted between the two layers of thread at this point.   This construction explains (1) why the pattern in

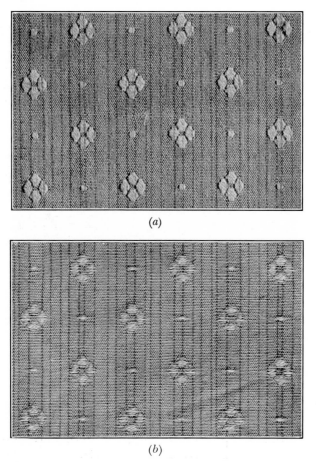

(a)

(b)

PLATE 9.   *a. Armure—front of cloth.   b. Armure—back of cloth.*

an armure always looks like warp satin, as it is formed by the warp threads; (2) why the patterns are always small.   Although a flower or petal seems to be solid and of fair size, careful examination will show that actually it is broken down into several smaller sections, so that there is really a firmly woven cloth instead of one with too many parts made of two layers of thread lying loosely on each other to make a firm web of cloth.

Historically, armures were much used during the eighteenth century.   During the first quarter of the twentieth century, when interest in antique furniture was at its zenith, many old armure patterns were copied, or adaptations were made from them.   The same method

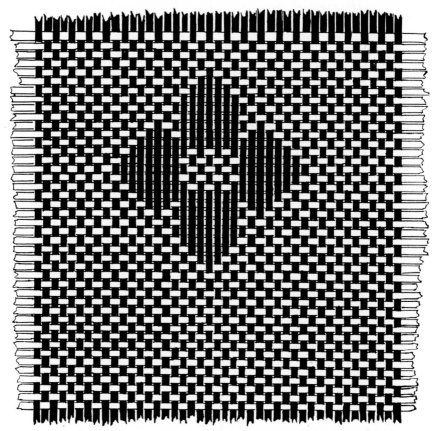

PLATE 10.   *Diagram—armure.*

of weaving was also used in making many less consequential fabrics in cotton and linen.   Most of these patterns had small, inconspicuous geometric figures quite different from the old standard floral patterns. Usually, armures are self-colored, although in some novelties the warp appears on the surface in a contrasting color.   Frequently such a cloth is not a true armure; it is called a "detached armure."   If the material is turned over, the extra color will be found on the back, running in loosely caught strands up and down the cloth, except where it is carried forward onto the face to make the pattern. Properly, these are not armures. They somewhat defy classification as they are definitely not brocades either; hence the term "detached armures" is common. Armures appear and disappear from the market periodically, influenced by the style of the moment.

WHAT ARE THE DECORATIVE USES OF ARMURES?

For the most part, armures are essentially seating materials. The small patterns can have great virtue, decoratively. They may also present a problem. When the figures are geometric and self-toned, they make little more than a small variation of texture on a surface of any appreciable size and thus present no problem. But the small floral patterns have both texture and scale aspects. On a chair seat that is of the size of a medium or small Louis XV chair, they have dainty charm. On a large piece of upholstered furniture, on which they are misused far too often, they may appear picayune, irritating. The same effect is produced when these patterns are used for curtains. However, occasionally a room problem will present itself where a material of the general damask aspect is needed but for which the usual figures of a damask are too large and bold. A plain material would appear too plain, too solid. One of the self-toned armures may give just the little vibratory quality that will lift the curtains from stolidity without making them too prominent because of the movement of a marked pattern. When the pattern is in a contrasting color, the effect is always small and is practically impossible to use except on sharply defined, small surfaces. On the larger surfaces, such a pattern grows wearisome because of its repetition and may even prove rather dazzling due to the movement of so many small parts over so much surface.

The small geometric-figured armures in cotton and linen often make excellent bedspreads as well as slip covers. Some can be used to advantage as casement curtains.

4

Combination Weaves in Fabrics
of Medium Weight

DAMASK

DAMASK—WHAT IS IT?

Damask is a combination weave. See Plates 11 and 12. Linen table cloth damasks are usually woven so that the background is a warp satin and the figure weft satin. As the light falls on the strands of linen running in opposite directions, it picks out the pattern and makes it visible, due to this difference of direction in the lay of the threads. Occasionally, damasks in the decorative field are woven in the same fashion. The majority of them, however, have the background in a warp satin and the figure in plain weave, in taffeta style. Often, the weft threads are spun so as to give the shikii effect, thus reducing the luster. Infrequently an all-taffeta damask or a damask with taffeta ground and satin figure appears. Both are rare, especially the all-taffeta type. However, regardless of what the weave variations may be, a damask is always a flat surface in which all the threads are essential to the web of the cloth. There are no extra, non-essential threads. As you run your hand over the surface of a damask, even though it may look bumpy to the eye, you will feel an essential flatness. The figures are not padded; they do not rise from the surface with an embossed effect. This statement is true even where the figure is done with nubby effect as in some modern types. Theoretically, damasks are reversible. Practically, they can be reversed satisfactorily only if the reverse side has been well finished and the thread character is equal in interest to that of the front surface. The pattern is woven through; it must be because there are only two sets of threads, warp and weft. However, the fact that it is woven through does not make the cloth reversible for practical purposes. The word reversible is often confusing to students in the definitions of damask.

In some damasks, the effect of the pattern is emphasized by the use of warp threads of one color and weft threads of another. Some-

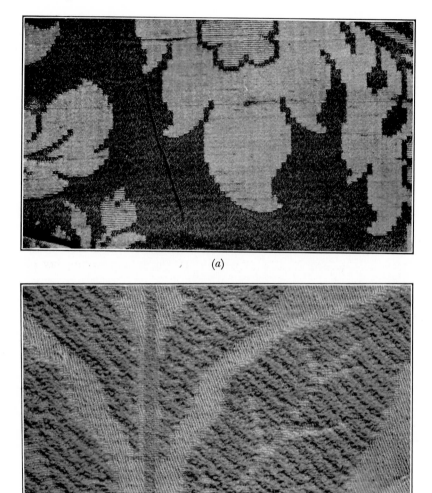

(a)

(b)

PLATE 11. *a. Silk damask. b. Cotton damask, modern type.*

times the background of the satin weave is varied by a strié or a jaspé effect. Less often, one of these variations appears in the figure, or in both figure and background. Rarely, two colors are used in the weft in such a manner as to give a definite colored pattern suggestive of brocade. As both threads are essential to the web of the cloth, the fabric is still damask, not brocade. Most of the standard damasks, whether of the old or the new type, are either self-toned, with warp and weft the same color, or two-toned with warp one color, weft another color. They come in a great variety of scale and character of design, from the big flowing figures of the Renaissance through the

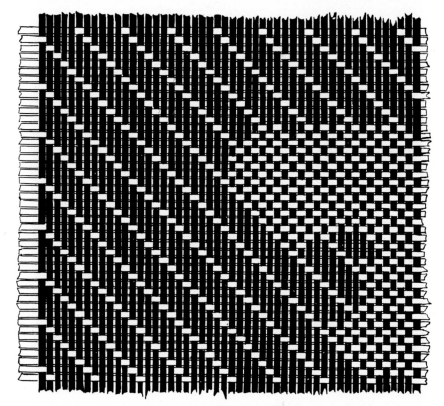

PLATE 12. *Diagram—damask.*

various modulations of the eighteenth century to the delicately drawn interpretations showing the revival of the classical interest in the latter part of that century, through the stolid, isolated-figure types of Empire influence to the modern, bold, over-scaled interpretations of floral forms. Even from early days, wherever damasks were used, the smaller-figured patterns were also in evidence. These small-figured damasks up to the time of Napoleon I are easy to distinguish. But later types, even those of today, often prove confusing to students because of the large amount of the satin weave ground. The pattern appears in small, isolated spots. However, if the definition is kept clearly in mind, the analysis can be made accurately.

All the historic damask types have been much reproduced, although few of them are exact period copies. Most of them are adaptations made up of motives from various periods. Many are beautiful; some are a mere hodgepodge of mismated motives. It requires much skill to interpret their design expression correctly so as to use them consistently with furniture on which they will look well.

Damasks are made of a great variety of materials from cotton to the synthetic fibers and their combinations.

WHAT ARE THE DECORATIVE USES OF DAMASK?

The uses of damask are many, depending largely upon their almost innumerable aspects. Some are thick and heavy; some are light and thin. Some of the heavy ones are useful only as upholstery; others can be used also for curtains when windows are large in scale. Most damasks make excellent curtains. The durability of damasks for upholstery depends upon the actual quality of the threads rather than upon the fact that the material is of silk, wool, linen, cotton, rayon, or nylon. A good quality of all-silk damask may outwear many other types. With linen added, it may wear still longer. But in the cheaper grades, a good cotton thread can make the fabric more durable especially if the silk is not of the best quality. It should be remembered that all degrees of wear cannot be provided in all types of cloth at a price to suit all pocketbooks.

Among the light, thin damasks, a slightly rough silk one is sometimes obtainable that is sheer enough to be used as a casement curtain in rooms where a nice effect is needed, but where long curtains are not desired—nor short curtains of very positive decorative aspect. Some of the small patterns in these raw-silk damasks are also especially pleasing when used as lamp shades in rooms where the general effect is solid and heavy. They also are excellent for pillows where some pattern movement seems to be necessary but where the luster of the usual damask would make the pillow too prominent. They are lovely for bedspreads also.

The smooth, lustrous damasks—the more common type—make excellent curtains, upholstery, pillows, bedspreads—more rarely lamp shades or dressing-table draping, as the texture and pattern needs of the room scheme demand.

None of the modern damasks have the brilliance of coloring of the finest old ones. The cost would be prohibitive. If you examine the background of some of the old materials of this type, you may be surprised to find that the glowing green, for example, which seems so incredible in its richness and vitality of tone, is not obtained by one set of warp threads of uniform color. The warp is varicolored, made up perhaps of a few brilliant yellow threads mingled with some blue and, of course, the green ones that form the basis. These other colors are not discernible to the naked eye; the green looks like one solid tone of particular brilliance. We would scarcely be willing to pay for their reproduction today.

Some damasks have a bare, uninteresting aspect because the figures look very flat and hard with the contour obviously outlined against the background. Others are full of vitality and interest. Close examination may reveal the fact that in the interesting ones the weave has been slightly varied either within the pattern or at the edges so that there is no uniformly hard edge against the background. This effect is achieved in various ways. One of the most common is running the warp threads over two of the wefts to give the aspect of faille, thus changing the flow of light over the surface. This variation of weave may occur just at the edge of a design, somewhere within the design, or at various places in irregular fashion to provide added interest. In the loveliest damasks the threads are so fine that the edges never give a bare, bleak, flat appearance. Then these subterfuges are unnecessary. But in the medium grades of the better type, they are fairly common. Usually these more interesting damasks cost a little more. They are worth the difference.

In many modern damasks cotton is much used. Often in this newer type the figures are in roughly twisted thread, sometimes bouclé (looped) which gives fascinating contrast to the satin-weave background. In these cases, the figures are, for the most part, large, bold, and sprawling, with wide open spaces of the background showing The drawing is clear and interesting. They are a welcome addition to the decorator's palette. Few can be used on traditional furniture if the tempo or theme of the room has been kept strictly traditional. However, if the furniture is traditional but the coverings, curtains, walls, and floor have been "styled"—treated in modern fashion either with keen sharp contrasts and definiteness of contour and mass or in close harmonies featuring the newer color nuances—then this type of modern damask, when selected with due regard for expression types to suit the furniture, has splendid possibilities.

Damasks are one of the most useful of all the decorating materials, especially in traditional rooms. They provide pattern that makes subdued motion, particularly in the self tones, where plain or even textured material would seem too solid and monotonous. They have kept many a sofa placed in the center of a long wall space from seeming to drop through the floor, because the damask pattern had sufficient movement to excite and hold the attention in that place and at the same time to lead the eye to the next item. They also have served to hold many a sofa in its proper place under similar conditions, when a plain lustrous material would have been too prominent and caused the sofa to bounce up into space, and a plain material with little or no luster would have been too flat in relation to the rest of the upholstery in the room. In the contrasting tones they often give the little accent needed where a chair should lead the attention toward other items; a plain fabric would leave the chair unduly conspicuous, holding attention exclusively on itself because of its plainness. At windows, damasks save many a room from stodginess and heaviness, because their flowing patterns have motion and thus keep the color and texture sufficiently vibrant to make it possible to regulate the importance of the curtains more easily. Somber masses of plain material against the walls are often difficult to manage. Damask may be as emphatic or as unemphatic as desired, according to the color, texture, and amount of movement in the pattern that is chosen.

Damasks are by no means always dressy. In general, whether modern or traditional, those with the high luster are the dressy ones. The exceptions to this rule are, of course, the rather hard, shiny damasks that are sold at low prices in "ready-to-wear" curtains and over the counter in the cheaper types of stores. They are so bad that they can scarcely be considered in decorative terms. All the references throughout this book have been to the better grades. If price is a consideration, there are so many fascinating effects that can be obtained with the newer cottons—effects excellent from the decorative standpoint as well as those of common sense, budgeting, and wear—that it seems foolish to ask people to put money into cheap imitations of a material that in its rightful aspect is so lovely.

Wool damask, whether made from sheep's wool or the wool of the Angora goat (mohair) comes in good variety of patterns, both large and a few small, filling a place that has been vacated since the depression by some of the imported heavier cloths. It comes in a fine range of colors and wears well. In the larger patterns it is especially good for large chairs and sofas. It also hangs well, making good curtains for rooms that can take its characteristic weight at the windows.

There is also a linen damask, used mostly for curtains, that is very decorative. It has an excellent surface and comes in good colors. It is not so expensive as some of the other materials. It wears well and looks well. Lined and trimmed properly, it is an excellent solution of many curtain problems in rooms where refinement, but not necessarily dressiness, is the theme. As upholstery, it is not quite so satisfactory. When tightly stretched over the edges of sofas or chairs, it shows soil quickly.

HOW DO DAMASKS HANG BEST AS CURTAINS?

The answer cannot be detailed because of the many types of damasks. In general, the lighter ones can be either draped or hung straight; the heavier ones, the stiffer ones, and those not of silk, usually are at their best hanging straight in simple dignified folds. The very thin ones—usually unlined when serving as casements—should be French-headed and used with a traverse to get the best results.

BROCATELLE

BROCATELLE—WHAT IS IT?

Brocatelle differs structurally from damask in that it has an additional and non-essential weft thread, which is used to pad the figure. The thin flatness of the typical damask has disappeared. In its place are thick, padded figures against a thinner, plain background. This additional weft thread, in a brocatelle of good quality, is of linen. In some of the cheaper types, jute is substituted for the linen. Its presence is immediately discernible because of its stiffness. A piece of brocatelle in which there is jute, when held in the hands, has a wiriness and hard stiffness. Even when the filler linen threads are stiff they never give this particular harshness and wiriness.

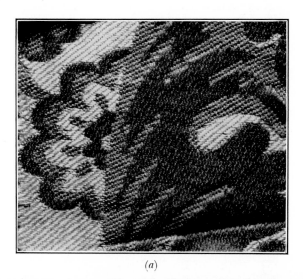

(*a*)

(*b*)

PLATE 13. *a. Brocatelle, large pattern. b. Brocatelle, small pattern.*

The figure in a brocatelle is always in the satin weave with the background in twill, another easy way of distinguishing brocatelles from damasks.

The material is an old type much used during the Renaissance. Since the depression, owing to the cost of production of the better grades with linen thread, and the poor appearance and poor wearing qualities of those with the jute substitute, the material has been little used.

The patterns follow closely the general types of the damasks, especially the damasks up to the early eighteenth century, and, like the damasks, they are usually self-toned or show one additional color.

WHAT ARE THE DECORATIVE USES OF BROCATELLE?

Brocatelle has been used mostly in the past as an upholstery material, particularly on large chairs and sofas. There still are occasionally small patterns of lighter quality that are usable on chairs of the later eighteenth century and on some of the smaller upholstered pieces. However, the majority of the standard patterns are derived from the earlier period types and belong with the heavier furniture forms.

Brocatelle, even when the linen padding thread is very flexible, is seldom used for curtains, unless the windows are of very large scale. The padding tends to make the folds rather clumsy. When the padding is of the jute, the material is impossible as curtains as it is too stiff. Nor is the jute type of brocatelle wholly satisfactory used as upholstery. The tender silk of the rest of the material is easily worn by being rubbed against the jute padding. The only way to tell whether a piece of brocatelle will drape well is to hold it in your hands and see how the folds fall. Even then, it is difficult to ascertain with certainty unless the piece is long enough so that you can see the fall of the folds as affected by their weight. A short piece, a half-yard sample length, for example, may give a very poor idea of the usefulness of that particular piece of material for curtains, although it might be adequate if it is being considered only as upholstery.

Sometimes a fabric that looks somewhat like a brocatelle, but which leaves one in doubt, appears on the market. The padded figure is missing, but the weave looks like the conventional brocatelle. The effect is produced by means of an extra warp thread, although this thread is not *under* the figures padding them. It is strung on the loom at a different tension from the other warp threads so that, when the cloth is released, it pops up, simulating the effect of the thicker, genuine brocatelle, but without the firm, substantial body supplied by the additional linen weft thread of the true brocatelle.

BROCADE

BROCADE—WHAT IS IT?

Brocades have a colored pattern on the surface of the cloth. This pattern is produced by means of additional threads, threads that are not essential to the web of the foundation cloth itself. All these threads could be snipped out, and the foundation cloth would still be there. In the older types of brocade, gold and silver were used in tiny strands wound around other threads to make them flexible. The threads which made the pattern ended—in manner similar to old-time tapestry threads—directly in back of the figures they produced on the surface. Sometimes this type of brocade is referred to as a *broché*. To avoid the controversy among the experts, remember simply that broché is the French word for brocade. In many places in the trade, if you ask for a broché, the salesman will bring you a light-weight brocade—often on a taffeta base—with the threads of the pattern ending, as described above, in back of the figure. See Plate 17*b* for ordinary type.

In most modern brocades, the additional colored threads which form the pattern are carried from selvage to selvage across the back, caught into the web of the cloth sufficiently to present a flat, smooth surface, but never brought forward to the front surface of the cloth except where the pattern occurs. Across the back of the cloth, instead of the loose, fuzzy aspect of the so-called broché, a neat woven colored background runs in stripes from selvage to selvage. Thus these threads are taken care of without becoming an integral part of the base or background of the brocade.

The essential point for the student to remember is that, under modern conditions, brocade is a cloth that has a colored pattern woven on it and that the colored threads, which form the pattern, are not essential to the original web of the cloth. Therefore, the cloth has a padded feeling where these threads are superimposed on the original cloth base. The pattern is woven in at the same time that the web of cloth is being woven by means of the *Jacquard* loom, which stops out the colored threads where they are not wanted and utilizes them where they are required. This is accomplished by an elaborate system of punched cards and hooks which govern the appearance and use of the threads.

Brocade is not necessarily of silk: there are brocades of cotton and other materials. Those that are not of silk, however, are often given other trade names.

WHAT ARE THE DECORATIVE USES OF BROCADE?

Brocade has many uses, although, in the decorative field, it is primarily an upholstery material. The softer, more flexible ones, of suitable pattern, make beautiful curtains. They can be used for bedspreads, pillows, sometimes for shades.

There has been a constant tendency to cheapen brocades, due not to desire but to the economic conditions arising with the depression period. They consequently have grown flatter and flatter with fewer and fewer colors—and threads. They are correspondingly less and less rich and sumptuous. In their finest interpretations, they are the most luxurious of all the fabrics with the possible exception of some of the Genoese and Venetian type of patterned velvets and, under traditional furnishing conditions of fine quality, are indispensable. Their color notes make easy transition of the attention from place to place in the room when they are properly used.

LAMPAS

LAMPAS—WHAT IS IT?

Lampas is a material that is seldom seen today. It was used commonly in the eighteenth century. During the heyday of decorating in the twenties it reappeared, and it may again. It is a colored material similar in effect to brocade, but softer, more flexible, and flatter. The flexibility is due to the fact that all the threads which form the colored pattern are an integral part of the web of the cloth. It is not a pattern woven so as to appear on top of the cloth, as in the brocade, thus producing a raised effect. The colored threads themselves form a portion of the cloth, and none can be removed without destroying it. Usually there are only a few colors, occasionally only one or two.

WHAT ARE THE DECORATIVE USES OF LAMPAS?

Lampas is usable both as curtain material and for upholstery, usually for upholstery, because the figures are apt to be too small to repeat well in the sweeping folds of curtains. They tend to be lost and to count for little.   Exceptions to this statement include the rare one or two tone types which appear at times in patterns characteristic of damask.   In these cases, the weave variations are of utmost importance.   Lampas of the ordinary type is also usable as bedspreads, pillows, and occasionally for dressing tables—under conditions where period furniture provides the decorative key.

5

Heavy Fabrics

MATELASSÉ—WHAT IS IT?

Matelassé is a thick material that has been much used since the depression. It resembles in one way the old ingrain carpets in that it is woven with two sets of threads, each making a complete web of cloth—one in front, one in back. These two faces of cloth are caught together at prudent intervals, so that there is no slipping of one surface against the other. In matelassé, where the two parts of the cloth are woven together the pattern appears. Sometimes the pattern is in another color—often a thin, sparse, trailing vine and flower effect that barely makes an outline on the plain surface of the fabric. At other times the pattern is smaller and closer. The interweaving of the front with the back may be done so as to cut the pattern into a great many small parts, although the figures themselves, in their entirety, may be either large or small. In cases where this is done the pattern usually has a bunched-up, padded effect like quilting. Sometimes there is no pattern of this sort, but the two parts of the cloth are held together by means of geometric forms made by the weave, such as a diamond shape where the weave goes through both sets of the cloth.

Much of this material is made with cotton, which probably accounts for its popularity; the depression wrought havoc with our exchange with foreign countries, and the importation of many of the fine brocades, tapestries, damasks, and brocatelles has been prohibitive since then, because the price has been practically doubled. Some matelassé is made of silk and the synthetic fibers.

WHAT ARE THE DECORATIVE USES OF MATELASSÉ?

Matelassé is sufficiently thick to give marked effect of substance and, therefore, is useful for large chairs that never will look right with thin-looking covering. It gives the impression of "a lot of fabric," an aspect that pleases many people.

In some of the modern-styled patterns matelassé is bold and effective. In most patterns that can be used with traditional furniture it

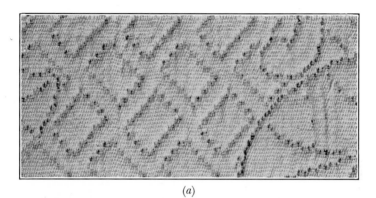

(a)

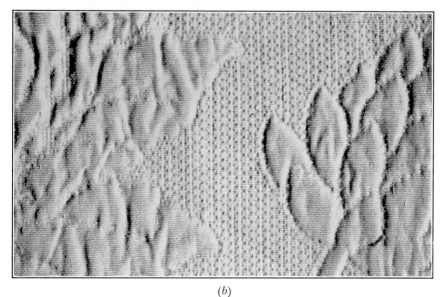

(b)

PLATE 14. *a. Matelassé, small geometric pattern. b. Matelassé, large pattern.*

is somewhat less satisfactory. The figures lack for the most part the definiteness that is a requisite of good decorative quality; they have a tendency to be nondescript and bunchy. When not well-designed matelassé has a pudgy aspect. When designed with sufficient boldness and clarity of effect it is a valuable asset in the decorative field.

As a seating material it has one fault, even at its best; the portions of the cloth that are bunched up, due to their looseness and height as compared with the parts that are interwoven, have a habit of catching the dirt from out-of-door clothing that comes in contact with them. On the other hand, the cloth usually is closely and firmly woven and will withstand many cleanings.

Some of the matelassé patterns, especially those that have long, bold figures in free modern style, lend themselves well to curtains. Overdrapery made of matelassé is always thick and heavy—a fact that is sometimes helpful, sometimes not. In modern interiors, where the furniture and walls constantly emphasize plain surfaces of broad and bold aspect and in large rooms, this heaviness may be a pleasant adjunct, providing a texture contrast that is very agreeable. If the pattern is not too bunchy, the material gives quiet and dignified motion and a texture softness as well, due to the way in which the light flows over the undulating levels of the surface. In traditional rooms matelassé is seldom attractive for curtains because its texture and heaviness as they are emphasized against the light on the walls are apt to be over-emphatic in contrast to the other furnishings.

Sometimes matelassé works well as portieres of interesting quality when the room balance demands hangings at the doors. Some rooms need the softness of textured fabric in a wide doorway in order to avoid an unpleasant gauntness of aspect. Sometimes too, door hangings of this sort are desirable in order to hold the attention within the room itself—to retain the feeling of the unit that it really is— instead of allowing the eye to wander far afield. It often is much nicer to look into a hall or a dining room as into a vista, rather than to have the doors so large and bare that one wonders whether it would have been better to have the rooms combined as one instead of having them partitioned.

The matelassé made of silk or of synthetic fibers has a luster that changes the texture aspect markedly. This type with its slicker, smoother, and quicker motion, is often usable with traditional furnishings, especially as hangings, curtains, and portieres.

VELVET

VELVET—WHAT IS IT?

At the moment, I am using the term *velvet* in the sense of velvet weave, not as the cloth that we call velvet. As a weave it covers a great many other types of cloth. The essential characteristic of the weave is the extra thread that is woven through the cloth—at right angles to it—thus providing an upstanding pile. Sometimes this thread is woven over little rods, which when withdrawn leave the ends in loop form at even height above the background of the cloth. Sometimes these rods have little knives in them that cut the loops as they are withdrawn. Then the ends of the pile stand free. This is the effect most people think of when the term velvet is used. The majority of the material with uncut loops is called frisé. Some velvets are double woven, that is, facing each other on the loom. Then the pile thread is cut by a knife before the cloth is removed from the loom, thus separating the two pieces.

FRISÉ

The term *frisé* is used ordinarily to designate a material of uncut, looped velvet weave made of cotton, linen, or mohair. The same process is also used for silk velvets, but they are usually referred to merely as uncut velvet. Both are the loop versions of the velvet weave.

The most common frisé is made of mohair. Mohair is the wool of the Angora goat. It is a firm, tough fiber, smooth and resilient. Frisé, in its newer interpretations, has lost most of the cheap, ordinary aspect of the old Pullman-car upholstery. It now appears as a heavy ribbed fabric, sometimes patterned and sometimes with slight suggestions of irregularity reminiscent of shikii. It has remarkable wearing qualities and a good deal of decorative interest. In the older forms it was so monotonous, hard, and rigid as to be uninteresting as a decorative texture.

The patterned versions of frisé are made either by combining the cut and the uncut pile, or by "voiding" part of the pile so that the background of the cloth shows, or by having the pile of different heights as well as different colors. In some cotton frisé and in the less common linen, the patterns are genuinely interesting. In most patterned mohair frisé the hard quality of the material itself counteracts the effectiveness of the pattern and results in a material with little genuine decorative quality. It wears forever. In some patterns it looks a little like some of the quaint old Victorian fabrics one could use in a country house— on little Victorian rockers, for example. However, for the most part, the cotton and the linen versions seem to have more texture variety and interest.

Frisé should not be confused with *frieze*. Frieze is a heavy cloth made in Ireland and used mostly for overcoats.

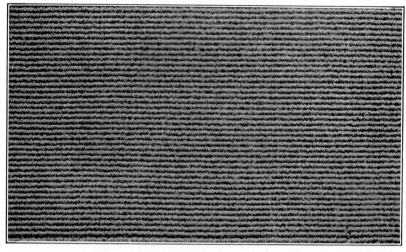

(a)

(b)

PLATE 15. *a. Frisé—plain.   b. Frisé showing alternation of cut and uncut pile.*

The silk velvet known as uncut velvet—with the looped pile—appears only occasionally in the market. When well patterned, it is lovely. I recall one that was current some years ago in the old flame pattern of the seventeenth century. It ranged in color from light cream to brilliant reds and deep blues and was beautiful. More often, however, uncut velvet (silk) is plain or in very subdued stripes. The sheen is softer and the texture more agreeable than is true of the other uncut pile fabrics. Sometimes it is woven so that the loops form little

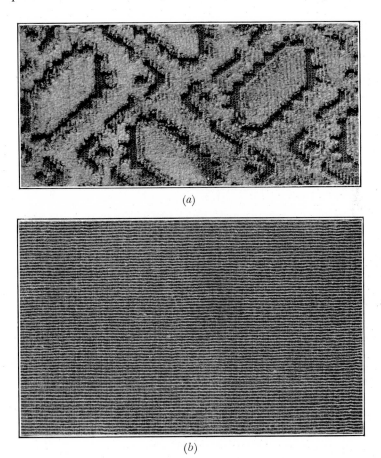

(a)

(b)

PLATE 16. *a. Cut velvet showing use of uncut pile at edge of pattern to give variety and interest. The background of the cloth shows where there is no pile. b. Uncut silk velvet.*

blocks, separated by slight, just discernible breaks. This type has been much used on fine furniture of the late eighteenth century in rooms of traditional period style.

In patterned velvets, the uncut loops are often used in conjunction with the cut pile to make the pattern and give variety of texture. See Plate 16a.

WHAT ARE THE DECORATIVE USES OF FRISÉ AND UNCUT VELVET?

Both frisé and uncut velvet are definitely upholstery materials.

CUT VELVETS

CUT VELVETS—WHAT ARE THEY?

These are the so-called velvets familiar to all of us. They may be made of silk, mohair, cotton, linen, or synthetic fibers. In the ordinary range used by decorators under normal conditions, the all-silk velvet stands at the top of the list for excellence of quality. All silk, in this case, means that the cloth itself as well as the pile is silk. Usually it is thin and soft and takes on beautiful colors—lights and shadows. Some are sufficiently heavy in effect to be usable with the dark oaks and walnuts of the seventeenth and early eighteenth centuries; others are so delicate that they are suitable only for the late eighteenth-century furniture. The suitability in each case is not entirely a matter of the color of the dye. A dark brown all-silk velvet may be delicate in effect, and a soft light blue may be heavy. It is the effect of the fibers themselves and the manner in which they are used together in one weave that determine the result. One must learn to distinguish differences in order to do fine decorating.

Probably the velvet with silk pile and cotton back is used more than the other type. It comes in a wide range of weights and thicknesses. Some of it is very flexible, some quite heavy and unwieldy. It looks well, and it wears well. If you ask for a silk velvet, the salesman will assume that you wish this type. Sometimes it is almost as soft and light in the hands as all-silk velvet. As you run your hand across the back, you can feel the silkiness of the pile threads, because the threads that form the back of the cloth are relatively so small. This is true also of some of the heavier varieties of this cotton-back, silk-pile velvet. There is also one of these silk-cotton type velvets in which the body of the cloth—not the pile—is made with silk warp and cotton weft.

It is unfortunate that, during a period of imitation antiqueing, this velvet with the cotton back and silk pile was often used as a base. Parts of the pile were omitted so as to make the surface look as though it has been through the wear and moth ravages of years. The effect may have satisfied the same sort of taste that was satisfied by some of the so-called antique furniture of the time which was produced with the aid of bird shot and was supposed to bring to mind the work of worms through the centuries. But such fabric is at least of questionable decorative value.

Occasionally in velvets, especially those of this grade, with silk pile and cotton back, there is a strié effect. Strié that is not overdone so that its lineyness counteracts the natural smoothness and softness of the velvet surface, is useful as well as good-looking. For example, there may be a small chair in front of a sofa. It is desirable to use velvet on it, but all the samples brought into the office seem to make it too solid, too flat, and heavy. The chair doesn't hold its position in front of the sofa as it should. Light tones seem to make it too prominent. A little strié effect in velvet of the right tone may provide just enough "lift" so that the chair takes and holds its place easily. The same effects may be apparent when velvet is being used as pillows. Indiscreetly used, however, strié may give an effect that is too indefinite. For example, a long sofa that holds the attention at the center of a wall opposite a fireplace may need the plain, smooth surface of plain velvet in order to be sufficiently bold and interesting as a key piece to keep the chairs back in their places.

Another commonly used type of cut velvet is the all-cotton type. This has both a cotton pile and a cotton back. It is thicker than the other velvets and has a hard, dry feeling as you run your hand over it. As the strands of the pile are coarser and thicker than in silk pile, and are without luster, a hard greyish light that modifies the color is at times apparent, quite different from the soft shimmer of the silk pile. This aspect is less noticeable in the medium and darker tones than in the lighter ones. All-cotton velvet is an exceedingly useful material, however, especially when the budget is a marked consideration. It is one of the best surfaces of its kind to use under these conditions. It seldom looks as well on a chair as on a sofa, whether the chair is large or small. For a small chair the surface is too flat, too thick, and the light on the changing surfaces is apt to display the least desirable qualities of the velvet. It is also too thick and clumsy on many of the turns of seat, back, and arms. On sofas, however, where the surfaces are longer, this difficulty seldom has to be considered. For chairs, most workers turn to velveteen.

WHAT ARE THE DECORATIVE USES OF THESE CUT VELVETS?

The statement has to be a general one owing to the great variety within each one of the three classifications given above. Their major use is as upholstery. They can be used as curtain material, although for the most part velvet curtains belong to the Victorian era. The two better classes, especially all-silk and the silk on cotton back, can be used successfully as portieres. The all-cotton is very uninteresting in this capacity, and its over-use on cheap work has been one of the reasons for the elimination of portieres by many people who can visualize only this type when the word is mentioned. Bedspreads are sometimes of velvet—in the better grade and in the thinner aspects. For pillows velvet is used in all its grades.

VELVETEEN

VELVETEEN—WHAT IS IT?

Technically *velveteen* is not velvet. However, as the difference is a matter of whether extra threads in the warp make the pile or extra threads in the weft, the visual aspect being the same, we shall not quibble over the statement.

Velveteen is another all-cotton pile fabric in which weft threads form the pile and the pile is much lower than in regulation velvets. This combination results in a thin and flexible material, and the low pile, closely sheared, has none of the hard cottony look of the regular cotton velvet.

WHAT ARE THE DECORATIVE USES OF VELVETEEN?

Velveteen is used a great deal for chairs as well as for hangings, portieres, and spreads. It works easily, is flexible, hangs in good folds—not clumsy like cotton velvet—and has a pleasant surface. It comes in a wide range of lovely colors, both traditional and modern in character.

On small sofas, or sofas of marked stylistic character, it looks well as upholstery. On large ones, it may lack the texture and body that another form of velvet could provide better. It has been much used on French Empire and English Regency furniture, although its value, decoratively, is by no means limited to these two types. It is excellent for many late French chairs and works admirably in many high-style settings.

VELOUR

VELOUR—WHAT IS IT?

Properly, *velour* is French for velvet. However, on the market, at times, a special form of velvet goes under the name Velour as a trade name. Our grandmothers used this type of velvet often on those old red or green chairs in the parlour. They bought it because they expected it to wear for years. It did. It was made with mercerized cotton pile and plain back; thus it had a slight luster. It can be distinguished readily by the slight effect of horizontal lines running across it, and the pile shows a tendency to lie down instead of standing upright. The sheen also is definitely not that of silk.

WHAT ARE THE DECORATIVE USES OF VELOUR?

Velour is most valuable for sofas and large chairs, padded generously, of the general Victorian type. It is much less satisfactory for smaller chairs and definitely undesirable where lean smoothness of surface is important—there velveteen is at its best—or where the surfaces because of their modeling change shape so much that the shine, with its hardness, becomes tiresome.

As curtains, portieres, or pillows it is seldom attractive; it is too clumsy. Other materials are much more interesting in their surface textures.

PLUSH

PLUSH—WHAT IS IT?

Plush is seldom classified as a velvet, although it is a pile (velvet) weave. The pile is much longer than that of velvet.

It is made from various materials, cotton, silk, mohair, and synthetic fibers. At one time, the modernists used a great deal of it for upholstery and for bed coverings. However, it has now practically disappeared from the market, except for automobile robes, for which it is often pressed and brushed in order to give the surface more variation. For upholstery it occurs both brushed and unbrushed, according to the style that is current at the time.

PATTERNED VELVETS

PATTERNED VELVETS—WHAT ARE THEY?

When *patterned velvets* are obtainable in the market, as they were during the twenties, the majority of them follow historic patterns. The large patterns follow Genoese and Venetian models, French Baroque of the Louis XIV period, and some of the Spanish types. The small patterns vary from those of the Italian Renaissance to those of the late eighteenth century—the type that might have appeared as a waistcoat on a French dandy of the Court of Louis XVI. The large ones are mostly floral effects, rich in color and fine in drawing. Often large areas of the background cloth show—usually in satin—and the pile is concentrated in the portion of the cloth that forms the pattern. The pattern is ordinarily made up of both cut and uncut pile handled with great adroitness to give varying shading and textures. The smaller patterns consist of many kinds of figures from the bold leaves and animal forms of the Renaissance to the dainty flower or small geometric forms of the Louis XVI period. In geometric patterns, especially, the uncut pile in contrast to the softer texture of the cut pile gives a delightful effect.

WHAT ARE THE DECORATIVE USES OF THE PATTERNED VELVETS?

The large patterned velvets are suitable under present-day conditions for dressy and luxurious drawing rooms with fine pieces of furniture. When the scale of the room is suitable and the decorating key sufficiently luxurious and lovely, they are welcome additions to the decorating palette. In the past, they were used also as wall coverings, as well as hangings.

The smaller patterns have a wider, more general use, and, if it were not for the high prices resulting from the depression era, probably would be in as great favor as ever for traditional work.

These small patterns run such a gamut of expression from the forceful vigorous ones of the earlier type to the delicate later ones that they cover a wide range of possibilities as upholstery for chairs, stools, sofas (small), chaises, and, more occasionally, for pillow covers. They seldom look well over large areas, as the repeat becomes monotous and one is too conscious of the incongruity between the scale of the large chair or sofa and that of the small pattern. The majority are too definite to count only as texture. The existence of the raised pattern caused by the pile sometimes makes the scale very apparent. On the other hand, on a chair with an upholstered back and seat, the back framed in wood as in so many of the chairs of the Louis XV and Louis XVI periods, the limited space, carefully framed, often makes these small-patterned velvets an asset. They are definite; they hold their own within that limited space and do not allow the attention to wander. Thus they frame well. The motion is controlled. One is not confronted with the aspect which suggests the question, "When will it stop?" as is so often the case when damasks are used under these smaller-framed conditions.

The "little" velvets also have great value as intermediate transition notes in a room composition, leading the attention from one piece of furniture to another by breaking up the surfaces so that they get a little attention but are not too active or too important.

Under ordinary conditions, it is well to be cautious about using these small-patterned velvets on sofas with the exceptions of some of the smaller, stylistic types. They can become very monotonous.

CORDUROY

CORDUROY—WHAT IS IT?

Technically, *corduroy* is not a velvet. Like velveteen, it is a pile fabric in which the pile is a weft pile. In this case, the pile appears in vertical ridges. In the heavy types, it is rather coarse. Lately, many variations of this material have been introduced, some of which have low, narrow wales, as the little ridges are called. They seem almost like velveteen in their thinness, lightness, and flexibility. In fact, some of them really are velveteens in which the pile has been cut so as to be of alternating heights.

WHAT ARE THE DECORATIVE USES OF CORDUROY?

Most of the finer corduroys are very nice in appearance and form an interesting variation for some of the lighter chairs and sofas when silk velvet is out of the question because it is either too expensive or too dressy. The material with the larger wales can be used satisfactorily only under the simplest conditions. The small-wale types come in ample range of good colors from light to dark; the large-wale types are usually limited to a few of the more common tones.

CHENILLE

CHENILLE—WHAT IS IT?

Chenille is a fabric, originally used in decorating only in the cheaper grades for portieres and couch covers, which, in the search

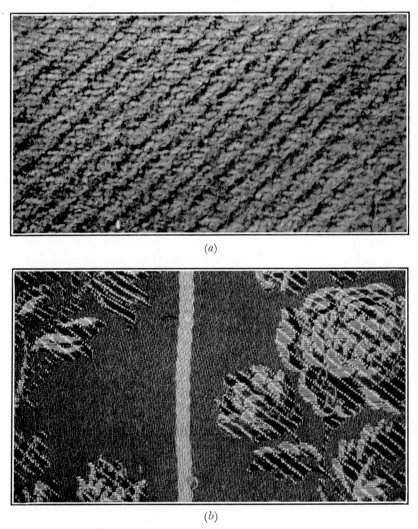

(a)

(b)

PLATE 17.   *a. Chenille.   b. Brocade with satin background.*

for new texture ideas both as adjunct for modern furniture and as replacement of the expensive imports during the depression, has reappeared in new forms and with new uses.

It is made with a specially constructed thread for the weft or filler. Instead of the usual round twisted thread, the chenille weft is made up of two parts. There is a horizontal thread and, standing out from this at right angles at the top and the bottom, are other threads of heavier weight that are held in place by this horizontal thread. These heavier threads are pushed up toward each other in a V-shape, with the horizontal thread holding them together at the bottom of the V. The result is that the thread has a brush-like effect. This aspect is responsible for its name, caterpillar. It is this caterpillar that is used as the regular weft thread in chenille cloth. The loose ends of the caterpillar form the surface of the cloth which thus is softer than an ordinary flat surface yet does not have the finish of the velvet-pile fabrics.

WHAT ARE THE DECORATIVE USES OF CHENILLE?

The irregular aspect of the ends of the caterpillar on the surface of chenille also gives the fabric a rather bunchy, not very convincing decorative effect. Chenille appears in the market, now and then, in interesting colors, some of which are excellent for use with the simpler types of furnishing. Some pieces of chenille can be used satisfactorily for upholstery, but for the most part the indefiniteness and bunchiness of the surface make it unattractive for this purpose, especially when the upholstery is snugly fitted. On chairs with loose pillows it is more satisfactory. For bedspreads and for hangings, it may be very effective.

TAPESTRY

TAPESTRY—WHAT IS IT?

One more material, under normal market conditions, is common in both simple and luxurious settings. This is *tapestry*. It is not the type of tapestry that was hung on walls in the later Middle Ages and Renaissance. These were decorative paintings done in wool; today they are priceless. Nor is it the modern descendants of these, nor the less elaborate types of the old ones destined for humbler purposes than wall decoration, such as the work of the Beauvais factory for the furniture of the French court. I am referring only to the ordinary type of upholstery tapestries that are found in the market and are used in our homes today—the usual yardage goods. Description of the others belongs under historic textiles.

In the regular market three types of these upholstery tapestries are commonly found: (1) The best grade which is all-wool, except possibly the warp threads that, for the sake of strength, may be cotton or linen. These fine wool tapestries are heavy, well-designed, and handsome. (2) The wool-and-cotton type which, unlike the preceding, is made by machine. Sometimes the tapestries of this grade are excellent; sometimes they are discouraging. (3) The all-cotton type, usually very discouraging, although occasionally a pattern is so characterful and interesting that one wonders why good designs do not appear more often in this lower price range.

WHAT ARE THE DECORATIVE USES OF THESE TAPESTRIES?

TYPE I

The patterns are usually large and richly colored, and the material is deep and soft because of the thickness and softness of the wool. The pattern in the best examples is woven by hand, the threads being drawn through the back and finished where they came through. This process accounts for the shaggy bunches of wool that appear on the back. The colors in most fine-wool tapestries are soft and subdued—variations of green, dark browns, dull reds, deep blues, with small notes of ivory, tans, and mild yellows. For the most part the designs are rather heavy—floral or verdure patterns in the style of the late seventeenth and early eighteenth centuries.

As the description indicates, these all-wool tapestries are best used in rooms with heavy furniture—the oak and the walnut of the periods represented by the designs themselves. They are definitely upholstery materials. A few lighter patterns appear, but they are more frequently found in the needlework types.

TYPE II

The imitations of the handmade tapestries seem very flat compared to the handmade ones. They are woven with two sets of warps and wefts. In the better grades many are in good colors and are well-drawn, although the contours always show a certain amount of monotony due to the mechanics of the woven cloth as compared with the freedom that is possible in the shading and modeling of the handmade products. Their decorative value depends entirely upon the inherent quality of the design of each piece.

On large chairs, wing chairs, and large, heavy sofas, they may prove, in their best interpretations, more successful than many of the thinner fabrics. Unfortunately, many of them are hopelessly non-descript with poorly drawn, sparse, badly balanced designs. They are "spotty" and commonplace. To make them even worse they are usually done in drab "safety-first" colors—dull taupes, drab blues, and sad rose with little or no sparkle and life. It requires a good deal of discrimination to select good decorative material from this group, but such material can be found.

Type III

It requires still more discrimination to select the good examples from among the many poor ones in the third group. The patterns for the most part are of the same sort—a little less well-drawn. Due to the all-cotton effect, and its resulting thinness, as compared with the roundness and softness of the wool, these Type III cotton tapestries look even more sparse than the poorer ones of Type II. At their worst, the cotton gives an increased flatness, a dryness of aspect, that seems to remove from them the last vestige of interest. However, at their best, either in the small, compact, geometric forms or the quaint little florals, they are very entertaining. They are as good, within their range of expression, as the best ones of Type II.

The best ones may be used to advantage on small surfaces—perhaps in the living room on a little old Victorian rocker, or in the bed-room on a not very large upholstered chair of interesting shape. On large surfaces they are apt to look either very flat or "spotty."

It pays to keep alert for the "finds" in this group when budget considerations loom large.

Tapestry Fillers

tapestry fillers—what are they?

Usually some plain tapestries, with no pattern, which are known as *fillers,* are also on the market. Ordinarily they are available in a wide range of colors among the darker tones and in a variety of textures from heavy to light.

Fillers have been used a great deal for large chairs in heavy rooms of handsome aspect and for large sofas where velvet would have been too dressy, damask too thin, and no other material has seemed to have the body, the substance, to hold the piece of furniture in its place. Some tapestry fillers have been manufactured to match exactly the background of a good, handmade wool tapestry, or one of the finer machine types, both of which are fairly high in price. Thus the more expensive figured material may be used on the parts of the chair that are constantly in evidence, as the front of the chair back, the seat, and the arms, while the plain matching filler covers the back which is usually a large expanse in any chair that is big enough to look well in one of these heavy tapestries. The handling of this combination of tapestries has been greatly abused; some pieces of furniture have come out looking like Jacob's coat. Properly handled, however, this practice is a good old English custom and can be used to advantage, if it is not overdone. It is applied particularly to chairs, such as the large wings, club chairs, or to large sofas.

EMBROIDERIES

Among the heavy materials that are used for upholstery and hangings are also some embroideries. They are mentioned here only because they have been copied in machine work.

English crewel work is the most commonly copied type. English women, long before the Renaissance, made beautiful embroideries. In the late seventeenth century the type known as crewel work was in its heyday and was one of their favorite forms, especially for bed hangings. Its exotic figures and long trailing vines seem to have been inspired by Eastern patterns, which at that time were being imported in quantity. The influence of the East had appeared earlier, due in part to the returning Crusaders. But crewel work was primarily the fruit of the imports brought in by the East India Company established by Queen Elizabeth.

Crewel is usually worked in wool on either cotton or linen. That is the most common type and the one that has been most often copied.

Sometimes the figures of the pattern are heavy and massive in bold greens, blues, and browns with smaller notes of brighter colors. At other times, the pattern is thin and delicate, covering very little of the background material as it meanders over it. Always, however, it belongs in rooms with the heavy types of furniture. Its bold curves and sharply silhouetted masses are quite out of keeping with the subtlety of lighter furniture. The machine copies of crewel work have little of the charm of the old handwork. They are apt to be hard and set. The irregularity of the long and short stitches, of which it is composed, are never approximated successfully by a machine. The one is soft, varied, and interesting. The other is hard, monotonous, and obvious. When designs are too obvious they are seldom interesting.

WHAT ARE THE DECORATIVE USES OF CREWEL WORK?

For fine decorating where the interiors have beautiful old furniture and it seems desirable to use crewel, most decorators send to England to have the embroidery done by hand. Only a few people in this country can do it skillfully. Crewel makes beautiful curtains against wood-panelled walls or rough plaster. It is excellent for some of the heavier types of wing chairs that are of genuine, early-period inspiration. Likewise, it looks well on some of the big club chairs that can be used in rooms where heavier furniture styles set the key. It is also usable as bedspreads in rooms of this early type, and as bed hangings.

GROS-POINT AND PETIT-POINT

GROS-POINT AND PETIT-POINT—WHAT ARE THEY?

Gros-point and *petit-point* are two other embroidery processes that have been imitated by machine work and are fairly common in the upholstery field. Most women are familiar with both, and many have made seat covers in one or the other stitch. Some have made purses or handbags. Both types of embroidery are made in the same way on a coarse background of linen, or more often canvas, and the stitches are pulled through the interstices and over the threads of the foundation cloth so that the background is completely covered. When the work is done on rather coarse canvas, it is known as gros-point; on finer canvas, petit-point. Gros-point runs from 12 to 18 stitches to the inch; the petit-point runs 18 and over. Fine examples run about 22 to 24. The resulting squarish blocks on the surface are imitated by the machine in various ways in tapestry-like materials. The simplest of these look very much like the tapestry fillers already described. They are in little blocks, both large and small in size, and they usually are in dark colors, such as dark brown. The more elaborate products are of the lighter weight, usually in standardized medallions enclosing flower patterns such as were in use during the latter part of the eighteenth century. Unfortunately, most of these are rather commonplace in design, and the flatness, due to the machine work, fails to lift them out of the ordinary into the fine decorative field. In the better ones, the designs are good, well-drawn, of excellent colors, and the flatness of the machine work is not unpleasantly apparent. Even in the modern handwork, it is difficult to find interesting, thoroughly well-drawn patterns that, decoratively, are worth the time spent on them.

WHAT ARE THE DECORATIVE USES OF GROS-POINT AND PETIT-POINT?

Both gros-point and petit-point, whether in the plain "filler" form or the patterned form, are essentially upholstery materials.

TURKEY WORK

TURKEY WORK—WHAT IS IT?

Turkey work is another handwork form used in England during the late seventeenth and early eighteenth centuries. It was made on a canvas back with coarse wool drawn through the canvas to resemble the pile of Oriental rugs, or Turkey rugs, as they were called. The patterns were bold; the colors were bold, sharply featured because of the coarse wool used; the general effect was rather rough but characterful.

WHAT ARE THE DECORATIVE USES OF TURKEY WORK?

Turkey work was employed especially for chair seats and backs on the smaller areas such as those of the Cromwellian chair types—both side chairs and armchairs. Its coarseness and roughness look well with the heavy turnings and bold proportions. As far as I know there are no machine copies of this work.

6

Printed Fabrics

UNDER THIS HEAD ARE INCLUDED THE CHINTZES, CRETONNES, AND LINENS. The method of printing determines in large measure the value of the product, decoratively considered. If the colors are printed on the fabric in quick succession, as in ordinary roller printing, the result is apt to be quite commonplace. No color dries before the next one is applied; thus there is a lack of fine, clear definition, such as we find on the handblocked products. Also, to keep the expense down, few colors are used; they meet the "general market" conditions that, decoratively, are always a compromise; both the drawing and the modeling of the patterns lack character and distinction. However, there are some good patterns in this low-priced group.

The handblocked materials, whether chintz or linen, are the handsomest fabrics of this type, and they cover the whole decorating field in terms of expression and suitability for different periods.

Chintzes are always relatively thin, light cotton, of even weave, which takes the colors well. They are available unglazed, semi-glazed, and highly glazed. Most of them are the two latter types. The glazed finish is produced by means of a coating of paraffin or resin and calendering. Calendering is the process of pressing a fabric between heated rollers to give it a gloss. The difference between semi-glaze and full-glaze is as the words imply. The semi-glazed chintz has been lightly calendered. The full-glazed type has been more heavily calendered. Unglazed chintz is not common.

Chintzes of the present day appear in all sorts of patterns, large and small, formal and informal, bold and quiet, quaint and sophisticated. The original connotation of the word has long since been lost. The basic idea which resulted in chintz came from India, and, for many years, both in England and France, the term was applied to the importations of a fine cotton cloth with flower sprays or meandering vines and leaves and Tree of Life design. It was likewise applied to the results of rather crude Western attempts to copy them.

Chintz patterns of today vary from the small, insignificant, and sometimes quaint effects suitable only with the simplest cottage furnishings to the large, beautiful ones of much dignity that belong in handsome interiors.

Linens, meaning handblocked linens, have a bolder base than the chintzes because of the characteristic appearance of the linen thread that is used, and thus require also bolder treatment of the designs in most cases.

Handblocking—whether on chintz or linen—allows the designer the greatest possible freedom. Each color is printed from a separate block and allowed to dry before the next color is printed. As there is no limit, other than expense, to the number of colors, and the tones come out clear and fresh with clean outlines, real beauty of modeling and coloring is possible.

There are three ways of identifying a genuine handblock, other than by the general aspect of the design and its decorative quality: (1) Each block has little markers, called pitch-pins, which guide the worker to place each succeeding block in the right position. Sometimes these markers pick up the color as the block receives its load of dye and leave little round marks at some of the strategic points of the design. If you see little round dots, which seem to have nothing to do with the design itself, at the termination of a leaf or a petal, for example, you may be fairly sure that your are looking at pitch-pin marks and that the fabric has been handblocked. Unfortunately, dishonest people have sometimes tried to deceive the public by crude imitations of this technique. A cheap material, or one that is priced higher than its real worth, may be dotted with marks to make it look like a genuine handblocked fabric. It does not require a great deal of discrimination to detect the spurious marks. Usually the dots are placed in such hit or miss fashion, and there are so many of them, that the effect is almost ludicrous. Furthermore, the fabric itself is likely to give the hoax away, because the design and the drawing are not worth the effort and expense of handblocking. That is not a question of being elaborate; it is a question of fine quality in even the simplest of patterns. (2) In a handblock the colors are seldom, if ever, exactly placed. There are variations, which to the trained eye are quite apparent. If the material had been machine-printed, each color would have been placed with exactness, or the studied variations used for deceptive purposes would be obviously studied. This is one of the surest ways of distinguishing the genuine handblock from the imitation or from the well-done roller print. (3) There is a cleanness of color that the cheaper processes never even approximate. This effect is due, of course, to the fact that each color dries before the next color is applied so that there is no mixing or slurring.

Handblocked linens come in a great variety of patterns to fit every period style.

Cretonnes are cottons with a horizontal ribbing, similar to repp, and printed by the roller method. They are seldom handblocked because of the repp-like surface. They appear at times, usually in the mass-production market. The ribbing makes the material look like "more value for the money" to many people. Occasionally, they appear in the decorative market.

A development of the chintz that appeared in Western Europe during the latter part of the eighteenth century should also be mentioned. I refer to the *toiles*—usually called toiles de jouy—as the first were made in the little French town of Jouy. All the earlier Western efforts to reproduce the Indian "chint," as it was called, had sidestepped the Indian method of "resist" printing. As the Indians employed it, the process was slow and laborious, but it resulted in beautiful products, and the dye was permanent. The Western imitations were merely printed, in outline, then the colors were either blocked in or painted in by hand, with dye. Some colors could not be blocked successfully. These dyes were not permanent if washed. The Eastern method was first used by Oberkampf, in France, with one color only; i.e., the pattern was blocked out in matter to resist the dye, and when the fabric came out of the dye vat the background was colored, whereas the pattern remained white. Soon followed the reverse method—printing the blue on the white. Later the early forms and methods were modified, and the printing was done from copper-plate rollers, the pattern being all in one color on a plain ground. These were beautifully drawn, and their reproductions today are well known.

WHAT ARE THE DECORATIVE USES OF CHINTZ, HANDBLOCKED LINEN, CRETONNE, AND TOILE?

All these materials have wide ranges of use. All are excellent for curtains, bedspreads, dressing tables, screens, and pillows. The linens and toiles make excellent upholstery. The cretonnes and chintzes are better as slip covers, except on cushion-type seats. As tight upholstery they soil quickly.

Chintzes, as curtains, may be either lined or unlined. Often the sun through their colors is lovely, although for the more formal effects it is customary to line them. Linen must be lined owing to the breaking of the color over the rough texture of the linen as the light shines through it.

NEW PROCESSES

Although there has been no specific effort to stress the types of yarn or fibers in the foregoing chapters, it seems wise to make special

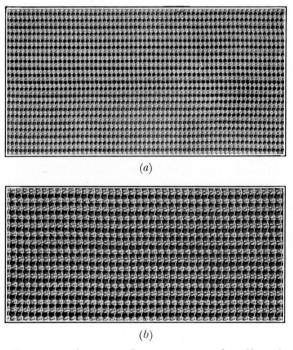

(a)

(b)

PLATE 18a, b. *Two marquisettes of the new process glass fiber—Coronized Fiberglas—showing close and open weaves for different types of work.* COURTESY THORTEL.

mention of two new ones that are making rapid strides in their development.

Glass appeared first as a material to be used in some of the thinner glass curtains. The earlier designs, although interesting and characterful, were rather limited in usefulness, because their texture seldom seemed quite right in combination with the traditional fabrics in most homes. In modern and high-style settings they worked well, and, in large scale settings, commercial, institutional, etc., they were admirable.

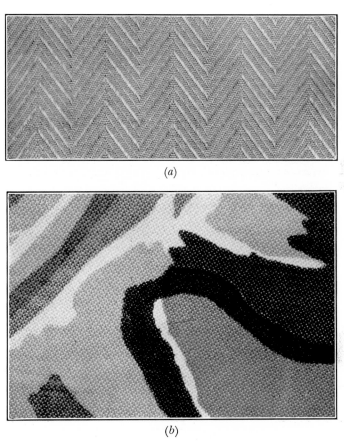

(a)

(b)

PLATE 19. *Two Coronized Fiberglas materials for overdraperies.* (a) *Twill and* (b) *printed material.* COURTESY THORTEL.

The earlier fabrics of glass that were printed for overdraperies had a rather uncomfortable sheen.

Now, however, a new process has been perfected which has made marked changes in the texture effect. The hard sheen and the stiffness have gone. These new products are known under their trade name, Coronized Fiberglas Fabrics, and are being recommended specifically for large scale, modern-type installations in offices, night clubs, hotels, etc. They have the marked advantage of being absolutely fireproof. A few of them are excellent for modern domestic settings, and undoubtedly there will be many more before long. Plates 18 and 19 show two marquisettes of different openness of weaves, a twill, and a piece of one of the highly styled designs for overdraperies. All

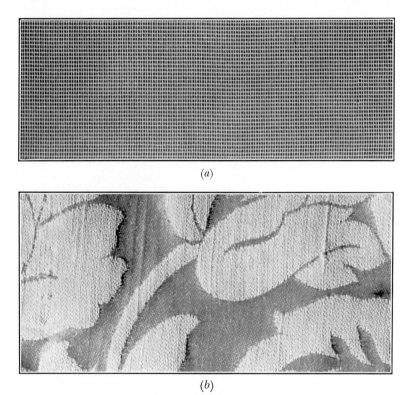

(a)

(b)

PLATE 20. *Two materials in nylon. (a) is a fine thin marquisette. (b) is a damask.* COURTESY J. H. THORP & CO.

the materials are exclusively curtain material and should never be used for upholstery.

Nylon, the second of these new materials, has come into the decorative field now in many forms. Like the glass material it is still in the early stages of its development, is still experimental, but it is progressing rapidly. It is being made in a great variety of forms from gauze and marquisette to damasks and frisé. (See Plate 20.) It is usable both for curtains and upholstery. Sufficient time has not elapsed to determine its wearing qualities. In appearance, its decorative quality varies. The thin materials, gauze and marquisette, have a fine, sheer quality with a very slight luster apparent. In damask, the luster is very evident and the surface lacks something that the older materials have. In modern settings where texture is emphasized it has great possibilities. When one considers the rapid developments made by rayon from its early days to the present, it is safe to predict confidently the future value of this other new fabric to the decorating field. In frisé, it is already more interesting than wool.

SECTION TWO

The Characteristic Expressions
of Historic Fabrics

Introduction

EVERY FABRIC USED IN INTERIOR DECORATION HAS ITS CHARACTERISTIC decorative expression, somewhat comparable to the individuality of people. Just as individuality is intangible and cannot be measured by height, weight, age, color of eyes, length of nose, or shape of jaw, but transcends all of these, so fabrics within their narrower range transcend the incidents of motif, leaf or flower, scale, and manner of repeat.

We may classify a brocade as belonging to the Louis XV period, recognizing it by its forms, scale, type of patterning, color, and, if we are textile experts, its weave. Decoratively, however, we still know little about it. Until we perceive, understand, and appreciate keenly this dominating, inclusive, over-all expression—which in the last analysis makes the fabric what it is—we are standing outside the door to its intelligent employment in the decorative field. The other contributing factors of aspect, taken alone, fail to explain what they are saying and why they have been used in given ways, though we do have to read them, too, to achieve this final expression.

A particular Louis XV brocade may look extremely well on a Louis XV chair of harmonizing shape and scale. Being "of the period," it automatically expresses a similar general character. Thus its use under these particular conditions is a simple matter of decision. But that brocade may have other possibilities. It may be very effective and satisfying on an English chair of the same or even a later period. It may be very nice on one of our upholstered chairs of the present day. Why? Because in addition to these lesser, obvious harmonies of shape and scale, the intangibles of expression—those general character qualities—have subtle underlying likenesses. These likenesses form a sound basis for employing the fabric as upholstery for these pieces of furniture so far afield from the original period types. They have some of the same harmonies, too.

If it were bound to the obvious academic employment of period fabrics with furniture of the same period, decoration today would lose much that is vital. It would become a matter of stale repetition and stereotyped mannerisms. But no creative designer in this field is ever bound by these decorative aspects that are limited by dates. Always he sees fabrics in terms of their inherent fundamental expressions and senses where these expressions coincide with others of whatever period.

Often, he will place together two items of widely varying source. This is an important phase of the decorator's creative work. Commonplace, stupid, and uninteresting results are usually due largely to blindness on this score. They may be "correct," but are they vital and rich in interest?

There is, of course, danger for those who merely seek to be "different"; lacking an educated viewpoint, talent, and native sensitiveness, such people blunder into bizarre effects. But these blunderers are not likely to be found among serious workers in the decorative field, who have been trained to perceive and understand these fundamental expressions; such workers know that these underlying expressions are basic to all fine work.

7

The Development of Silk Fabrics in Italy during the Early Renaissance

DECORATIVE FABRICS AS WE KNOW THEM TODAY HAD THEIR BEGINNINGS for the most part during the Renaissance in Italy. Historically, the steps in their development are a fascinating story. The details of that story belong to the historians. They would help us but little in our present narrower inquiry. Our only reason for going back to these periods is to have contact with the standards, the classics of design in the purity of their source expressions and thus be able better to measure our responses to the modern adaptations that are our everyday problems. Relatively few so-called period fabrics in the decorating market are exact copies of the older ones. There is no reason why they should be. There are many, however, that are classified as belonging to a certain period because their dominating expressions have their source there, even though several of their motifs have been drawn from other, later periods and combined with the earlier ones to make new designs. If we can read the expressions of the pure period types with sensitiveness and accuracy, we shall find little difficulty in applying the same skill to any adaptation or even to fabrics in our modern mode of design. Our perception has been trained to keenness by contact with the standards that have stood the test of generations. Furthermore, we have a fund of valuable information that can save us from making quite ridiculous mistakes.

HISTORY

Italy was the home of the beginnings of the story of modern fabrics. Its early fabric history may be divided roughly into three periods as follows:

Period 1.   Early—from approximately the middle of the eleventh century to the third quarter of the fifteenth century.

Period 2.   High—from the third quarter of the fifteenth century to the middle of the next century—about 1550.

Period 3.   Late—from about 1550 to approximately 1650—a period which includes the Baroque.

After this, the leadership passed from Italy, never to return. France was the immediate successor.

Divisions of this sort are always very arbitrary. The important thing for us as students to see is the sequences in the stages of development, regardless of where the dividing lines are drawn. The only reason for using these props is to assist us in isolating the dominant movement of the sequences.

PERIOD 1

The fabrics of Period 1 are of several well-marked types which are classified as follows for the sake of simplification.

1. The designs of the earliest fabrics are for the most part, crudely drawn human, bird, and animal figures in enclosing geometric forms. They show several influences—Byzantine, Persian, Turkish, East Saracenic, and West Saracenic, or Spanish. The designs are symmetrical—very often with figures placed right and left of a center—either facing each other or back to back. Plates 21, 22.

2. These earliest designs were soon accompanied and followed by another type, influenced by Chinese art, with both similar motifs and new ones—notably flowers—in symmetrical and asymmetrical balances without enclosing frames. Plates 23, 24.

3. These two types were accompanied and followed in turn by designs with feudal subject matter, castles and hunting scenes with animals. Some were in symmetrical balance—without an enclosing frame. Others were in free asymmetrical balance. Plate 25. Religious subjects also appeared at this time.

4. By the first part of the fifteenth century, these early forms, whose production had covered some 350 years, were showing marked improvement in several aspects: (1) in drawing; (2) in design—now essentially weaving designs; (3) in the general technique

of handling sizes, shapes, motions, etc. New motifs were appearing. The fully developed ogival forms as frames were replacing the other geometric frameworks. Free asymmetrical balances continued and showed interesting progress in more skillful handling of shapes, of placing, and of consistency in motion. The floral forms, especially the pomegranate, were in process of development as central interests within ogival frames, but they did not reach their full expression until the third quarter of the century, close to the borderline of the next period. Plates 26, 27, 28, 29, 30, 31.

HISTORICAL BACKGROUND OF EARLY PERIOD

The silk fabrics of Western Europe from which most of the later ones have developed from the sixteenth to the twentieth century were first produced in Sicily in the eleventh century. The fine silks produced in Spain, during the heyday of the early Moslem occupation in the eight, ninth, and tenth centuries may seem to be an exception. Their use, however, was confined at that period mostly to the territory where they were made. Little is known about them in detail. Commerce between the Moslem and the Christian countries was not encouraged. The Mediterranean was ruled by Moslem pirates. The Italian maritime city-states had not developed, and there were no trade routes such as were established later.

This early Moslem civilization in Spain centered in Cordova and brought to the Western Moslems in Spain the best of what the East had to offer in terms of knowledge, skills, and culture. But, elsewhere in Western Europe, the countries were in bad condition without commerce, industry, or culture. There were few trade routes and very little interchange of goods from country to country. There were no manufactured articles and no surpluses of agricultural products with which to trade. Europe was at its lowest ebb.

Thus this isolated Moslem center of production and prosperity in Spain had no influence on the major line of the development of the very early silk fabrics of Western Europe. That development began in Sicily. The Italian effort in Sicily, sponsored while the Normans were at the peak of their power there, later moved to the mainland of Italy, Lucca being the first city to develop it. Lucca was followed by others—Venice, Milan, Pisa, Sienna, and Bologna.

It should be remembered that Italians had been handling cloth, either weaving it or finishing it, for some time, in fact, ever since the early days of the rebuilding of commercial and industrial relations between countries. Much of the prosperity of the people, which provided the power to fight against the feudal overlords and gradually gain the freedom of their communities, had come from the cloth industries. But fine silk textiles were another story. Western Europe had known these only through imports—mostly from the East—with the exception of the Spanish products.

It was not until the eleventh century that Norman adventurers, returning from the Crusades, plundered and took the south of Italy, were recognized by the Pope, its feudal overlord, and were given feudal control over that district and Sicily. Just how much weaving was done during the early years of the Norman kingdom that resulted from this conquest of Southern Italy and Sicily is unknown; authorities disagree. The Norman kingdom, centering in Sicily, was for nearly 200 years, the richest and most enlightened of all the western Christian countries. In 1133, under Roger II, it is known that silk weaving was given great emphasis by the importation of Greek weavers. The industry remained in full swing until Sicily, always a political pawn, was given in 1260 to Charles of Anjou, brother of Louis IX of France, as part of the papal defence in the long struggle for power between popes and emperors.

The work on the mainland seems to have started at Lucca sometime in the twelfth century. Lucca was near the seaport Pisa, one of the three great maritime powers of Italy at this time. To further their trade, all the great maritime powers had established workshops in settlements in foreign ports. Venice traded mostly with the East; her settlements were in Thebes and Athens. Genoa traded mostly in the Western Mediterranean at first, later in the East as a rival of Venice. But Pisa, and Lucca through Pisa, traded mostly to the West, and the Lucchese workshops were in Akkon and Barcelona. Barcelona had become the great trading and shipping point of Spain. It was natural, therefore, that the Lucchese work should be inspired by the Spanish designs, just as those of Venice—and to some extent those of Genoa— were inspired by the Byzantines and, later, by the Chinese. The influence of the Chinese was intensified by the Mongolian conquest of the Near East by Genghis Khan, after which time Chinese products found easy entrance into Europe through Venice.

Plate 22   *109*

example, (1) there is an appreciable effort to make the birds the dominating, central interest with correspondingly less emphasis on the alternating figures within the framework. (2) There is some rather immature effort to adjust the bird shapes to the size and shape of the central field. This is shown primarily in the placing of the body and its angle, and the placing of the feet and their shaping. Although not entirely successful, it is an improvement over the majority of these early fabric designs with their loose decorative thinking and almost

PLATE 21. *Early textile showing Byzantine influence of enclosing geometric forms.* COURTESY METROPOLITAN MUSEUM OF ART.

complete disregard of spatial relations of size and shape. (3) There is obvious, intentional balancing of the light and the dark values to draw the attention to the central interest and hold it there, easily. The dark of the bird is silhouetted against light, thus giving it force and power. Conversely, the intermediate figure, although also dark against light, is cut into smaller parts which exert less pull upon the attention than the more boldly silhouetted bird. Furthermore, the size relations are sufficiently well handled to establish a fairly reasonable motion relation between the bird and the secondary figures. If the secondary figures were larger, they would throw the bird into such marked relief that the existing balance, even with the aid of the well-handled subdued tones of the frame design, would be upset.

PLATE 22

This design, thoroughly characteristic of this early growing period, indicates an attempt at greater freedom than that seen in the older roundels and other geometric enclosures—but with not very successful results. A good deal of decorative ingenuity is displayed in the details

PLATE 22. *Early textile, twelfth century, Sicily, showing Persian characteristics in the placing of the birds.* COURTESY METROPOLITAN MUSEUM OF ART.

of the filling forms between the birds and animals as well as in the way in which sub-divisions of areas are handled on the wings and tails of the birds. New decorative conventionalizations are beginning—but they are very crude. There still is almost no understanding of the

Plate 23   *111*

spatial relations. Motifs are crowded together haphazardly. It should be noted, however, that the drawing of some of the smaller details shows a good deal of movement and freedom.

PLATE 23

In some respects, this design shows quite astonishing skill. In others, it shows how far the designers still were from understanding

PLATE 23. *An early fourteenth century pattern showing vigorous rhythms.* COURTESY METROPOLITAN MUSEUM OF ART.

the value of space against space and the elimination of non-contributing detail.

The movement of the principal birds is finely considered. There even is evidence of subtlety in the rhythms of wings and tails, in the sweep of the curves that climax at the turned heads. There are freedom, interest, skill in drawing, and much ingenuity in the secondary portions of the design. But to get these two portions of the design working together in perfect harmony still was beyond the ability of the designer. The gay sweep of the bird movement dominates, but the spotting—the sizing and placing—of the intermediate figures still tells of clumsiness and immaturity of decorative thinking.

PLATE 24

This design shows the same qualities although with very different motifs. It has none of the gay lightness of motion of the preceding

PLATE 24. *Venetian, first half of the fifteenth century.* COURTESY METROPOLITAN MUSEUM OF ART.

fabric (23) although there is plenty of action. The contradiction of emphasis between the boat and the intermediate figures blocks the unity. And, of course, there is absolutely no conception of scale—considered either from the standpoint of actual appearance or decorative

Plate 25   *113*

use. However, those big figures are superbly drawn. So also are some of the smaller ones. Compared with the stodgy setness of the figures in Plate 21, a great advance is in evidence.

PLATE 25

This typical "castle" design reverts to symmetry and, although the handling of the new motifs is far from being mastered, it should

PLATE 25. *An early fourteenth century pattern showing characteristic feudal motifs.* COURTESY METROPOLITAN MUSEUM OF ART.

be noted that there is evidence of a keener sense of balance in space than has been apparent before. It shows in the size and placing of the castle and moat areas. And the subordinate details, although still crowding the space, are beginning to be reduced a little in emphasis.

It still is untamed decorative ingenuity. But like the designs of Plates 23 and 24, there is a new vitality, new vigor—something worth taming and using. It is these qualities that led to great things later.

PLATE 26

The fabric shown in Plate 26 is a direct forerunner of the great designs that came out of Florence in the middle and last of the fifteenth

century. Much learning through making and correcting mistakes had preceded this definitely decorative product. Although the spacing and the sizing of the parts still lacks the masterly handling that was to come a little later, there is vast improvement over all the preceding work. There is an entirely new grasp of pure decorative quality. This should not be attributed to the new use of the ogival form, to the consolidation of the smaller field detail within its confines, nor to the use of the pomegranate within its concentric enclosures. The reason goes deeper than any of these. The design shows, in the more ordered thinking, the control that no longer allowed ingenuity and fertility of invention to run wild but had reached the point of making careful selection for greater power in over-all expression. And the result is correspondingly much more satisfactory.

PLATE 26. *A design of the early ogival type.* COURTESY METROPOLITAN MUSEUM OF ART.

The contradictions that exist here in terms of still unmastered space and size relations do not detract from the peaceful aspect of the design as a whole and its unity. This is an example of clear decorative thinking, as far as it goes. The next 50 to 75 years saw these elements adjusted so perfectly to each other and drawn with such skill that they became some of the classics of the world of fabric design.

Plate 27 115

PLATE 27. *A handsome fifteenth century Venetian velvet.* COURTESY METRO-
POLITAN MUSEUM OF ART.

PLATE 27

The fabric shown in Plate 27 marks a further advance over the decorative quality of the fabric shown in Plate 26, because, at last, the spatial relations are beginning to take on their rightful emphasis. They are not perfect yet; the central figure is too small and cramped, the cusped figure enclosing it is too smug and tight, and the intermediate figures in the field spaces outside the ogival framework are still too important both for the size of the frame and for the central motif. The detail of the frame also is too closely matted. Note, incidentally, the rather timid use of the acanthus. Yet, compared with the fabric of Plate 26, this is a masterly production, bold, vigorous, full of interest, skillfully drawn, and thoroughly impressive in its decorative quality.

It has great dignity. In fact, it is rather somber and definitely massive and heavy. It is much more than an accumulation of ingenious motifs. There is present now a well-knit unit, a dominating and powerful over-all expression of decorative character—an intangible quality that makes the fabric what it is. This is the quality for which we search when considering its use in combination with other designs.

PLATE 28

This fabric shows an effect similar to Plate 27, although the motifs are repeated alternately and only on one side of the ogival framework—thus giving the continuous S form. Patterns of this and the preceding type are always very large in scale. They are really "large-scale design thinking" and would be ridiculous if made very small. This fact alone is clear indication of the advance made in decorative thinking.

There is another interesting note in connection with this fabric. It has a richness of aspect that is lacking in the fabric of Plate 27. Plate 27 has great dignity; there is some richness in its texture (velvet) but, on the whole, in its over-all expression, it is rather simply severe. In Plate 28, however, there is a quality that, in the hands of a less honest, less skillful designer, could be called ornate. Every part is filled with fascinating variation. Yet the fertility of invention never gets out of hand. The design is all finely ordered, skillfully balanced, and it maintains the clear and dominant expression of strength, vitality,

Plate 28 117

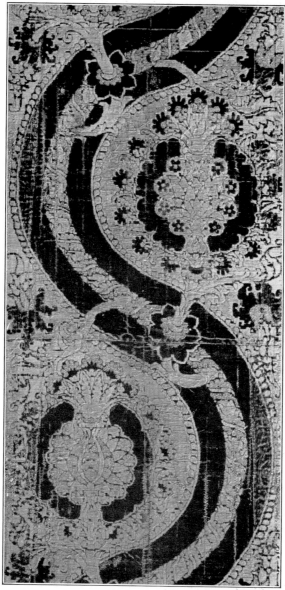

PLATE 28. *A distinguished design of the last half of the fifteenth century.* COURTESY METROPOLITAN MUSEUM OF ART.

vigor, that has now become the hallmark of the Italian genius for design. But it also has ease. It is a masterly design unit, handsome in the balance of its emphasis and spaces. Note how perfectly the placing of the shapes and of the darks—and their sizing—all concentrate the attention on the central motif, the artichoke, while the broad S band weaves its way up and down without becoming over-emphatic or oppressive at any point. Its perfect balance and the adroit handling of the other spots and areas keep its importance in proper check.

This careful, skillfully handled richness brings a new element into the story of the development of characteristic expression and shows clearly that we cannot base our "use" judgments solely on period dates. These two fabrics would serve widely divergent purposes because of their divergent over-all expression, even though they had appeared on the market the selfsame day.

PLATE 29

The fabric shown in Plate 29 belongs to the same general group as the two preceding ones though it is much simpler. Underlying its ordered planning is about the same degree of decorative skill and understanding. It is somewhat nearer to Plate 27 than to Plate 28 in its not quite mastered sizes, in its shape contours, and the feeble, rather tentative handling of the fine connecting lines. One should remember that these fine lines show the background of the velvet; the dark areas are the pile. Maintaining wholly fluid, vigorous curves in fabric woven under these conditions requires much more than skill in drawing.

There are many such designs—some more ornate, some less so. Many are much cruder in execution than this one, some much less so. But, taken as a group, they are pleasant decorative units, dignified without the excessive, massive heaviness of the fabrics of Plates 27 and 28. They are usually very beautiful in color.

PLATE 30

Plate 30 is one of the small-figured velvets that came into common use in the fifteenth century and were based on the long-used free asymmetrical balance. The handling of the motion shows marked increase of skill over the earlier ones. The balancing of parts, however,

Plate 29   *119*

PLATE 29. *A much-used velvet design of the fifteenth century.* COURTESY METRO-
POLITAN MUSEUM OF ART.

still has been no better mastered than in the large-figured fabric of Plate 27. Some of the small-figured velvets of this period show much greater advance in this respect than the one given here.

It should be carefully noted, that, although this is a small-scale pattern, it is not a light and delicate one. In its small way, it is as vigorous and forceful as were all the larger-scale fabrics. It belongs with them; its over-all expression is exactly like theirs. There is noth-

PLATE 30. *A small but forceful design. Velvet, fifteenth century.* COURTESY METROPOLITAN MUSEUM OF ART.

ing light, delicate, nor suave about it. It belongs in rooms that are as forceful, forthright, and heavy as itself, even though the design, measured in inches, is so small.

PLATE 31

The fabric shown in Plate 31 is an excellent example of the finest work of the period, the fruition of the trials and experiments that had preceded it in the earlier part of this Period I. It stands at the borderline of the next period—a striking example of perfect weaving design of its type. Careful analysis shows how the designer finally mastered the problem. Note, for example, the following points:

1. The elimination of all unnecessary parts so that every bit of the final design is essential for its complete expression.
2. The well-adjusted movement of every part, giving proper emphasis to the central motifs and carrying the attention easily over the field.

Plate 31   *121*

PLATE 31. *A beautiful example of the ogival pattern at its best.* COURTESY METRO-
POLITAN MUSEUM OF ART.

3. The delightful use of light and dark with carefully modulated emphasis at the proper places to re-express the unity of the form design.
4. The skillful gradation of the sizes of the parts which harmonizes the over-all movement of its forms.
5. The well-considered drawing, so perfectly handled to achieve decorative unity and interest that we are scarcely conscious of it.

The over-all expression of this fabric illustrates clearly all that is best in Italian Renaissance design of this period. It is dignified and bold, vibrant with vigor and vitality, fluid, and graceful, the very essence of Italian Renaissance design. These are the characteristic dominating qualities that mark all the early Renaissance design—which must be considered carefully wherever these designs are used.

8

Silk Fabrics in Italy during the High and Late Renaissance

PERIOD 2   HIGH RENAISSANCE   1492–c. 1550

It was during this period that Italy fell under the heels of new invaders in the three-cornered struggle for power by France, England, and the Empire—specifically Germany including Austria and, later, Spain. The Empire had already reached out her tentacles under Ferdinand, so that, when Charles I (of Spain, who was Charles V of Germany) took the reins as Emperor, his regime was but a continuation of what had preceded. This period saw also the short-lived return to power of Tuscany under the newly created Grand Duke, Cosimo I, a Medici of the lesser branch. It saw, too, the palm of achievement in the arts pass from Florence to Rome and thence, toward the end of the time, to Venice.

The effect on fabrics was twofold. Industry and commerce lagged during the worst of the fighting but later came back to full vigor. As they revived, fabric production was renewed and extended. The patterns showed both greater freedom and versatility than hitherto. They were very luxurious. However, they lacked something that had been present in the earlier, more austere productions. The close, clear thinking, the intensely serious and honest thought that had produced the type of design shown in Plate 31 was no longer present. In its place appeared facility and technical skill, leading by gradual stages to very ornate, though well-executed, patterns. Too many, however, were weak in design and over-all character expression. The spirit had gone from the product. Only ingenuity and skill in manipulation—both in design and production—remained. By the end of this period, the finest quality of the Renaissance had passed as far as fabrics were concerned.

Patterns showed marked variations from the earlier types. The major changes were as follows:

1. The classic motifs were used in much greater number and with more freedom than previously—until they were discarded in favor of newer styles.
2. Vases appeared in common use. Sometimes they were filled with highly conventionalized flowers, sometimes not. Both gadrooning and masques were used as part of the vase ornament.
3. The pomegranate with its cusped enclosure gradually disappeared, although the ogival framework remained. Sometimes the framework was in band form; sometimes leaves and flowers were used in rather free fashion to maintain its semblance; sometimes it was merely suggested in the general movement instead of being drawn in detail—thus retaining the ogival as the basis of the mechanical repeat without its former definition of contour.
4. Leaves and flowers appeared in innumerable forms, both large and small. The large ones, especially in the velvets, were flowing, ornate patterns, symmetrical for the most part. The smaller ones were mostly all-over patterns based on the earlier lively rhythmic effects. Both types became increasingly naturalistic in aspect. These are the types that set the standards during the last part of the period and that were copied later by other countries, especially France.

HISTORICAL BACKGROUND

After the death of Lorenzo the Magnificent in Florence (1492), during the rule of his son, Pietro, the French started the invasions that were to completely demoralize Italy for years to come. Not only Florence, but most of the rest of Italy during this period changed radically. One invasion followed another; Germans under the Emperor Charles V (Charles I of Spain) followed the French. For a short time, Rome held its own, only to fall and be disastrously sacked at the end, owing largely to the duplicity and avarice of Pope Clement VII who finally so exasperated the Emperor that he allowed its destruction (1527). The majority of the prosperous, thriving, independent city-states became subject either to France or to Charles, as German

Emperor and King of Spain. The rulers assigned to Florence after the death of Pietro were hopelessly decadent, unbelievably corrupt even for a corrupt age. Until the advent of Cosimo I in Florence, conditions there were chaotic. After early grasping of power by ruthless means, Cosimo, however, proved to be a capable ruler, and, as a result, Tuscany later took a leading place in an Italy still for the most part under the domination of foreigners. Charles held Lombardy for Germany and Spain. The north of Italy was again a devastated waste. He also held Naples and the Sicilies—the south of Italy. The Papal States stood by themselves. Venice managed to hold her own and made steady progress. Genoa, Lucca, and a few small states were still held by great families. It was no longer the glorious Italy of the fifteenth century.

The prosperity that came to Florence and Tuscany through the work of Cosimo was a superficial brilliance, even though it marked the peak of their greatest wealth and material power. The prosperity was no longer the result of the vital power that came from the many as during the fifteenth century. Nor was the patronage of the arts of the sincere type evidenced from the earlier Medicis through Lorenzo the Magnificent. It was already decadent because it was rotten at the core.

Fabric development, in terms of decorative quality, followed the trends of the major arts—architecture, sculpture, and painting. It was at its best when these were at their best. Their formative period had been during the earlier years of the fifteenth century when the classics and classical sculpture and architecture were being discovered and cherished. Men's efforts were bent on a new goal of expression that challenged all their best endeavors. Improvement piled upon improvement. Every opportunity was given for steady growth as both political and religious leaders employed these talents to the full. Until the beginning of the invasions, there had been—relatively speaking—peace and prosperity. Leader had vied with leader, popes with nobles, to achieve fame through patronage of the arts.

But by the end of the invasion period, the greatest architects, sculptors, and painters had died. There were a few notable exceptions. Following them, came a long line of men who tried to work in the grand manner but who produced only the shell. They had little to say. It was natural, therefore, that the vehicle itself, the shell, began to assume undue importance. In architecture, for example, the shell became exaggerated, in many cases extreme. Proportions lost their finesse; ornament became overdone and meaningless as structural enhancement. The effects produced tended to the bombastic. Before the end of the century—the sixteenth—the Baroque, the bizarre, was in full swing. This is what was happening in most sections of Italy. In terms of its own technique, each of the arts was passing through the same changes.

But the Baroque had not reached Venice as yet. Venice had not figured largely in the earlier Renaissance, owing primarily to commercial connections and difficulties. Her hitherto exceedingly prosperous trade with the East began to dry up because of the Turkish successes and their conquest of Constantinople (1453). However, during the quarrels of the fifteenth and sixteenth centuries in the rest of Italy, while the land was being overrun and devastated by the invaders, she managed to remain independent, avoiding the destruction that befell other powers. She had also avoided the disturbances of warring factions within her own borders. She had been continuously well, if sternly, governed. Prosperous merchant princes had built their great palaces in relative security compared with its lack in other city-states. She had turned from the East and developed her commerce and industry in other directions. It took time, but, when, at the turn of the century, the rest of Italy was prone at the feet of the foreign powers in their territory, and their arts were on the downgrade, Venice came into her own, especially in painting. Her architectural style— her earlier work had savored of both the Gothic and the Byzantine— showed signs of the approaching Baroque rather quickly. But in painting, she came forward with great men—Giorgione, Titian, Tintoretto, Veronese. They were working when the great men of Florence had for the most part passed.

This High Renaissance outburst in Venice was thus unlike what had preceded it in other sections of Italy. It was based only in part on the sequential progress shown elsewhere. In Florence, which had set the lead, hitherto, classic art and ornament had been used in native, original interpretations at first. The buildings were heavy and massive. A later stage, typified by the works of Bramante, after nearly a century of study of classic models, marked the beginning of the "correct" use of these motifs—along with notable changes in the shapes and proportions of the building themselves that were based, in a measure, on the old Roman models. It should be remembered that the Roman remains used as models were themselves but interpretations of the work of another race—the Greeks—and often fell far short of the beauty of the originals. Later, in Italy, this "correctness" became almost a fetish. Bramante and some others of his period, Raphael and Peruzzi, for example, were great men and could use these Roman motifs with great skill and effectiveness in results that were neither Greek nor Roman, but Italian. In the hands of lesser men, however, results were dry and stereotyped. They lacked the largeness of creative thought and expression for which earlier years had laid the foundation. It was natural that there should be a revolt against this dryness. Michael Angelo, too, was working at the time of Bramante. Sculptor, painter, architect—he defied the conventions that were closing in on the arts and gave the world new heroic expression—as in the ceiling of the Vatican and the great figures on the Medici tombs at San Lorenzo. But he, too, was a genius. When lesser men tried to follow him, they produced large empty curves and shapes, which, though monstrous, were weak and vacuous. In a narrower sphere of decorations, fabrics changed similarly. The vitality and vigor that had produced patterns such as those of Plates 31 and 32 slowly seeped away. The incentives for that type of achievement had gone. It was natural that Venice, coming into her own so much later, should have avoided much of this empty exaggeration and become a leader in her own right, with a type of expression that was lavishly rich, but still had a vitality that was to last for a long time, until it, too, fell entirely under the Baroque influences.

Fabrics and furniture did not follow these lines of development simultaneously. At the end of the period we are discussing in fabric development, furniture was at its peak in the quality of its design. Fabrics, however, had already begun to show the decadent influence of the Baroque.

In furniture, classic motifs had begun to be used "as such" in the fourth quarter of the fifteenth century. Where they had appeared before there had been a freedom comparable to that shown in their use in the other arts—as far as one can judge from the meager sources that remain to us. Chests, for example, by the turn of the century, were definitely inspired by classic study. They had not become the finely coordinated pieces of design that were achieved 30 to 40 years later. There was a rather naive clumsiness about their proportions and about the placing and use of the ornament. The degree of skill displayed was vaguely comparable to that shown in the architectural field some 50 years earlier. But the results were honest, straight-forward, serious, and dignified design. Later, in the early half of the sixteenth century, these proportions and degrees of emphasis in the use of ornamental accent were mastered; and between 1540 and 1550 or thereabouts, furniture design marked its height in finesse and sin-cerity. The development of fine design in furniture was much slower than in the greater arts; much slower, too, in accepting the general creative trends than the fabric designs. But soon the baleful influence of empty exaggeration struck, and in only a few years the proportions lost their fitness and firmness, shapes became exaggerated, and orna-ment was not only excessive but also badly placed.

In connection with this variation in time of development of furniture and fabrics, it may be well to recall the fact that in Italy fabrics and furniture were not associated as we luxury-loving moderns associate them. Even the finest fifteenth-century palaces were bare of the luxuries that we consider essential. Few fabrics were used on furniture except beds and for accessories such as pillows. They were used rather as hangings. Italy did not begin to manufacture her own tapestries until the time of Cosimo I. Fine silks were also used as costume fabrics, of course, and some of the changes in the character of patterns and scale were due to sharp changes in costume styles. Chairs were of wood; benches were of wood; the ancestor of our sofas, the casapanca, was of wood. A few chairs had a back strip of material, sometimes fabric, sometimes leather, with a loose cushion on the seat. But in these early years, upholstery as we think of it was nonexistent. The huge upholstered chairs popularly considered Italian Renaissance chairs belong to the next century—the seventeenth—and were Baroque. Upholstery in Italy belongs mostly to the decadent periods.

ANALYSIS OF THE DESIGN DEVELOPMENT

PLATE 32

The velvet shown in Plate 32 is a fine example of the High Period before there were any indications of weakness. It illustrates the full vigor and power both of the drawing and the design of the period. It is Italian Renaissance fabric patterning at its best.

Note the power of those classic inspired scrolls, their perfect pro-portioning, the fine balances of the spaces and of figures against the

Plate 32

129

PLATE 32. *Velvet band. Italian, showing vigorous use of classical motifs.* COURTESY METROPOLITAN MUSEUM OF ART.

background, and the unerring flow of the movement. This is masterly design with much greater freedom and more varied skill than we saw in the earlier handsome velvet of Plate 31.

PLATE 33

In Plate 33 we have a finely drawn, beautifully designed example. It is much lighter than most of the Italian patterns and is very lovely. Of its type, it, too, belongs to the peak of the Renaissance.

PLATE 33. *An interesting design showing how the vigor of the period was expressed even when the parts were small and thin as compared with the types previously shown.* COURTESY METROPOLITAN MUSEUM OF ART.

Plate 34 131

PLATE 34

As we compare Plate 34 with the two preceding fabrics, it is easy to see how decadent thinking began to creep in. In many respects the design is good, and it illustrates clearly the new use of conventionalized

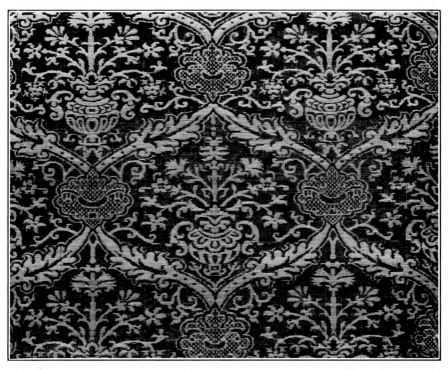

PLATE 34. *The design shows clearly the beginning of the weaker drawing that characterized much of the work at the turn of the century and later.* COURTESY METROPOLITAN MUSEUM OF ART.

flowers and the vase form, along with the changing aspect of the enclosing ogival. The forms are well distributed; they could have been produced only by skillful and experienced designers. There is an easy grace about the spotting of the flowers and the handling of their stems that is pleasant.

But there is also an awkward flattening of the big curves of the ogival frame. And, if we wish to be very critical, we could say that even the flower stems show some of this awkwardness, though the flattening is not nearly so pronounced as it is in the enclosing ogivals,

PLATE 35a, b, c, d. *All these four patterns show the same deterioration evidenced in the pattern on the preceding plate.* COURTESY METROPOLITAN MUSEUM OF ART.

which unquestionably border on being flabby. A good free curve springs from a starting place, and its motion ends in a climax. These curves merely travel lazily from place to place. The spirit has gone that made those earlier strong, vigorous designs.

PLATES 35A, B, C, D

All these designs of Plates *35a, b, c,* and *d* belong in the same group as Plate 34. All have interest and show skill, yet the parts have weaknesses. Curves flatten, and details are carelessly placed; they are far from the vigor of the fabrics of Plates 31 and 32.

PERIOD 3   LATE RENAISSANCE   1550–c. 1600

The fine textiles of the Late Renaissance are a little confusing unless we hold firmly to decorative standards, refusing to be swayed by show, by ornateness, and by technical skill. Many exquisite fabrics were being produced—richer and more luxurious in many instances than those we have been discussing. Their production was still one of the main sources of the prosperity of some of the Italian states. But, as noted in the preceding paragraphs, elements of decay were at work. They grew increasingly active and eventually caused the end of the leadership of Italy in the design of fine silks.

During this period, motifs and pattern types changed markedly.

1. The pomegranate and its drawn or indicated ogival disappeared.
2. The use of classical ornament was rare, i.e., in its previous forms.
3. The vase form continued.
4. Flower forms were more often naturalistic rather than conventionalized. Some of them began to show modeling—the appearance of the third dimension or roundness.
5. The crown, specifically the ducal crown with the fleur-de-lis at the front, appeared—not only in Florence but in other centers as well.
6. Small patterns of marked rhythmic character continued to be used, but the motifs showed more naturalism than before.
7. The large flowing patterns typified by the Geneose and Venetian velvets appeared, definitely floral and unlike the earlier designs.

Such were the characteristic Baroque fabric patterns whose influence on the developing industry in other countries was widespread.

HISTORICAL BACKGROUND

In 1569, peace was signed between France, England, and Spain, and Italy was quiet for the next half-century. Spain still held the North and the South. Tuscany held the center, under Cosimo I, until his death in 1574. He left Tuscany more prosperous and in better condition than it had ever been. Venice had stayed independent and was both wealthy and powerful. The Church still held the Papal States and ruled them as a lay sovereign. France gave up Savoy, which became an important independent buffer state between France and Italy.

The struggle between the Catholics and the Protestants waged hot. The popes instituted the inquisition in their search for heretics. For a time, Rome was again the center of great activity and power. France was torn with the same struggle while Catherine de Medici held power and did not begin its long journey upward until Henry IV ascended the throne, re-united the nation, and put her well on the road to recovery before his assassination. Spain was ruled after 1555 by Philip II, son of the great Charles V, and saw its heyday of glory and success. In England, Elizabeth came to the throne and re-established its unity upon solid foundations.

But the next 50 years saw great changes. All Philip's successors were weaklings, and the Spanish power diminished rapidly. Many of her possessions passed to Austria, that is, to the powerful Hapsburgs. Both England and France continued to grow, vigorously and healthfully. But Italy continued on the downgrade. The successors of Cosimo were weaklings, too, for the most part, and, although there was a show of magnificence, it had little structure to sustain it. Gradually Italy became the tourist Mecca of the time—the show place of the world. The majority of its states were under the Hapsburg power. The old spirit of fervent endeavor had entirely departed. Artistically, too, the Baroque had passed its best days. Yet these were the days during which the products that inspired the workers in France, who under Louis XIV helped to make that country the style center of the world, appeared. They were, however, only the starting point for the French creative genius.

Plate 36 135

PLATE 36. *Characteristic use of the ducal crown and of natural forms.* COURTESY
METROPOLITAN MUSEUM OF ART.

ANALYSIS OF THE DESIGN DEVELOPMENT

PLATE 36

The fabric of Plate 36 shows clearly the typical changes in motifs and the weakening power in both drawing and design. The curves are definitely flabby. Yet the aspect as a whole is not bad.

PLATE 37

Plate 37 shows a very lovely small pattern in which the reverse movements are handled most successfully.

PLATE 37. *A small-figured velvet with movement skillfully handled.* COURTESY METROPOLITAN MUSEUM OF ART.

PLATE 38

Plate 38 is a typical Baroque pattern. With all its luxurious movement, it leaves us with the feeling that "someone has been saying too much"; it is tiring in its lack of restraint.

Plate 38   *137*

PLATE 38. *One of the flowing patterns of the period of the Genoese and Venetian Baroque type, seventeenth century.* COURTESY METROPOLITAN MUSEUM OF ART.

9

Silk Fabrics of the French, English, and Spanish Renaissance

FRENCH

During the early period of fabric development in Italy, specifically during the fifteenth century, France presented a rather sad picture. For a hundred years, she had been the battleground whereon were settled the rival claims to her lands of the English and the French monarchs. Not until 1453 were the English finally driven out—except from Calais and two small villages—leaving the land badly devastated, its commerce and industry broken. Her people still were thinking in terms of the Middle Ages. Feudal conditions to a large extent still prevailed. Living conditions were very crude. Castles were bleak fortresses. There were few luxuries anywhere and these were, for the most part, imported. Fine silks were among these imports.

The buildings were still Gothic, for example, the lovely Palais de Justice in Rouen, which was built in that century. The sculpture still followed the traditions of the Middle Ages as did painting—what there was of it.

It was Louis XI, son of the Charles whose way to success—and his crown—had been opened by Jeanne d'Arc, who drew France together again as a stable unit and laid the foundations of the French prosperity and leadership that were to persist until the Revolution some 300 years later. Louis (1461–1483) broke the power of the great feudal lords and centralized the government. France became a nation. He encouraged both industry and commerce with marked success.

It was Louis who started the move toward the future great silk industry of France. Fine imported silks had been entering France through the marketing center, Lyons. Louis, wishing to keep the money spent for them within France, tried to have the same type of weaving done there in Lyons. Italian weavers were brought in to do the work. But the merchants made it so uncomfortable for them that for the most part they went back to Italy. Lyons was the home of merchants not of producers, and at this time the merchants were in no mood to change their already successful modes of living and making money.

The few Italian weavers who remained were moved to Tours. There were too few of them to make much headway in this particular field. Nevertheless, Tours became a silk center producing the simpler types of silk fabrics—not the elaborate damasks, brocades, brocatelles, and velvets of Italy.

The weaving of silk was being done in one other place in France, but the contacts with the remainder of France were too slight for the industry to have much influence. When the French popes made Avignon their center, weavers were needed to provide the rich materials demanded by church and clergy. Accordingly, weavers were brought from Italy and did a thriving business within that territory. But Avignon was not France; it was an isolated religious center that had been bought outright by the Pope.

Some of these weavers did remain in Avignon after the final settlement of the rival claims and the return of the Pope to Rome. Eventually, under Henry II (1547–1559), about a hundred years later, they were given a charter, and their work spread along with the work that by this time had been started in other centers. But in the early days, the weaving that was being done in France, considered as a national industry, with the exception of Tours, was not of silk.

However, new ideas were on the way. Louis left the country in excellent condition and with a full treasury. Both these conditions were incentives—in those days—to look abroad for new conquests. The three monarchs who followed him cast longing eyes on Italy and with little valid excuse invaded her. The invasions were without permanent territorial results for France. But they did bring marked changes of thought to the thousands of Frenchmen who came in contact with all fields of Italian art, then at its height. Renaissance motifs began to appear in the new French buildings, though the structures were still medieval. By the time of the third of these monarchs, Francis I (1515–1547), the structures themselves were showing the Renaissance influence. So, too, did the sculpture and, to a very limited extent, the painting.

In the field of fabrics, until the time of Francis fine decorative silks were still imports from Italy. Then, the merchants of Lyons made a right-about face. They had been letting their own weavers practice in making these silks, but progress had been too slow. Now they wanted permission to import weavers from Italy both to produce and to teach their own French weavers. This proved to be the real beginning of fine silk weaving in France.

Francis was followed by his son, Henry II, who reigned until 1559. The religious wars of Catholics versus Protestants upset the country again after the death of Francis. They began in 1562 and continued until the end of the century. Conditions were again chaotic. Prosperity was not restored until the reign of Henry IV (1589–1610). Commerce and industry then received wise encouragement and aid. Silk weaving was started in various centers, although Lyons kept its lead.

It is not surprising, considering the manner in which this type of weaving (fine silks) was started in France, to find that the designs were Italian, produced either by Italians working in France or copied by less skillful Frenchmen. For this reason the earlier French Renaissance fabrics are scarcely distinguishable from the Italian fabrics of the same period. What has already been said about the Italian patterns applies to French designs of this period.

The Italian influence persisted until well into the seventeenth century. Typically native French silk designs began to emerge in the early part of that century. But it was not until the first part of the reign of Louis XIV (1643–1715) that they grew to full stature. By that time, Italy had run its course and was rapidly going downgrade. French products were setting the styles for all the world. What Versailles did, the world did, too. Louis' reign was a long one. It was only to be expected that, by its end, forms and patterns would again begin to show sharp changes completely apart from all the Renaissance influence. French Baroque was on its way out—the last of the French Renaissance. The new types were forerunners of the designs that were to prevail in the early eighteenth century.

Although France did not develop her decorative woven silks until late, she had earlier done some beautiful work in an allied field—embroidery. These were distinctly French in feeling and over-all expression. They show clearly the basic qualities that have always marked French design—and still do. There is an exquisite justness of proportion, a restraint, finesse, and a quick pointing up of accent peculiar to French work.

Plate 39 141

PLATE 39

No one could mistake the early Renaissance embroidery of Plate 39 for anything but French. It is bold, as all Renaissance design was bold. But in the elegance of the shaping of the curves, in the restrained, almost piquant handling of the little tendrils, there is something distinctly French. Compared with Plate 32, this French embroidery shows much reserve, whereas the Italian fabric has a robust enthusiasm spread throughout its length.

PLATE 39. *A fine example of French Renaissance embroidery.* COURTESY METROPOLITAN MUSEUM OF ART.

In this comparison, we see an illustration of what was meant in the foreword to Section Two by the word intangibles. Here are two fine expressions, one French, one Italian. They make use of somewhat similar forms. Yet they are very different in expression. Both are bold; both are sufficiently massive and dignified to be limited to furnishings of like character. As far as their expression is similar, both belong to the over-all expression character common to all Renaissance products. But there is, too, a difference based on countries, on people, and their ways of thinking. The quality of this aspect at times is the determining factor in deciding whether a particular fabric is usable on a given piece of furniture, i.e., usable with wholly satisfactory results. We shall see more clearly later why these aspects are so important.

ENGLISH

While France was being put on the road to recovery by Louis XI, England was in the throes of civil war, the Wars of the Roses. Only after the civil war ceased with the accession of Henry VII to the throne, did peace reign and the foundations were laid for later growth and prosperity. It is an interesting fact that the change was based partly upon the skill of the English weavers and the production of fine wool. But the Court and the gentry still had to buy their fine silks from Italy, Spain, and the East—and later from France. The English weavers could not make the rich damasks, brocades, brocatelles, and velvets. The weaving of these fine silks was not accomplished until 200 years later, and then only in limited form. When Louis XIV repudiated in France the supposedly irrevocable Edict of Nantes that, from the time of Henry IV, had given immunity to the Protestants of France, thousands of these Protestants fled from their homeland. Many were skilled weavers, the best in France. Of these, a goodly number found their way to England where the sovereigns, William and Mary, set them to work at Mortlake. England thus began the production of fine silks. With the establishment of the looms at Mortlake, England began to build this production into an industry, though slowly. The output did not equal the demand, and she still imported extensively for many years, notwithstanding the efforts of the textile workers to have the competition stopped. Earlier, under Edward III and Henry VII, a few weavers had been imported. But the production had never equaled the demand, nor had the product been on a par with the quality of the imports.

Renaissance art forms had come slowly to England, too. Not until the death of Henry VII, when an Italian workman was brought to England to design his tomb, did they get a foothold. But from that time on, details of Renaissance work began to be mixed with the earlier forms and finally resulted in a complete change of the forms themselves. But England was nearly 100 years later than France in really accepting Renaissance forms.

Thus, for all the Renaissance years in England, we again have the story of Italian influence—coming either directly from or by way of France or Spain. The great expense of imported silks during all

these early years had stimulated handicraft among English gentle-
women, with the result that English embroideries had become famous.
As in the discussion of French work, it seems worth while to turn for
a moment from woven fabrics and ascertain what the English were
saying in their famous embroideries and what the dominating characteristics were.

PLATE 40.   *Bedspread design.   English crewel work, late seventeenth century.*
COURTESY METROPOLITAN MUSEUM OF ART.

PLATE 40

The example shown in Plate 40 is crewel work of the late seventeenth century; it illustrates vividly the thoroughly English qualities of expression. It has none of the suave formality shown in Plate 39. It is free, full of life, thoroughly vigorous—almost untamed, decoratively speaking. Yet it shows remarkable skill in the apparently very casual placing of spots and lines so that the word "crude" has no place in analysis of it. The parts of the design go where they will, but they get there with a good deal of distinction—in fact the result is really handsome. This type of design was inspired by the Indian designs that had been coming into England for some time before the crewel work reached its height.

SPANISH RENAISSANCE

Although many fine fabrics were produced in Spain during the height of the Renaissance, they were for the most part the result of Italian influence and often cannot be distinguished from the Italian fabrics. The Christian Spaniards were not craftsmen. They owed all their success in these fields to the Moslem workers who remained in the country after the Moslem rule ended and who worked, first under the name of Mudéjars later under the name of Moriscos. With their final expulsion, Spain lost one of her greatest industrial assets. Furthermore, as Spain gradually lost her place as a first-ranking power, after the seventeenth century, both quality and production in the specific field of silk production dwindled. Her influence waned and the creative incentive in the design of fabrics passed from Italy to France and thence to England. The Spanish contribution was a short-lived one.

MOSLEM RULE—ELEVENTH TO THIRTEENTH CENTURIES

A complete reversal of pattern types in silk production from those of Moslem inspiration to those of Italian followed the political and economic fortunes of Spain from the eleventh to the thirteenth centuries and from the thirteenth to the fifteenth centuries.

From the eleventh century until close to the end of the thirteenth century, Spain passed through great turmoil. The Christians, who had been driven back into the northernmost sections, were determined to regain their territory. Meanwhile the Moslems had begun to fight among themselves. Civil war weakened the unity of the Cordovan caliphate, and Moslem Spain became a country of small states, each under its own independent chief. Thus weakness laid the Moslems open to constant—and successful—harassment by the Christians from the North—from León, Castile, and Aragon. Many of the weaker Moslem chiefs fell, and their land was taken by the Christians. To further the downfall of this older Moslem civilization which had been so prosperous, a recently converted group of fierce Berber tribesmen from Africa came into Spain at the call of some of the small local chiefs who needed their military prowess for aid in fighting neighboring chiefs. Soon these new, cruel, and fanatical Berber Moslems overran the whole of the Spanish Moslem territory as conquerors, putting to death huge numbers of the former inhabitants.

These later Moslems were in turn conquered by the Castilians and the Aragonese. By 1276, the Christian kingdom of Castile held all of Central Spain from the Pyrenees to Cadiz. Its northern neighbor, Aragon, held all of the eastern coast down to Murcia—and also the Balearic Islands. Portugal had become an independent kingdom. The Moslem rule was concentrated in a small section on the southeastern coast below Murcia—in Granada. Murcia had become Castilian.

During these centuries, silk production had continued in spite of the turmoil and the gradual encroachments of the Christians into the Moslem territory. The work had early spread from Cordova to Almeria in the South as its main center, and at the beginning of the twelfth century, to Seville, Murcia, and Malaga. At the end of the thirteenth century, when the Moslems were finally conquered, they took their work with them and continued vigorous production in Granada.

However, all the conquered Moslems did not leave the new Christian domains. Some of them remained and, for many years, were well treated and allowed to ply their usual trades. Their great skill and fine craftsmanship were of the utmost value to the less skilled Castilians and Aragonese. These were the Moslems known as Mudéjars.

Thus silk production flourished continuously as the Christians made steady advances into the Moslem territory, and later, both within and without Granada. Little is known in detail about the designs of these centuries. The West Moslem designs (Spanish) seem to have been influenced by the East Moslem designs of Asia Minor, Egypt, and Persia. Asia Minor and Egypt in turn had been strongly influenced by late antique forms. The Persians never gave up their own art forms. They were never thoroughly Arabianized and continued the animal, human, and floral units in their designs, even though the Koran forbade their representation. These same Persian forms contributed largely to the development of the West Moslem patterns in Spain. Hence appeared the roundels and the polygonal shapes with lions, gryphons, and peacocks facing each other or with a man in the center strangling a pair of lions. They persisted in varying forms until the Italian Renaissance drove them out. The Persians, in turn, adopted some of the motifs based on antique art—the foliated vines that developed into arabesques, as well as the palmette and the lotus. They also used Arabic lettering—often merely as a decorative motif without religious significance.

In Spain, during the rule of the fanatical Berbers, these Persian-inspired types were frowned upon and true Islamic types that were wholly abstract were developed. They were composed largely of inter-laced bands and geometric figures. These are the so-called designs of Alhambra type; they were thus named because of their likeness to the designs on the stucco walls, the ceilings, and the tiles of the Alhambra. Arabic lettering also was used freely, in decorative fashion but for religious purposes. Its meanings were unmistakably religious this time. It should be recalled, however, that the Christian kingdoms were meanwhile making steady inroads, that not all the Moslems were under Moslem rule in Granada, and that the Moslems were producing fabrics for Christians as well as for themselves. Thus the Persian types persisted steadily also.

During this period, the old barriers to trade were broken down. The seaports on the eastern Spanish coast became thriving centers of both commerce and industry, carrying on a prosperous trade with the East, especially Italy. It will be remembered also that the Lucchese had established workshops in Barcelona; thus in the early Lucchese designs some of these Spanish types and motifs appeared. However, Italy soon made more contacts directly with the East through her own maritime trade and had little need of the Spanish interpretations, and the Spanish soon began borrowing some of the Italian motifs.

Through the Moslems, both of the East and of the West, new Chinese influence brought about by the conquests of Genghis Khan, began to modify both Spanish and Italian work. Their influence was revealed in the manner of using the vine and scroll patterns, in the pointed oval design—later to become the typical Renaissance ogival base—in the parallel oblique scrolls, and in the animals now drawn naturalistically. From the Mid-East also, in the latter part of the period, came bold stripes, often combined with Arabic lettering. Such work formed the basis of some of the Christian designs in which castles, lions, and heraldic devices were repeated at intervals in the stripes, sometimes, too, with diagonal vines combined with lotus flowers.

CHRISTIAN RULE—THIRTEENTH TO FIFTEENTH CENTURIES

The thirteenth to the fifteenth centuries were a period of consolidation for the Christian kingdoms and of further decline for the Moslems. The Moslems, within the confines of Granada, during the earlier part of the period continued to prosper in terms of material wealth. But the social structure grew increasingly weak with great contrasts of wealth and extreme poverty and suffering. Many of these wealthy Moslems left Granada and went back into Christian Spain as Mudéjars. Christian Spain continued to treat them leniently for some time longer. They had their own courts and law and were allowed to retain their own mosques. Commerce and industry were almost entirely in their hands—or of those of foreigners or the Jews. Mudéjars were treated with honor and respect.

Silk production continued both in Granada and in Christian Spain. Commerce with Italy grew apace. The coast cities of Valencia and Barcelona rivaled the importance of the Italian maritime cities.

In silks, the types of design that had begun to emerge in the preceding century were continued—those of the pure Islamic inspiration, those that showed the new Christian types, and the new ones with the infiltration of Chinese types in Persian adaptations.

At the end of the period, the Spanish conquest of Sicily and Sardinia and the occupation of Naples (Southern Italy) gave Spain a foothold in Italy and direct contacts with the full sweep of the Italian Renaissance. She began to extend beyond her borders—following a program which, in the end, led to her downfall two centuries later.

THE RENAISSANCE AND LATER DECLINE— FIFTEENTH TO SEVENTEENTH CENTURIES

The great days of Christian Spain were those of the last of the fifteenth century and the whole of the sixteenth century. During this period came the American conquests with great resulting wealth. There came, too, further great extension beyond the peninsula which proved fatal, however, in the end.

Castile and Aragon in the last part of the fifteenth century came under the combined rule of their respective sovereigns, although each country retained its own identity and political institutions. Ferdinand of Aragon had married Isabella of Castile. Tremendous impetus resulted from their joint rule.

Their successor, Charles I, was their grandson. From Ferdinand and Isabella, he inherited Spain, the Italian possessions, some parts of newly conquered territory in Northern Africa, and all the American conquests. From his father, Philip of Burgundy, son of Emperor Maximilian of Austria, he inherited the Low Countries, Luxembourg, Burgundy, and Austria. A little later he also became Holy Roman Emperor as Charles V.

Charles was followed by his son, Philip II, who died at the end of the sixteenth century. With him passed the greatness of the Renaissance in Spain. Neither Charles nor Philip had been able to hold the enormous domains. Wars had been incessant and expensive. Even the wealth that poured in from America was wholly inadequate.

Philip was followed by three weaklings under whom the decline was rapid. The next king was a French Bourbon, the grandson of Louis XIV.

Under Ferdinand and Isabella, the country progressed. Both manufactures and commerce were encouraged. Unfortunately for Spain, most of it was still in the hands of the Mudéjars, the Jews, and foreigners. The Jews were expelled in 1492 as a result of the growing fanaticism in the country. More foreigners came in to take their places. Valencia and Barcelona gradually lost much of their trade. The bulk of the seafaring changed from the East to the West coast on account of the traffic with America and the new water routes. The Mediterranean no longer held its old importance.

Ferdinand, in 1492, conquered Granada, the last of the Moslem kingdoms, and drove its occupants to Africa. Civil wars and forays into Christian territory by the Moslems had been a constant source of irritation. The Moslems took with them into Morocco their silk manufacture where it continues in some measure today.

The Mudéjars, according to the treaty made at the time, were not to be disturbed. In Aragon, especially, and in Valencia and Catalonia, they formed a large and important part of the population, vital to commerce and industry. In Castile, however, they were meeting constantly increasing difficulties due to fanatical hatred. In 1502, all Mudéjars in Castile were ordered either to accept Christianity or to leave the country. After that date, there were officially no Mudéjars. Those who accepted Christianity and remained were called Moriscos. They continued to be the mainstay of the financial well-being of Spain as far as her own efforts in production were concerned. Ferdinand tried to protect the Mudéjars of Aragon, and they remained as before for a while longer.

In 1525 in the reign of Charles so much pressure was brought to bear that Charles was forced to acquiesce in the expulsion of the Mudéjars from Aragon. Again, many went to Africa. But thousands accepted Christianity and became Moriscos.

Feeling against Moriscos, especially in Castile, was still bitter. They were placed under the most severe restrictions. Soon these same restrictions were applied to the Aragonese territory. In 1609, matters came to a head, and Valencia, first, expelled them en masse in the most brutal fashion. Other states quickly followed suit. A few remained and became outlaws in the mountains. With these expulsions went one of Spain's greatest assets. Rapid decline in all types of commerce and industry followed.

Philip II lost the major part of his father's possessions. Constant wars drained Spain dry. The conditions under the three weaklings who followed him, Philip III, Philip IV, and Charles II, grew rapidly worse. The prestige and power of the great Spain of the sixteenth century faded out.

Silk production held its own during the sixteenth century and as long as the Moriscos with their skill could do the work. After their expulsion in 1609, the products deteriorated rapidly.

In design, the silks followed the Italian lead for the most part. Some of them made by and for the Moriscos, especially in Granada, still carried the strong color and some of the aspects of the Moslem types. But by far the preponderance of design was Italian in character and, as already noted, was often not distinguishable from it.

SUMMARY

The attributes of expression that are thoroughly characteristic of the Renaissance should now be clear. They vary in some respects from nation to nation, but fundamentally, as compared with all later products, they tell the same story.

The words that describes them are familiar. "Bold, vigorous, massive, heavy" are perhaps the dominating ones. Fabrics that can be so described never rest peacefully as upholstery on furniture that has not at least some semblance of the same qualities. The tyro in decoration places a small Renaissance design on a light and exquisitely formed Hepplewhite chair and considers that he has been very original. To the trained eye, the association is a resounding discord. Another, a skilled designer, places a small Renaissance design on another Hepplewhite chair—and it fits. There is sufficient lightness in the motion, in the forms, of this second fabric and sufficient lack of delicacy in the more clumsy Hepplewhite chair for the two to find a common meeting ground of expression. Discernment of these fundamental likenesses and the ability to reject unlikenesses come only with much study and experience. They cannot be gained by reading. After the reading—which can open the door—must come practice, continued until the necessary skill and perception are really attained.

A brief analysis of some of the elements of designs in Renaissance patterns that justify the given adjectives may not be amiss.

Consider, for example, the velvet design of Plate 31. Let us take the adjectives one by one and see how they apply to details of the design.

(1) Bold. The sharp definition of the forms against the light background leaves no vague borderlines. Nor does the drawing of the shapes; they are clearly expressed without entangling fussiness of unnecessary parts. Every form, every line, every curve is working to one clear end. A blockiness of shape, echoed by the proportions

both in the detail and in the design as a whole, is also a strong element contributing to the boldness of expression.

(2) Vigorous. A few lines put together may express ease, grace, delicate gradations of movement—suavity. Or they may denote boldness, robustness, vigor, and power. The proportion of the shapes may express qualities as far apart as do the lines. In this plate, as we look at the proportion of the parts, individually and in combination, we see nothing gentle in movement. The effect is robust and vigorous. We move from shape to shape with forceful action. The lines are moving our attention with determination. There are no weak moments. All is vigorous and determined.

(3) Massive—heavy. Both of these qualifying words already mentioned contribute to the over-all heaviness. But there are other contributing factors, too. If we examine the curves carefully, we see that not only are they clearly defined, determined, vigorous, and bold— they have a slightly ponderous aspect because of their degrees of curvature—all of which are very full. They round out into space boldly. Even the contours of the smallest parts show the consistent repetition of this aspect. At no point is there the slightest suggestion of attenuation or approach to straightness. They are "heavy" curves. Their proportions within themselves as curves repeat this fullness— this heaviness. So, too, does the slow movement from size to size as we move from part to part in the design. All together, these aspects give us that feeling of heaviness and massiveness.

If we compare this design with the one on Plate 38, which is heavy as compared with a light Louis XVI design, we can see a difference. The one on Plate 38 seems perceptibly lighter. Its curves are less stubby and forceful. They are larger and more sweeping. The shapes and the proportions of the shapes show greater contrast and move the attention faster—making for less weight and none of the ponderous quality. It is easy to see why these later Renaissance velvets could be used—and still can be—on some of the English and French furniture of the late seventeenth and early eighteenth centuries, whereas the pattern on Plate 31—also Renaissance—although its design is finer in many ways, would look much too heavy.

10

French Fabrics of the Louis XIV Period, 1643–1715

IN THE LONG REIGN OF LOUIS XIV IT WAS ONLY NATURAL THAT THE character of fabrics should change markedly. In the beginning of the reign, they came to the first full power of French expression—based on the Italian but done in the French manner. By the end of the reign, the designs were in transition again, this time strongly influenced by the Eastern patterns that were coming into Western Europe through the various East India companies. As this last phase did not, in turn, reach its full fruition until after Louis' death, it will be considered in the next chapter, under French Fabrics of the Régence. In this chapter, we shall concentrate on the patterns that reached their peak during the Louis XIV period.

HISTORY

We have already seen that French fabric designs followed Italian patterns from the time of Louis XI until that of Louis XIV. It should be recalled that the later Italian designs made liberal use of naturalistic plant forms. Lace also had appeared sporadically as a part of these later patterns. So, too, had the crown as has already been noted. Vase forms had been in continuous use from the end of the fifteenth century. The large Baroque velvets of Genoa and Venice were mostly floral in character. All these types had been carried into France and had been in process of gradual evolution away from Italian patterns and toward French ones—with varying degrees of excellence in design. This process had been going on approximately a hundred years when Louis came to the throne.

By that time, the French had made the lace form their own; it became the basis of a very characteristic Louis XIV design. The big

Baroque velvet designs of the Italians likewise were adapted to French ideas. They became a little smaller, less flamboyant, more compact, and better drawn—yet still grandiose. The Baroque of Louis XIV was in no sense the decadent Baroque of Italy. Large in scale, often overloaded with ornament, but never weak nor merely blatant. It contained the seeds of great skill that were being most intelligently nurtured. Although the patterns were built on the old forms, the French used them in a new way. There are a tightness and rightness in the drawing of the floral forms; no sloppiness, no lazy, slack curves, no bigness for the mere love of bigness. The large-scale forms are made up of a multitude of small parts, each delicately, exquisitely, designed and drawn—with the familiar justness and precision of French work clearly apparent. The lace, when it appeared, was well controlled; it was used as supporting motifs and kept well in the background. The patterns were still symmetrical; they were held together with these long bands of lace but were kept flat as part of the background and made into interesting shapes that supported the remainder of the design. The keen sense of fitness that characterizes so much of French art was evident in all the best of these designs.

Historical Background

Perhaps without the religious wars that made havoc for so many years in France, fabric development would have come more rapidly. Actually, however, industry did not begin to muster its forces and start anew until, as we learned in the preceding chapter, Henry IV again consolidated the country and laid the foundations for the stability and prosperity that Colbert, Louis' great minister, brought to full fruition. Richelieu, during the reign of Louis XIII, had furthered the process indirectly by starting France on the road to being politically the most powerful western nation. At the death of Richelieu's successor, Mazarin, who had practically ruled France during Louis' minority, Louis XIV took over the reins of government himself. He inherited a kingdom that had become a great power in Europe. Moreover, within the nation itself, the last vestige of the power of the great nobles had been broken. The provinces were administered directly from the throne, and Paris was truly the center of the government. The task that Louis XI had begun was completed. All power was in the hands of the king.

Colbert, Louis' minister of finance, had been trained by Mazarin. His passion to make France a wealthy nation was as great as that of Richelieu to make it powerful among the other nations. Richelieu tore down the castle fortresses of the nobles, destroying any possible extension of their power as a military caste. Colbert, on the other hand, encouraged old industries and proceeded to build new ones, too, in order to make France wealthy. He went on with and enlarged the work that Henry IV had fostered; the weaving industry was one of his developments. He drew into the country more skilled foreign artisans, who both produced and taught. He encouraged native French craftsmen to produce better work by offering money prizes—large enough to be incentives. He made loans to leaders of industry to help them build new factories and to purchase the raw materials necessary to run them. Further, he safeguarded the quality of the product as a necessary and sound measure to ensure steady trade, making certain that the French products really were "the best" and wholly reliable. He further built up this trade by improving transportation facilities to increase the flow of both materials and finished goods. Consciousness of success, with its attendant power, was bound to bring forth latent native talent, which could scarcely brook such complete dependence upon another country for its designs as had been evidenced previously. It is easy to see why the designs of Louis' fabrics blossomed in a truly French idiom.

Louis reigned for 72 years. One of the industrial experiments of Colbert during the early years of the reign had been the formation of an East India Company patterned after the English and Dutch companies. This Company brought into France new design concepts which took root through the long years. Thus, by the end of the period, the heavy, symmetrical patterns with their large masses, intricate flower and lace groupings, and heavy scrolls were disappearing. They were being replaced by designs that were radically different. Fruits and flowers were being rendered "in the round," no longer conventionalized as before, and no longer flat. They were skillfully modeled, very full, very round—with the third dimension powerfully represented. Further, these forms were being tried out in the characteristic asymmetrical repeats—spot balanced against spot in space. Many of these new patterns were experimental and lacked the smoothness and power of the older forms which had been so thoroughly mastered. Sometimes these new floral interpretations were bunched with obvious effort and with very unstable effect. The attention moves from spot to spot in uncomfortable jumps. It was a new idiom that would be mastered a little later—during the Régence, after the death of Louis and while his great-grandson, who was to follow him as king, was growing up. When it was finally mastered, it became such a distinct phase in the development of French design that it has been accorded a place of its own as the Régence type. However, we must not forget that it was during those long years of the last of Louis' reign that it was being tried out.

Analysis of Typical Design of the Early Part of the Period

PLATE 41

Plate 41 is an admirable illustration of the Louis XIV lace type of pattern at its best before it had begun to be modified by the new modeled flower forms and the new balances. Notwithstanding the multitude of parts, there are remarkable coordination and concentration of emphasis. The detail gives constantly alluring play for the imagination, yet it is held perfectly within its positions of relative importance. The drawing, too, is exquisite in its finesse. It is a masterly product within its particular range of over-all character and expression in fabric design.

One may easily see from this plate, with its typical pattern, that the Louis XIV designs are large, massive, and rather grand and can seldom be used with furnishings other than those of the period. They are formal too and rather unbending in their dignity; this statement is perhaps especially true of the damasks and velvets based on the Genoese and Venetian types. Yet they have such a wealth of delightful, delicate detail, thoroughly controlled and exquisite—a forerunner of what was to come once the Italian type of pattern had slipped finally and completely into the background.

Summary

Compared with the designs that had gone before—regardless of the country in which they had been produced—these new French types of the early part of Louis' reign mark a general lightening of effect. They are still heavy—but not with the compact massiveness of the

PLATE 41. *A remarkably handsome Louis XIV type design with detail coordinated in masterly fashion.* COURTESY METROPOLITAN MUSEUM OF ART.

earlier Italian design of the last of the fifteenth century, for example. The force and power that characterized the Italian designs, the robust quality, has disappeared completely. The largeness of scale and heaviness now apparent are rather of the quality that causes one to think in terms such as "formal, grandiose, important." They never unbend. They still retain the setness of symmetry which, added to the formality, limits them to furniture and settings that retain a goodly amount of the heavy rectangular aspect of the Renaissance forms.

The same statement is not true of many of the patterns of the latter part of Louis' reign. With the advent of the asymmetrical balance, the freer rendering of form with its lessened conventionalization, came also a lessening in formality, an easing of rigidity—which allowed them to be used a little more liberally. They were still large; they were still heavy. How this new aspect can be used with furniture will be seen later. For the present, we shall merely note the possibility.

11

French Fabrics of the Régence Period, 1715–1723

IN THE PRECEDING CHAPTER, WE LEARNED THAT THE NEW TYPE OF DESIGN, which had started toward the latter part of the Louis XIV reign, came to its full fruition during the Régence. To that statement, we now add that it continued beyond the Régence period into that of Louis XV. Thus this particular type really was in evidence during three reigns—the latter part of the Louis XIV reign, the Régence, and the early part of the Louis XV reign. This type of pattern was copied in England as well as imported; it was used during the last part of the seventeenth century and through the early part of the eighteenth. We are familiar with it as a "Queen Anne" pattern. Anne reigned from 1702–1714. This period illustrates again the folly—and danger—of trying to catalogue human growth and development within sharply marked limits. Rather, let us say, the tide was turning quite definitely to the new ideas and design types, away from the old ones, during the eight years when Philippe d'Orléans was acting as Regent for the young Louis. The Regency lasted only a short time—1715–1723. Louis was declared of legal age when thirteen years old. The Duc d'Orléans died in that same year. Fleury succeeded him as adviser but not as Regent.

The design types show several variations of which the following are the most important:

1. Bunches of naturalistic, well-drawn, beautifully modeled flowers and fruits in symmetrical formations that had begun to express some of the aspects of the new type but still retained some of the old forms.
2. Scattered bunches of flower and fruit forms in asymmetrical balance, beautifully modeled. The balance varies greatly in

quality of design—from instability due to tentativeness to marked stability and beauty.

3. Motifs from Eastern design, treated in the manner of (2).
4. Native French motifs treated as (2).

A sharp change in scale also occurred in this period. Except the patterns in the (1) classification, which follow the older type in general form but with new shapes, the units were much smaller. The formality that had remained partly as a result of the previous large scale, began to disappear. By the middle of the Louis XV period it had gone completely. The entire expression character of the patterns showed obvious movement from formality toward gaiety and informality— which in turn forecast what was to follow during the rest of the century until the time of the Revolution.

HISTORICAL BACKGROUND

Louis XIV's ambitions and struggles for the aggrandizement of France left the treasury badly depleted. Colbert's great work in building up the finances of the country came to naught in the end because of a spendthrift king who wanted power, more power, glory, and more glory. Colbert, before he died in 1683, had lost control, and France had again started on the way downward financially, because of the tremendous drain, for the most part, of Louis' many wars.

After the death of Philippe d'Orléans, the Regent, in 1723, the young king Louis XV (aged 13) had to have an adviser. Fortunately for France, the man who held the reins until his death in 1743 was an able man, Cardinal Fleury. To a certain extent, he repaired some of the damage that had been done. But when he died, Louis, then in his thirties, made pretence of governing without an adviser or minister. That attempt and its results are beyond the scope of this chapter. For the moment, we are concerned only with that brief interval between the two reigns and the early part of the Louis XV reign, when the patterns we are discussing were in vogue. France continued to be the center of the style world. It is interesting to note here that Italy, so long the leader, had now begun to copy some of these new French motifs.

The reaction from the austerities of the last part of Louis XIV's reign was sharp. The immorality that had been seething—temporarily under cover because of Court disapproval—a belated disapproval—came to the surface with much encouragement from the Regent. The grand days of the "Grand Monarch" were over. Gaiety and license ruled while Philippe was Regent and afterward. Such a reaction was bound to show in the designs that people wanted, the designs that pleased them and suited their new ways of living. Thus, along with the changes in motifs and pattern types that had been coming naturally, due to new contacts with the East, came new incentives for doing away with the stiffness, the formality—the grandiose effects. It was only natural that the patterns should begin to show freer movement, livliness, less pompous formality, and more gaiety. These are precisely the characteristics that appeared during this time, and they continued for a long time after this brief interval.

ANALYSIS OF DESIGN DEVELOPMENT

These new designs, albeit the forms were so different from what had gone before, still showed their derivation in evolution from the massive, heavy forms that had preceded them. The short, round, full curves of fruit and flowers, the rolling surfaces, the slow movement from part to part through slowly changing sizes could never have appeared suddenly. They moved directly out of the past. But there was a new type of rolling movement, too, from spot to spot quite different from the old static effect within the stiffly set frames. This new movement synchronizes perfectly with the new curving forms in furniture that were coming into vogue—in England as well as France.

One cannot but admire the technical skill that could produce the well-designed fruits and flowers that, although so round, were still such thorough-going textile design—not pictorial. It was a very high type of conventionalization, based on the natural forms but far from the copying that came later. Yet the repeat mode is often very clumsily handled, apparently little understood. Flower groups tumble through space instead of being poised in space. Fountains and figures—simulating the Eastern subject matter—hold precarious balances against each other. Occasionally, however, we find a fabric in which the repeat is handled with great skill, and it makes us ask the non-answerable questions, "What proportion of the work at the time was fine? What, mediocre? What, poor? Were the heights reached only occasionally?

Plate 42 161

Or, in reverse proportion, were there plenty of the fine ones?" All that we can determine are the limits of excellent and poor quality. The rest is a matter of guesswork.

PLATE 42

The fabric in Plate 42 illustrates clearly both the weaknesses and the strength of these designs. As noted above, the flowers and leaves are beautiful bits of textile-weaving designs. Their shapes and textures grew out of weaving exigencies, adroitly, skillfully handled.

PLATE 42. *One of the typical forms of the early eighteenth century patterns in France, commonly called Régence. Note the skillful handling of the design details from the standpoint of expression in weaving and the instability of the placing.* COURTESY METROPOLITAN MUSEUM OF ART.

But the designer was not so successful in balancing spot against spot in space. There is much clumsiness and the positions of many of the spots are quite unsettled. Yet the detail of the design is so thoroughly understood and so perfectly executed that we cannot but accept the whole effect as exceedingly interesting and pleasant. In-

PLATE 43. *Another fine example of early eighteenth century design in France. Masterful in both drawing and placing.* COURTESY METROPOLITAN MUSEUM OF ART.

cidentally, this is the Régence type that has been adapted and used so much in modern fabrics of the last 25–30 years.

PLATE 43

In Plate 43 the spotting of the forms in space has been mastered. The movement is easy and finished. It is a superb piece of textile design, entirely free of the earlier conventions and motifs.

SUMMARY

Seen abstractly, without reference to what had preceded them in the design world, these Régence designs would be called heavy by almost anyone tuned sensitively to design aspects. Yet, in comparison with their precedents, they are definitely lighter. Perhaps a word of caution is in order here. The words lighter and heavier are relative terms. Lighter than what? Heavier than what? In this case, lighter than what had gone before and heavier than what was to come. It is important that this scale of relative weight aspects is clearly seen and used in connection with all the period fabrics. To appreciate the place of these Régence fabrics in the whole development of silk textiles, we must take care that we give these terms the flexibility due them. When all the evidence is in and we have surveyed the last period, then, and only then, can we get a true picture of the range of these relationships. Our background for thinking will have been set.

Thus we find that Régence designs are still heavy, but lighter than those that had preceded them. On light, delicate furniture, they will be ridiculous because of their weight; yet they can be used on furniture that will not take cheerfully the older still heavier types. Why? Because of the new rolling motion, this new freedom that is so far away from the old rectangular forms of the Renaissance furniture. Régence designs belong with those new curves—which are round and stubby curves, too. They belong with the smaller scale in furniture that has appeared, that in turn fits the smaller rooms and houses which begin to leave behind the dignity and stiff formality of the older ones. They come near to what we use today in traditional settings—not pure modern—and fit also many of the larger chairs and sofas that are not strictly period.

12

French Fabrics of the
Louis XV Period,
1723–1774

IN THE PREVIOUS CHAPTER, IT WAS POINTED OUT THAT AFTER THE REGENT
died in 1723 the young king appointed Cardinal Fleury as his adviser
and that as long as he, Fleury, lived (until 1743) France was in good
hands economically, and, to a certain extent, politically. As a matter
of fact, she actually reached a marked height of prosperity. At one
time, the budget actually balanced. Had the money been spent wisely,
there could have been continued prosperity. But Fleury had little
control over the dissolute young king and his extravagant court. The
money went out much faster than it could come in, even with industry
and commerce flourishing. After the death of Fleury, the situation
went from bad to worse.

Nevertheless, it should be remembered in connection with fabrics
that all this court extravagance, wicked and deplorable as it was in
its effect upon the lower strata of French society, was one of the reasons
for the production of so many fine silks. It put a premium upon
ingenious, interesting—and of necessity—constantly changing design
modes. When fashion vies with fashion in any field, designers are
busy. Thus it is easy to see why there was such a vast and varied
production during this reign. France was rotting but those who wanted
these fine silks did not care. Production went on.

HISTORICAL DEVELOPMENT

It is impossible to classify all the design types; they were too varied.
But, for the sake of as much simplification as possible and to provide
a basis for our special inquiry regarding characteristic expressions, the
silks are divided into three major groups. Group 1, the continuation
of the so-called Régence type; Group 2, an intermediate type, based

quite obviously upon Eastern forms and pattern types that were gradually modified by French taste and assumed a distinctive French aspect, becoming the basis of many of the designs of the next period also; Group 3, an outgrowth of the other two that took the form for the most part of the smaller floral patterns so familiarly called Louis XV.

THE EARLY MODE

We have already discussed Group 1 under the Régence. For many years, the patterns remained heavy, though they still were modeled skillfully. They were superb weaving designs, notwithstanding the clumsiness evident in some of the balances. This clumsiness began to disappear as the Eastern products continued to flow into France in great quantities and the designers began to get a better grasp of the new mode of thinking. Designers began to be correspondingly more skillful in adapting the new mode to their own French ideas and living needs. By the middle of the century, the mode had disappeared as such and had changed into those of Groups 2 and 3.

THE INTERMEDIATE MODES

Group 2 is really a transitional period in which several distinct design aspects appear. Some of them lasted for but a short time; others became the basis of the next major type, Group 3. These may be roughly classified as follows:

(*a*) Groups of flowers. These were light in appearance as compared with the earlier fruit and flower groups and the modeling was much reduced. They were accompanied by a great variety of connecting links, some Eastern in type, some pure French invention. Ribbands, intertwined stems, floating bits of lace began to appear in tentative fashion.

(*b*) Even well into the century, a few designs used a form much like the Eastern panels—with exotic birds, Tree of Life, and flowers. Sometimes these were drawn to look like the Eastern products themselves. Some were neither Eastern nor French but the result of talented French designers working with much freedom. They are one of the types that the famous designer, Philippe de La Salle (1723–1813) did with such skill. Some were large panels. Others were much smaller.

(*c*) Sometimes only the general idea, the asymmetrical balance, was all that remained of the Eastern type. The figures could be almost anything—people, landscapes, monkeys. As long as the general aspect of the subject matter in these smaller designs was Oriental, they were called Chinoiserie. Those, however, showing monkeys as a prime feature, were called Singerie.

It should be remembered that one of the many notions of the Court was the introduction of strange pets, monkeys among them. It belongs to the same kind of striving for "something different" that led the ladies of the Court to have their little black dwarf-slaves, the blackamoors.

Among the gayest and most charming of these whimsical part-French, part-Oriental new style patterns was the work of Pillement (1728–1808). His designs were delightful vignettes, poised in exquisite balance, using every conceivable type of motif.

In this phase of development (c) the little vignetted landscape scenes began to appear.

TYPICAL LOUIS XV FLORAL PATTERNS

The final form of the asymmetrically balanced flower groups inter-mingled with odd bits of lace, ribbands, and garlands also went through many changes. It grew out of the type characterized under Group 1 and, about the middle of the century, appeared in the fashion shown in Plate 44.

The design shows great care in both drawing and patterning; it is careful, thorough, well-considered design. If we look at a much later one, toward the end of Louis' reign, we see a marked change. Plate 45. Not only has the scale grown smaller and the general aspect changed to much increased lightness and daintiness but also there is a falling-off in design quality. The balances are not so well done. They are not clumsy, like those of the early part of the Régence; they are merely a little haphazard and nonchalant. The result is very carefree and gay. Also the patterns become increasingly naturalistic as they grow less consequential. They are still drawn with great skill but they simply have less to say.

This light, gay pattern type carried on into the next period, and it is impossible to draw a sharp line between the two periods. Some-times all one can say is, "It is either the last of the Louis XV period or the beginning of that of Louis XVI." These odd, asymmetrical, delicate flower spottings did not cease at the moment of Louis' death and stripes suddenly take their place, as is too often assumed in the popular conception of these fabrics. Incidentally, stripes had ap-

PLATE 44. *A finely balanced brocade design by Philippe de La Salle.* COURTESY METROPOLITAN MUSEUM OF ART.

peared, too, in the latter part of the Louis XV period, but they were not used liberally as they were later. Both the stripes and the floral forms continued into the next period—one to increase in importance, the other to decrease, but not to disappear as is popularly supposed.

PLATE 45. *Late Louis XV type showing marked changes in scale of detail, as well as in the character of the drawing.* COURTESY METROPOLITAN MUSEUM OF ART.

HISTORICAL BACKGROUND

For our particular purposes the detailed history of the Louis XV period is not important. There were wars with consequent further drain upon an already suffering country. The Court did not suffer, nor did a group of the upper middle class who made much money out of the Court. But everything and everyone below the upper middle class did. The lower the strata, the more miserable was the condition, because the added moneys were always squeezed out of them. They had no means of redress.

Louis kept the reins of government in his own hands but paid little attention to his duties. His ministers had to run the country with but occasional help from him. He was vain, idle, immoral—a sad travesty of a man.

Plate 44   *169*

In the field of the arts, little that is of great value was accomplished. But it should be noted that it was during this reign that the first indications appeared of the turn away from the Eastern influence with its apparently complete absorption in asymmetrical balance to the influence of the classic again. It was a slight change, and only at the end of the reign did it become at all marked. Strangely enough, the change was due to the influence of one of Louis' many mistresses, Mme. de Pompadour. When Pompeii and Herculaneum were uncovered in 1755, she evinced great interest and from that time on, bits of ornament and small articles began to show some of this type of influence. It should be recalled that, although these were Roman cities, the art work in them had been done to great extent by Greek slaves and showed much of the finesse of Greek thought and execution as compared with the coarser Roman work. Further, these cities were "play houses" where the Romans went for recreation as we go to our summer resorts. They did not have to have the dignity of city dwelling—nor did they. Their decorations are whimsical, gay, and done with much delicacy and finesse. Thus this excavation opened a new field of appreciation of the classic and also aroused new interest in the older forms already known. Bit by bit some of this new mode of thinking that tended to the classic in new terms of delicacy crept into the design picture during the days when Pompadour held her position as chief mistress. And the ideas persisted. The Petit Trianon built by Louis' best architect, Gabriel, is a fine example of the return of the classic influence.

ANALYSIS OF DESIGN DEVELOPMENT

PLATE 44

Plate 44 is still vigorous, handsome design, boldly done but with none of the heaviness that had preceded it. Note the beautiful balancing of the large spots against each other, the space movement over the whole surface. Note, too, the skillful sizing of the two intermediate spots and their perfect balance. Note also the manner in which the flowers and leaves are turned so that their lines of motion contribute to the dominant movement of the whole pattern. Then note the nice handling of the textures of the flowers and leaves—also how flat they are compared with the Régence flowers and leaves. Note the difference in tempo of the motion from part to part compared with what we saw in the Régence patterns. However, this tempo will look quite moderate later, when we compare it with that of the next period. The motion is set by size against size which acts to pull the attention along through the parts of the pattern. It is assisted, too, by the details of shape, such as the flattened (but not flabby) curves of the stems and the short flat silhouettes of the petals and leaves.

This is one of the designs of Philippe de La Salle.

PLATE 45

Comparison of Plates 44 and 45 tells the whole story of the change in expression that took place from the middle of the reign to its close. Compared with Plate 44, this fabric is a petty, trivial affair; yet it is "pretty"; it has charm—is a gay, graceful little thing. But it will not benefit by analysis from the design standpoint.

The general effect of the over-all movement is very agreeable and seems to be due largely to the nice handling of the background areas by the little waving bands of floating lace. They really make the design. The flower sprays are by no means so well handled; they do not balance either in space or in size. Yet our attention is swept on quite gaily and pleasantly because the floating bands dominate the situation. The lines of direction controlling the floral sprays are well handled even though the spotting and placing are so casual.

Note carefully in what manner the quick changes of direction in the lace bands and the stems of the flower sprays are used to give an effect of light, quick motion. Also how skillfully the same effect is maintained by the size changes in flowers and leaves. These are some of the aspects that account for the new lightness and delicacy that are becoming the new design idiom.

SUMMARY

If we glance back for a moment to the beginning of the Louis XIV reign and compare those static, austere designs with these very light designs of the last of the Louis XV reign, we see a strongly accented picture of expression contrasts. We must not forget to recognize always the French genius whether seen in the drawing and shaping of the flower forms in those early Louis XIV patterns or as we follow the continuous growth in freedom to its climax in the forms in all of the last half of the Louis XV period. They are one in essence of expression, reflecting the lives and thinking of a particular people, just as we saw in the case of the Italian design. We saw the same quality also in the French embroidery of the Renaissance. It is a common national expression.

But within this sharply defined national expression are aspects continually changing from heaviness to lightness, from massiveness to delicacy, from austerity to gaiety, from careful calculation to nonchalance with its resultant casual effect.

The story of these French patterns from the expression standpoint shows that they grow increasingly light, delicate, playful, as time goes on. The beginning of the reign of Louis XV to its end marks a vast change—a change that in England includes furniture as varied in its expression as that of Queen Anne and Hepplewhite.

We have almost reached the climax in the progress of fabric expression towards lightness and delicacy. By the time of the death of Louis, it was well on its way; it came to its zenith during the short term that followed before the Revolution—the reign of Louis XVI.

13

French Fabrics of the
Louis XVI Period,
1774–1793

LOUIS XVI, GRANDSON OF LOUIS XV, INHERITED THE ACCUMULATED DIS-
astrous results of the evils of the preceding reigns. Corruption was
current in every sphere of life, individual and national. Extravagance
continued. Steady trade and industry had brought wealth to many
of the middle class, the bourgeois. But suffering was acute among
the lower classes, particularly among the agricultural group that
formed the great bulk of the nation's population. As a nation, France
was on the verge of bankruptcy. In our narrow field, production
was still high, owing not only to the demands of the Court but also
to those of the wealthy among the commercial and industrial classes.

Fabrics continued to grow lighter, more delicate, and, at the same
time, much less sumptuous and formal than those of either of the
preceding reigns. Most of them had great charm. They were designed
and executed with the utmost skill and taste. There were now generations of skilled workers in back of the designers and weavers—and
traditions had been set with standards that were still maintained.
Sometimes the smaller patterns, because of their small scale, seem
trivial. Yet those trivial bits are often presented in exquisite fashion.

In general, the patterns followed five modes, although these should
not be regarded as completely inclusive. The designers displayed too
much ingenuity to be catalogued so easily.

> Group 1. This mode consists of floral patterns, the types in-
> herited from the preceding reign. Like them, they
> were in asymmetrical balance in space. The flowers
> grew smaller as did likewise the bowknots and the
> ribbons, the garlands and the lace. Scattered among
> them also appear new, wholly unrelated motifs, from

garden rakes to musical instruments. The former are merely the playful fancies that grew out of Marie Antoinette's effort to escape the heavy formalities of the Court when she played at being a simple dairy maid at Le Petit Trianon. It was natural that items should be put into designs in order to please her. The Queen set the styles for the Court.

Group 2.   This group was also inherited from the preceding reign—the little vignetted landscapes with people at play. Already, in Louis XV's time, these had begun to display bits of classic architectural detail, such as broken columns, balustrades, urns. It was part of the interest in the classic that Mme. de Pompadour had so carefully fostered. Now, these motifs began to take the place of the freer, naturalistic floral forms that had occupied the attention of designers, in one phase or another, since early in the eighteenth century.

Group 3.   This period saw the return of formal patterns in symmetrical balance, sometimes large, sometimes small, with classic motifs as their primary themes. They were drawn with great delicacy, having the light touch native to the French and savoring of that lighter touch of the workers of Southern Italy. The motifs were not Pompeiian, however. They were a mixture of the Roman with the delicate fancies of the Frenchmen who designed them. It was the quality of the work that echoed the Pompeiian— not the subject matter. That was to come later. Sometimes these patterns are very large, i.e., their units, made up of many parts, extend for long stretches. But they retained their essential lightness and delicacy regardless of the number of inches they measured. A very small Italian pattern perhaps only an inch or so in size may give the appearance of great weight and force, whereas one of these large Louis XVI patterns measuring 60 inches for the unit will seem light and delicate.

Group 4. The little floral groups developed, too, into a new
type. This consisted of a formal symmetrical design, combining the flowers with a framework that
often, but not always, was made up of classical detail.
There was great variation in this group. Most of
the designs were large in scale, although still delicate
and delightful. The units of repeat may show many
sub-divisions which run down to very small scale
in their detail; these appear in great variety. Then,
too, the motion in these large-scale patterns of this
type gives lightness of effect. Motion in a design,
as we have seen, may be slow or fast. If the parts
are large and the changes from size to size—of the
parts—are not sharply different but moderate, the
attention moves along in a leisurely fashion. This
motion may be assisted by shapes that are rather
simple and curves that are ample. The result is
heaviness. On the other hand, in a pattern fully as
large in scale, or even larger, if there are enough
parts of which both shapes and sizes show many
quick changes, if curves are active with more changes
within their shorter, flatter lengths, there is less
leisure. The attention moves quickly from part to
part; there is the aspect of lightness. This is the
characteristic aspect of these Louis XVI large-scale
floral patterns.

Group 5. The commonest mode of all was, of course, the stripe.
As already noted in the preceding chapter, this too
had made its appearance in the preceding reign.
In Louis XVI's reign, it appeared constantly, composed with all sorts of motifs. Little floral bands also
were common, and some of these are exquisite in
their balances. Combinations of straight-line stripes
with floral bands or with floral sprays scattered at
random were one of the common versions of the
stripe. Because the type was so common, it has
become known as *the* Louis XVI type of pattern.
It was only one of them.

HISTORICAL BACKGROUND

Louis XVI had to face a hopeless task in a country where everything below the surface was seething. Had he been a very wise and a very strong man, it is questionable whether the situation could have been rectified without revolutionary events. He did make efforts, but he was not strong enough to stand firmly against the intrigues and maneuvers of the nobility, nor to give his ministers the support that they should have had. Both of his ministers, Turgot and Necker, tried to stem the tide but were driven out by the nobility, especially those of the Court. The successor of these two ministers, Calonne, put the finishing touches to the bankruptcy of a great nation. By incessant borrowing, the Court for a time was provided with plenty of money, as long as loans were obtainable. Luxury was piled on luxury until all the extravagance had to come to a sudden stop.

During all the years that had preceded, while the people were being more and more suppressed and afflicted by this small group at the top, other changes had been taking place. The last elements of old feudal subservience were being eliminated in the thinking of most men—outside the Court and the nobility as a class, and even among some of them. The absolute monarchy was no longer a reality to the majority of thinking men. Somewhere, somehow, all this new thought centering around freedom of the individual had to come to the surface. The complete bankruptcy, the ruling class, and the King provided the time, the immediate causes, and the place. Thus, from 1789 on, efforts were made to turn France into a constitutional monarchy with the people represented under the rule of law—not subject to the whim of a monarch or the cruel edicts of his courtiers. After many false moves, many failures, and much distress, France did get a constitution, and, eventually, in 1791, Louis promised to uphold it. The period was one of turmoil, nor did it end with the agreement of Louis to become the servant of the State instead of its sole authority. Faction struggled against faction, the more fanatical unfortunately gradually gaining control. Outside the country, the nobles who had fled joined the ranks of those who wanted to see the Old Régime continued. War was declared on Austria for her troublesome meddling on that score. Marie Antoinette was an Austrian. She was found guilty of sending important military information to the Austrian Court. The Austrians openly declared that they were going to "rescue" Louis. Finally, in 1792, it was decided to write a new constitution, to suspend the king— now Louis Capet. Monarchy had gone.

For our inquiry, the background for the fabric story, it is needful only to concentrate on the fact of the continued luxury and spending that went on until the Revolution broke in 1789. Up to that time, the story of sustained and continued skill in production and demand

PLATE 46. *A late eighteenth century brocade of type used during period of Louis XVI.* COURTESY METROPOLITAN MUSEUM OF ART.

Plate 47   *177*

is clear. After that, for a short time, affairs were too upset to provide much background for the former luxuries and there was no money to pay for them. After 1792, everything was "out of hand" for a time. Many of the skillful artisans were lost; they had sided with their old patrons. When affairs quieted down sufficiently for new demands to rise, there would be new styles, new pattern types, and these we know in the next period as the Directoire.

ANALYSIS OF DESIGN DEVELOPMENT

PLATE 46

It is but a short step from the light, gay motion of Plate 45 to this one. The quicker, more accelerated motion and much smaller scale of all the parts illustrate perfectly the characteristic aspect of the Louis XVI work. It is worth noting, too, that this fabric is done with a care not in evidence in the fabric of Plate 45. It is delightful weaving design, fascinating in its texture variations that so skillfully follow and help to make the themes. Though small, it is too finely designed, too well considered, to be called trivial. It is exquisite and delicate—a beautifully balanced bit of work.

PLATE 47

In this fabric, we have one of the typical Louis XVI uses of classic motifs. The general effect gives the same delicacy and lightness as the preceding fabric. As pure design, it lacks some of the virtues of the former and displays clearly the tendencies that were to appear as major ideas in the design of the new period.

The manner in which the classic motifs are used is very French and decidedly of the Louis XVI period. This quality shows especially in the attenuated acanthus leaves and the oval-shaped scrolls, both types of interpretation peculiar to this period. It is a quality difficult to name. We saw it in Plate 39, the piece of French embroidery. We saw it again in the handsome Louis XIV pattern in Plate 41. It is the verve, the exquisiteness of precise thinking—always evident whether the design be heavy or light. No other nation has ever expressed this quality in the same way.

PLATE 47. *Typical use of classic motifs. Late eighteenth century in France. Period of Louis XVI.* COURTESY METROPOLITAN MUSEUM OF ART.

SUMMARY

The plates themselves have given us a clear summary. The period is characterized by the qualities of lightness, delicacy, and exquisiteness. When the work is not done well, these degenerate into triviality of expression, though they are usually still well executed technically.

Some of the patterns are gay, others run toward a little more formality, but never is there anything that remotely expresses the austere formality of the Louis XIV patterns—regardless of the weight aspect. Apparently, all is pleasant and happy in this world of design. Ease and grace are inherent; there is no self-conscious effort nor striving for effect. Design character is vastly different from what is to follow.

It is interesting to note that straight lines and sizes of spaces in juxtaposition can say so much. No one can mistake a Louis XVI stripe with its dainty lightness and ease. But how quickly, in the next period, it degenerated into a self-conscious mannered affair, and in the following period, into still bolder self-conscious insistence, often bordering on vulgarity.

14

French Fabrics of the Directoire, Consulate, and Empire Periods: 1795–1799, 1799–1804, 1804–1815

THE FABRICS OF THESE THREE SO-CALLED PERIODS, DIRECTOIRE, CONSULATE, and Empire, really present three not very clear stages of one period. The first two are merely part of the transition from the Louis XVI types to the new forms which finally evolved and were used during the Empire and which do represent a new style. Because of this fact, the historical background will be considered in this chapter before going into any detail regarding the fabric story.

HISTORICAL BACKGROUND

DIRECTOIRE

Briefly, the Directoire period was that short time (1795–1799) after the Reign of Terror, when reason and decency were trying to prevail. The monarchy had been overthrown in 1792, but Louis Capet and his wife were for a short time treated with reasonable consideration. In 1793, a new constitution was given France. But it was then a country in the hands of a fanatical, radical group followed and bolstered by an unreasoning mob. The more moderate men among the revolutionists were swamped, for the time being. The guillotine was doing its deadly work, increasing in number of victims rapidly as the radical elements gained more and more control. Fanaticism soon demanded the death of Louis as a lesson to the nobility—especially those who were with the armies of Prussia trying to recover France for the Old Régime. Louis was guillotined in 1793. Other nations, horror stricken, joined with Prussia in the war against this new and bloody Republic. France, through a period of horror, was governed only by the infamous "Committee of Safety," reporting supposedly to the Convention, the body that had been set up after the fall of the

180

Monarchy to write another constitution for France—without a king—
a Republic. Economic conditions grew increasingly chaotic. It was
literally a time of Terror, which lasted until the decent elements again
got some measure of control in 1794. In the new constitution of 1793,
provision was made for five Directors who would be the executive
control for the country. In 1795, these Directors became a fact and
for five years attempted to rule the country under that constitution.
Although it was a feeble attempt, some measure of peace did return,
and there were the faint beginnings of law and order, as well as a
semblance of return to industry and trade.

CONSULATE

But a new element was destined to enter the picture. During
the last days of the Terror, after Robespierre, one of its instigators and
later its dictator, had been guillotined, there was in some quarters a
movement toward monarchy—not the old absolute monarchy, but a
new type built on the liberties won by the first Convention. When the
current Revolutionary Convention tried to perpetuate its membership
by limiting the vote for the new legislatures to a large majority of its
own members, protests grew into action and insurrection. The insurrection was quelled by the army under the leadership of a young
officer, Bonaparte. For the future, the army with Bonaparte as its
leader was to be the deciding element in a still storm-tossed nation.

As the Directors made failure after failure during their tenure,
Bonaparte, the successful leader winning battle after battle against
France's enemies on the outside, became in effect the new leader, the
idol of the country. He returned to Paris from Egypt—en route to
India to strike a blow at England—in 1799, chased out part of the
Directors, and established a new executive force for France, the Consulate. Bonaparte himself was to be First Consul-Chairman—with the
army behind him. He immediately gave France another new constitution, elements of which are still in force today. It was a return to a
power as absolute as that of the Old Régime, but disguised under the
paraphernalia of Republicanism.

EMPIRE

The period of the Consulate lasted until 1804 when Napoleon
felt himself strong enough to be crowned Emperor. He already was

Emperor in everything but name. And he had brought France back to a reasonable measure of prosperity, law, and order.

This lasted until 1814 when he was captured by the English, whom he had never been able to conquer, and sent to Elba. He escaped, gathered his army again, but was finally defeated at Waterloo in 1815 and imprisoned for the remainder of his life on St. Helena.

DESIGN DEVELOPMENT

From this brief outline, it is easy to see why these three periods have been grouped together. The reaction against the Court, the King, and anything connected with them was bound to be deep and bitter. In the unsettled condition from 1789–1795 with its crescendo of murder, travesties of law and order, and disruption of former living modes and conditions, obviously little could be produced, although it must be remembered that it was only in Paris that the full height of the bloodshed and terror was found. The Revolution did spread in some measure throughout the land as was evidenced by the burning chateaux, the hounding and hunting of the aristocrats, and the smaller mass executions. However, out in many parts of the country and even in some of the smaller centers that escaped the particular attention and ire of the assassins of the government, approximately normal living did persist. Some factories stood; some worked throughout the period, though with much reduced output. But they worked only if they cast aside their traditional designs and played with the new ideas.

These new ideas included an idolatry of things "antique" on the basis that they represented "reasonable" ideas. "Reason"—or what passed for it—was enthroned in place of God and Church and was supposed to be the guiding star of the new dispensation. Because they were "antique," things were "correct" and "pure." Sources of information and inspiration being meager, the French designers were hard put to it in their "correctness" and "purity" and came forth with some strange results compounded of a few ideas based on the antique—Egypt, Greece, Rome, and farther East—and their own fertile imaginings.

The early efforts were bound to feel the effects of fine work that had preceded the cataclysm. Some of the old workers were still in their places; skill was at hand. New designers had not had time to come to the fore. Thus there ensued a simplification of the old Louis XVI types, the elimination—in furniture, for example—of moldings, and the adaptation of some of the characteristic curves and shapes of the antique. In six years of deadly turmoil, there could not be much headway. Nor did the following still turbulent years of the Directory give much opportunity.

In fabrics, the change was revealed in rather more marked fashion than in furniture. The shapes of chairs, for example, were still dominantly of the Louis XVI period. But they were simplified, and new curves replaced some of the old ones. The flaring sharp curve of the sides of the back, the mannered curve of the sides as they came down to the seat, the curve across the back, all suggested—in rather tentative fashion—antique models but still on the Louis XVI forms. And the old finesse, possible because of a few skilled workmen, remained to appreciable extent.

In fabrics, the new-old emblems became the new subject matter. The classic of Louis XVI was banned, replaced by new Republican motifs—or those that French ingenuity was beginning to manufacture as true to the "antique" ideas. Further, the patterning itself began to show change. Into the spotting and placing came a disregard of the finer design qualities. Later, this degenerated into the coarseness of the Empire. As a part of this break-up of the older skill, figures were often broken apart and isolated. The old easy, graceful flow of movement over the surface vanished. In its place were isolated units, placed at none too carefully related intervals over the surface of the cloth. At first, many of these were placed and drawn with the same care and exquisite consideration that the old ones had received. And it is to this earlier type that the name Directoire is usually given. Even though the motifs no longer reminded the purchaser of the hated aristocrats, the skill and taste that had served them were still working and serving. But that was not to last. Other forces were at work.

These new forces centered around Napoleon, first as Consul, then as Emperor. Money flowed like water. It is said that Josephine spent more on her wardrobe than poor Marie Antoinette had ever dreamed of. All the products must glorify the New France and Napoleon. A few designers, architects, and painters were given free hand and led the van with strange results, motivated in part by an unmeaning mixture of antique motifs, which were not understood, and in part by their own imaginations. Everything was heavy, uncompromising, and for the most part quite ugly. Articles were not only astonishing in design but also stiff and artificial, awkward and gauche, especially the furniture. The style was so artificially made to order that it could scarcely be free. Nor was it. Everything that even remotely suggested the Old Régime was eliminated. Case furniture was uncompromising in its squareness of corners, its bluntness of form. Its aspect of heaviness was due largely to the awkwardness of its proportions, which seldom showed any of the refinement that for centuries had been the hallmark of French taste. Chairs and tables had strangely formed supports, even more strangely put together—again with the clumsiness of lack of skill and refinement. Occasional pieces are found that belie these statements, but, for the most part, they are in a manufactured, artificial style developed by and for people whose taste had been so warped by conditions that they were apparently incapable of expressing for the time being those great French qualities that are in reality basic to the race.

Out of this confusing mass, it seems wise for us to concentrate on two of the three types already discussed, Directoire and Empire, grouping the Consulate with the Empire rather than setting up strained barriers in the effort to catalogue the fabric changes in more detail. The times were abnormal, and the products changed rapidly. But within these two groups there are clearly marked style variations.

GROUP 1—DIRECTOIRE

Fabrics followed the old types in general except that new forms were introduced and anything savoring of the Old Court was barred. Figures continued small, however, and were well drawn and executed with finesse.

New motifs included various "antique" elements—urns, torch, classic heads set within small enclosing geometric forms (Wedgwood-like), wreaths of laurel, the lozenge, the diamond—usually a horizontal one.

Noticeable is a lessening of the grace and ease of movement characteristic of the earlier Court patterns. These new motifs often are placed rather stiffly and without acute sensitiveness in their spacing and spotting, even though they are beautifully drawn. The step from these to the almost total disregard of beauty in spacing and spotting in the next group was easy.

PLATE 48. *The full expression of the Empire design mode with its isolated spots.*
COURTESY METROPOLITAN MUSEUM OF ART.

GROUP 2—EMPIRE

The isolated, unrelated spots placed without regard for interrelation of background space and unit size and shape characterize most of these Empire designs. This accounts in large measure for their clumsiness.

The trend in motifs continued with constant utilization of borrowed "antique" ideas very badly interpreted from the design standpoint. Everything is heavy, with the heaviness of awkwardness.

Characteristic motifs include the almost ever-present laurel wreath, stars, bees, eagles, a perverted form of the honeysuckle or palmette, another perverted form of the acanthus, the Greek fret—heavily done —the sphinx, torches, fasces, lamps, lions with wings, chimeras, griffins, and also bands with heavily massed leaves.

SUMMARY

If we take the Directoire type only as the forerunner of a style, a period of transition, we can still see the earlier aspects of design in the delicate, light patterns as well as the beginnings of definitely mannered and self-conscious effects that were to be predominant later. The lightness of the patterns is no longer free; there is no gaiety about it. It is firmly set, determined.

The resulting style, the Empire, is, as has been noted in the text, heavy and cumbersome. The fact should be clear, however, that, when the adjective heavy is applied to the Empire design, it does not have the same connotation as when applied to Renaissance design. One may ask, "Doesn't 100 pounds always weigh 100 pounds?" Of course, it does. But against what background are you considering that 100 pounds? Against a background of 25 pounds or 75 pounds? In the same fashion, if we consider these Empire designs against the really heavy Renaissance designs, they do not show the same weight aspect. But, if we consider them against the background of the Louis XV or the Louis XVI designs, they seem heavy. As pointed out previously, their heaviness is not true boldness and vigor like those of the Renaissance but is due rather to the stupid, clumsy handling of shapes and sizes. Thus, if we compare in detail the curves of Plate 31 with the curves found in so many of the Empire fabrics and pieces of furniture, we shall find in the Empire products circular curves with their monotony, ill-considered curves that blunder along without beginning or ending, a few very mannered curves that, when studied carefully, are often misfits within their own confines, but never the well-designed fullness, richness, of the Renaissance. Perhaps, if we substitute awkward and cumbersome for the terms we have been using we shall come nearer to an accurate statement.

15

Color as Used in Period Fabrics

IN THE TEXT OF THIS SECTION, NOTHING HAS BEEN SAID SO FAR ABOUT the expression of the period colors. The omission has been intentional because of the extreme difficulty of making words convey even an approximately accurate notion of color. However, for the sake of rounding out the story, the following brief summary is added. It should be interpreted, either with sample in hand or while one is standing or sitting in contemplation of a really old piece of material.

RENAISSANCE COLORS

Renaissance colors, like the colors of each of the other periods, re-expressed automatically the character of the design. Only when we moderns "copy" an old design in a color native to another era, other ways of thinking, are the colors misfits for the design.

Reds, blues, greens—to name a few tones—were richly vigorous. A real Renaissance green is a tone entirely different from a modern green, even when we think we are copying it. There is a rich vitality to the Renaissance tone that ours, brilliant and handsome as it may be, does not have. Even in the finest reproductions—and there have been many excellent ones—the expert usually can tell the difference in that tonal quality. Clarity with body and depth characterize the original.

It should not be assumed from this that all Renaissance colors were strong in chroma, like the brilliant red damasks and velvets, for example. Light tones were used, too, but a light Renaissance color is unlike a light Louis XVI color. A light-colored Renaissance velvet cannot be used on a Louis XVI chair—pleasantly. Nor can a Louis XVI velvet be used on a Renaissance chair. Whether light or dark, the same characteristics prevail—body, depth, richness, fullness—all

187

giving the essential aspect of weight to complete effectively the under-lying form composition of any given fabric. Thus if we describe a light blue Renaissance brocade as "light and delicate" we are mak-ing trouble for ourselves when we wish to describe a light blue brocade of the Louis XVI period. Actually, that light blue brocade of the Renaissance as compared with some of the red, green, and gold damasks of the same period may be more delicate, i.e., less heavy. But, as in the case of the patterns, if we reserve our extremes of possibilities to the range between Renaissance and Louis XVI, for example, then that light blue brocade of the sixteenth century is comparatively "light," but not delicate. On the contrary, it is quite forceful as compared with the paler, gentler Louis XVI light blue brocade. Clear understanding of this point and keen discrimination of the differences in these characteristic expressions would prevent many of the strange misfits that one sees in upholstery, as well as in curtains.

The commonest colors of the Renaissance were the reds, most of them rather purplish; greens, mostly a handsome slightly yellowish green; gold, usually slightly orange, which gives it weight; and blues. But we also find intermediates and variations, particularly in the brocades and the later velvets. There is a handsome rich purple, more likely to run a little blue than red; a beautiful light turquoise; a pale apricot, which tells plainly of its derivation from yellow, orange, and red; an occasional grey; an occasional pink, usually a warm one; and sometimes a clear yellow—not gold—used in connection with white. Definiteness is a major characteristic of all the tones, either light or dark. In combinations, the colors usually run a wide gamut from light to dark, a fact that also contributes to the forcefulness and the aspect of weight which synchronize with similar qualities in the drawing of the patterns themselves. Clear definition in the com-binations, as well as in the individual colors, is always present. Trans-lated into other terms, clearly defined color re-expressed the funda-mental boldness and vigor of Renaissance patterns themselves.

The first very marked change in color expression came with the turn of the seventeenth century into the eighteenth. In France, the period was the Régence; in England that of Queen Anne.

EARLY EIGHTEENTH CENTURY

We find the reds, greens, blues, and golds still the popular colors, especially for damasks and velvets. But, when we look at the brocades, another fact comes to light. The sharp definiteness of the coloring of the Renaissance has been modified to suit the expression of the new patterns. There is a richness of intermediate tones that helps the eye to follow the rolling, modeled forms. The colors are still strong, as they would have to be to re-tell the story of the forms. But there is more variety and more softness, due to less sharp contrasts. They are richly round and soft. The simple apricot of the Renaissance has become a series of more mellow tones—some yellower, some more orange, some more red. Other beautiful reds, with more orange in them, have appeared, influenced probably by the Chinese lacquer red which was in vogue for both walls and furniture because of the great interest in the importations of the East India Company. The blues too were in a wider range than hitherto—from exquisite green-blues to purpler ones. But always there was the soft roundness necessary for complete harmony with the underlying form that they were coloring. There were also richer dark tones, as for example the dark greens—both yellow-green and blue-green, suggested possibly by the foliage tapestries.

The next marked change centers around the middle of the eighteenth century.

MIDDLE EIGHTEENTH CENTURY

Either the forceful clarity of the Renaissance or the rich mellow roundness of the Régence colors would have been overpowering on the lighter designs of the middle of the Louis XV period or their vis-à-vis, the Chippendale in England. But the mistake must not be made of thinking of the characteristic Louis XV and those of the Chippendale period colors as "pretty or dainty." With very few exceptions they were not. The greens, for instance, that form the ground for many a handsome dress brocade are astonishingly brilliant and clear. But there is a new note, a thinness, almost a sharpness, that has not been seen before. It is this thin sharpness with so much less body that makes them seem so much lighter in aspect of weight, in sharp contrast to the heavy rolling nuances of the Régence. In general, the gamut from light to dark has decreased, too. More of the colors range near a middle value. There are lighter ones; there are darker ones; but, taken as a whole, the possibilities of motion suggested by range of movement due to value changes have decreased, another contribution thus being added to the effect of decreased aspect of weight. The vigor is tempered, no longer bold like that of the Renaissance. Its clarity is less forcefully impressed.

The colors in the brocades that were based on white grounds are usually more delicate than those based on the colored grounds. Perhaps they were an unconscious forerunner of the next change. We find examples of lovely pale greens, almost pistachio in effect, of exquisite pinks, soft and light greens, blues, lavenders, pale yellows. The effect of these combinations is often quite different from what we would expect if we had seen examples only of the damasks, the velvets, and the heavier brocades. They are flatter, lighter, with much-lessened contrasts in tones showing great variety of finely modulated nuances, but yet not weak, not really "delicate" in the sense of what we shall see as delicacy later.

The next major change brings us directly to the truly delicate colorings, often for the most part in the very light values.

LATE EIGHTEENTH CENTURY

The values in the late eighteenth century are light, but often with a few very dark notes, such as stems, which give piquant accent. There are seldom any brilliant tones. Delicacy of emphasis in color goes hand in hand with delicacy of form and composition. The color actually covers a wide range of hues with almost infinite variety of gradations, but they never have the sharp brilliance of the preceding reign nor the round fullness of the Régence. The colors are light, exquisite, really delicate, in a great variety of hues so gentle in their transitions that we scarcely consider their range. The close harmonies again accentuate the quick motion of the small shapes and sizes that characterize the pattern forms of the period. These represent the climax of the color story from the standpoint of growth and development.

EARLY NINETEENTH CENTURY

The next great change in color followed the downward trend of taste so plainly seen in the furniture and the fabric designs. Subtlety was a thing of the past. Obvious, heavy tones, rather flat and stupid, echo the forms—heavy, soggy greens, reds that lack both clarity and vitality, golds that tend toward the brazen—are the dominating colors.

Blues are heavily harsh and muddy. Nor are these colors any better balanced, one against another. Heavy-toned red silk may have a green figure, likewise heavy, that fails entirely to keep the attention moving over the surface or even to hold its own adequately against the background.

Unfortunately, the coloring of this period was what set the coloring for almost the whole of the nineteenth century. Most Victorian colors were muddy, heavy tones, and the conditions did not change until (1) there was a revival of interest in old furniture, (2) the moderns introduced a new note of hope and beauty. The Modern work, incidentally, will be treated in the last section as part of our current situation.

The Victorian and the other nineteenth century fabrics have not been considered here because they have little to contribute; they never were distinct creative types that could be called styles. They always were, even at their best, "made over" from these classic periods that we have discussed. To these latter we have to turn for our standards—to set a background against which to estimate present-day products and their legitimate and attractive uses—which in the last analysis is our problem.

16

Characteristic Expressions
of Furniture Forms
through the Major Periods

WE HAVE REACHED THE POINT AT WHICH FROM THE UPHOLSTERY STAND-
point we are ready to make our selections for specific pieces of furniture. But we must make sure that we can interpret what the furniture is saying, too, before we can make successful combinations. It
is not necessary here to go into the long story of the history of furniture. If we learn to see the furniture—period and modern—in terms
of its major expressions and character, we shall have sufficient knowledge for most of our work. From the practical standpoint, these
expressions are the aspects that form the basic a, b, c, of everyday work.
This does not mean that furniture history is not necessary. It is
definitely essential. But furniture history without this understanding of "what it all is saying" is a barren base for the composition work,
design, that is interior decoration.

We shall study briefly then, a few characteristic items of furniture,
both period and modern, to discover how their expression and character compare with those of the fabrics already considered. In the
first part of this section, historic fabrics are grouped in five major
expression types from the Italian Renaissance through the French
Empire. The Victorian and the Modern will be added. This is the
classification that we shall use for the furniture, too, when we are
considering specific chairs in relation to their upholstery.

GROUP 1

HEAVY

Group 1 contains all the Renaissance types regardless of country. Although Italian, Spanish, French, English, and Dutch furniture

PLATE 49. *A fine example of an early sgabello.* COURTESY METROPOLITAN MUSEUM OF ART.

showed marked variations, bascially they were similar. On these basic qualities we need to concentrate. Variations due to national characteristics appear only as sub-divisions in an over-all analysis.

All Renaissance furniture was rectangular, giving in essence bold, bulky, plain silhouettes. The ornament, whether carving, inlay (as on an Elizabethan court cupboard), marquetry (as the intarsia of Italy), or paint, partook of these same bold, massive, heavy aspects.

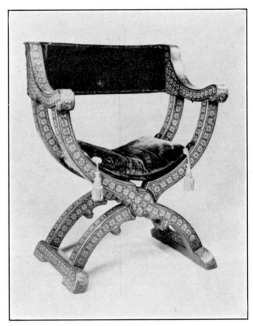

PLATE 50. *So-called Dante chair—crisscross. Of the Venetian type showing certosina work.* COURTESY METROPOLITAN MUSEUM OF ART.

Let us test that statement with respect to a few of the characteristic chairs of the period. Three thoroughly characteristic chairs of the Italian Renaissance were the sgabello, Plate 49, the crisscross chair—Dante or Savonarola—Plate 50, and the high upholstered arm chair of the Baroque, Plate 51, the seventeenth century contribution. They cover a period of approximately 200 years.

The sgabello, shown on Plate 49, is definitely angular though not rectangular. Though not large by actual measure, it gives, however, the effect of weight because of the awkward handling of its over-all dimensions and shapes. It makes a bold silhouette, too, with its angular contours jutting forth into space with such unquestioned vigor. In this particular early example, a very beautiful one, the forms are much smaller than those of the later ones, and the carving

PLATE 51. *An unusually handsome example of a large upholstered Baroque arm-chair.* COURTESY MUSEUM OF FINE ARTS, BOSTON.

in the finial shows exquisite care and taste. However, should we be tempted to describe it as delicate and then use the same word to describe the fluting on the posts of a Hepplewhite bed or the moldings on a fine Hepplewhite chair, the fact would become immediately apparent that the carving detail on this sgabello, though finely considered and beautiful, partakes of the essential quality of the rest of the chair and, in essence, is vigorous and bold, even though small in scale. The smallness of the scale, plus the great skill that made the small scale possible in such finely considered completeness and finish, may lead us astray for a moment.

The crisscross chair, Plate 50, is one of the Venetian types with typical ivory inlay, certosina work. Surely no one could deny massiveness, boldness, and vigor, with resulting effect of weight and power, to the bold shape and its little blunt ornaments.

The big upholstered chair, Plate 51, shows none of the fineness of the sgabello nor the power of the crisscross chair. It is unquestionably big. But, as in the case of the fabric patterns of the same period, its bigness is empty. However, it is massive, it is bold, it is heavy. The huge exaggerated finials, the bold rectangular back and seat, the massive legs and arms, all are obviously expressive of the period, though this particular example is much finer than were most of the type.

In England, the Jacobean, the Cromwellian, and the Carolean furniture types are usually included under the general late Renaissance heading—sometimes merely as Jacobean in contrast to the earlier Renaissance forms known as Tudor. We are concerned only with the last part of the period, the so-called Carolean of the last of the seventeenth century. This period includes the chairs of Charles II and James II, Plate 52*a* and *c*. Properly, from the expression standpoint, the chairs of the William and Mary period should be included, for they, too, come under the general classification of rectangular, massive, heavy. Plate 52*b*. The changes in detail of ornament and shape were Dutch in quality (still Renaissance) rather than leaning somewhat toward the French, as in the case of the Charles II chair.

In France, the chairs of Louis XIV also can be classed reasonably with the heavy Renaissance expressions. Those tall, ungainly products of the early part of Louis' reign are strongly reminiscent of the Italian Baroque. Surely no one can gainsay "rectangular, massive, heavy, and bold" when looking at them. However, the chairs of the latter part of his reign, Plate 53, show decided movement toward another type of expression. Grace and elegance begin to be evident in the curves of arms and legs, the shaping of backs and seats, and the modified proportions. Yet even these later examples are basically rectangular and heavy. The new expression was on the way but had not fully arrived. In France, it did not come until after the death of Louis

(a)

(b)

(c)

PLATE 52. *a. Typical Charles II chair (Carolean) late seventeenth century. b. William and Mary chair. c. James II chair showing transition.* COURTESY METRO-POLITAN MUSEUM OF ART.

(1715).   In England, it appeared a little earlier, during the reign of Anne (1702–1714).

PLATE 53. *Fine example of late Louis XIV chair with typical covering.* COURTESY METROPOLITAN MUSEUM OF ART.

GROUP 2

MEDIUM WEIGHT

During the seventeenth century, cabinetmakers had steadily been gaining skill.   Houses had been growing smaller; rooms were more varied.   Thus more furniture was needed; also, with new social customs, furniture of new types was in demand.   Chairs had assumed a new role in ordinary living. The social distinctions attached to the "great chair," upon which only the master or the person highest in authority sat, to tabouret, and to stool were disappearing; and chairs

PLATE 54. *A rarely fine Queen Anne armchair.* COURTESY METROPOLITAN MUSEUM OF ART.

were gradually coming into use in the homes of people who could afford them. Perhaps the increasing changes in social distinctions are one explanation why chairs about this time assumed proportions akin to those of the human body and why the inspiration for their design came mostly from the burghers of Holland rather than from court-ridden France. These new chairs lost the old, heavy rectangular aspect. They were built on curves, often very beautiful ones. There is a fine simplicity, a straightforward quality about these early curved chairs, especially those of the Queen Anne period in England. A few were fussily ornate, holding fast to some of the old type of thinking although following in part the new proportions and shapes. Others were masterly designs of bold and vigorous curvature, quite new in conception. Plate 54.

PLATE 55.   *Régence chaise, French, early eighteenth century.*   COURTESY MUSEUM OF FINE ARTS, BOSTON.

Compared with the designs of the chairs of Group 1, they were of much lighter aspect, due to smaller size, to better-considered proportions that eliminated awkwardness, to finely coordinated shapes, and to the suavity of the curves. Still they were far from light; they continued bold and vigorous, retaining a degree of weight and mass which was to disappear in the next 50 years. Because of this transitional aspect, a combination of qualities partaking of both types, it is not surprising to find that some of the fabrics that were suitable and had been used on late seventeenth century chairs fitted some of the new style, too, notwithstanding the curves and more humanly considered proportions. For the most part, however, the freer designs with their occult balances and vigorous modeling of light and shade were their best coverings.

French chairs corresponding in general aspect to these Anne types appeared during the Régence. They differ radically from the English type in the details of their designs. Yet considered from the stand-point of over-all expression, they belong in this Group 2. Chairs of the last of the long reign of Louis XIV that were so much better than those of the first part of the reign (such a long reign of 72 years) were still sprawling and awkward with high raking backs. Now, how-ever, the backs were lowered. Both seats and backs began to take on easier shapes, proportioned better to fit the body so that com-fortable sitting became possible instead of perching. The curving legs and arms of the late Louis XIV period were continued but were handled with much more skill and some of the subtle grace that was to characterize the best chairs of the next period. The austerity of the rectangle disappeared completely with the changes in its pro-portions. However, the fact should be noted that, as in the English development, the over-all aspect of these transitional pieces still showed appreciable weight and mass. Boldness was moving slowly toward subtlety. Plate 55.

Briefly, then, this second group introduces the rolling motion of the curved forms while retaining much of the vigor, weight, and bold strength that had been apparent in the earlier rectangular forms.

GROUP 3

LIGHTER MEDIUM

In Group 3, we see that curving forms and the new proportions have been really mastered. The chairs are lighter than those of the preceding period although still far from delicate. Vigor is marked, but in a new way. Comparison of the curves of a good cabriole chair leg of Queen Anne type with an equally good one of the Middle Georgian period tells the story instantly. The thickset stubbiness of the former has disappeared. Although the knee of the Middle Geor-gian chair is sharply defined, jutting boldly out into space, the sil-houette does not have the forceful roundness of the Queen Anne cabriole. Moreover, in the center of the shank of the Middle Geor-gian leg there is a tendency toward a straighter, less rolling curve. There is a longer stretch from knee to foot without marked change of direction than in the Queen Anne chair. This lessening of rolling curves has the effect of making the leg look lighter, less forcefully bold and massive, though it is still vigorous. The same difference is evident in the curves and carefully considered taper of the side rails of the back and in the serpentine curve of the top. The cyma curves at the sides of a Queen Anne chair seem very heavy in comparison.

PLATE 56. *Medium to small type of Louis XV bergère.* COURTESY MUSEUM OF
FINE ARTS, BOSTON.

French chairs of this period followed the general lines of the classification as outlined above, though the curves were a very different type in terms of expression of national characteristics. Plate 56. They were as French as the curves of Chippendale furniture were English—even when the English called them French. They follow developmental pace similar to the French Régence curves during corresponding time. Louis XV, like his predecessor, lived a long time. The designs of the latter part of his reign as compared with those of the first part changed markedly. Some of the later products could be put quite properly in Group 4. If, however, we strike an average, the major part of the work would be in Group 3.

In both the French and English chairs, there was great variation within this group but a bird's-eye view gives us an over-all picture of chairs characterized by moderate weight and mass, of graceful, moderately bold curves, ease and elegance—the elegance that comes only when the artisan has great skill and complete command of his materials and tools.

Briefly, these chairs were much lighter than those of the preceding group. They were still vigorous, still had some of the rolling motion that comes from generous though much modified curves.

GROUP 4

LIGHT AND DELICATE

Group 4 gives an entirely new standard in terms of lightness and delicacy. The vigor of the earlier curving forms of Groups 2 and 3 gave way to very mild, exquisitely considered motion, very gentle, very self-contained. In the new idiom some of the furniture made liberal use of curves; some of it had few curves or none. But, when the curves were few or when there were none, it should be noted that the proportions of parts to each other set up another type of motion, from size to size; the same mildness and gentleness of aspect were achieved.

To get a sharp picture of this emphatic change in expression, compare the sweeping curves of the side rails of the back of a Chippendale chair, or the bold flowing motion of its serpentine top of such generous proportions, with the thin and quiet curves of a shield-backed Hepplewhite chair. Plate 57. As the sizes of the chairs diminished, so did the amount of the roll, with the result that force and vigor were replaced by lightness and delicacy. Carefully considered changes of line within very small distances now occupied the attention; the delightful, delicate pieces of furniture of the end of the eighteenth century—late Georgian in England, Louis XVI in France —resulted. When curves were used sparingly, even sparsely, as in the many general Sheraton types, it was the proportion of the parts that produced these same aspects of lightness and delicacy. Shapes, too, even though not curved, seen in conjunction with other shapes,

PLATE 57. *An unusually beautiful Hepplewhite chair with shield back.* COURTESY METROPOLITAN MUSEUM OF ART.

told the same story. Their contrasts were very mild as compared with those of earlier groups.

As already noted, French furniture of the latter part of the reign of Louis XV, as well as that of the reign of Louis XVI, can often be classified under Group 4. It makes no difference whether the legs are straight or curved in terms of this expression classification. We are not discussing periods as such. It is the amount of the curve, the bold or less bold contrasts in the moldings, the flutings or channelings, the great or less great emphasis in size contrasts with resultant gentleness and suavity that place the furniture in Group 3 or Group 4.

Briefly, all late eighteenth century furniture, whether featuring curved or straight lines, is light in aspect, delicate. And some of the furniture of the latter part of the middle of the century reaches over into this group.

If we apply the test rigidly, both the Directoire furniture of France and the Regency furniture of England—at least much of it— belong in this group, too. The Directoire is of the last of the eighteenth century; the other belongs to the early part of the nineteenth century. They were offshoots, respectively, of the Louis XVI types and those of the Sheraton group as influenced by what was going on in France. In neither type did the Empire influence show in change of major proportions, except in a few instances of the Regency furniture. It showed for the most part in changes in detail. Thus the basic aspects of lightness and delicacy were retained.

There is, however, another facet to this part of the story. Both of these types of furniture had curves that, although light, were quite different in expression from any that had preceded them. They were sharply flaring, sophisticated curves, like mannered gestures. Sometimes they were very interesting. Sometimes they were so loosely designed that the flare seems to have neither beginning nor ending. This rather forced, artificial manner, in addition to the quality of lightness, demands special consideration in terms of fabrics, too.

GROUP 5

CLUMSY HEAVINESS

Group 5 includes only the heavy French Empire furniture and its derivatives of the nineteenth century. It is not massive, bold, and vigorous like the Renaissance furniture, but, as already pointed out in the fabric section of the book, it appears heavy because of its extreme awkwardness of proportion and the placing of parts. Where curves are used, they are stolid and clumsy. Finesse of proportion is seldom seen. Shapes are frankly experimental and labored. The furniture can be catalogued as clumsy rather than heavy.

GROUP 6

VICTORIAN RANGE—MEDIUM HEAVY TO MEDIUM

Furniture, in England, that corresponded to the Empire derivatives in France after the Regency period was Victorian. It covered a wide range of experimentation with display of much rather unwisely employed ingenuity. As a whole, it classifies as heavy, but never with the bold massing of the Renaissance. The best of it approximates rather the qualities of the furniture of Group 3—Middle Georgian and Louis XV. In fact, in many of its best interpretations, Louis XV shapes and motifs are used freely. The worst of it, of which there is a great deal, has much of the awkwardness that the French Empire furniture showed although it is definitely English in expression with abundant use of the vagaries of the machine age.

GROUP 7

MODERN RANGE—HEAVY TO LIGHT

The last group, Modern, cannot be catalogued as simply as the preceding ones. It has already run a wide gamut of expression and is likely to go much farther before it settles down into anything we can call a period style of definite expression. Experimentation and change have been its essence, owing in part to the very rapid technological advances and the development of new materials and processes that challenge the creative ability of many artists and artisans. Once it can be entirely freed from the earlier wordy propaganda, we shall get a much larger quantity of really fine production. More designers will see what they have produced unattended by the aura of words that too often have been tinctured with wishful thinking and rationalizing. Where the work has been free of this self-conscious doctrinaire quality, the results have been bold and stimulating with promise of great adventure and beauty.

The general tendency has been away from the earlier very heavy things to much lighter, more practical and usable ones. The lesson seems already to have been learned that we do not have to use ugly masses of great bulk and questionable proportions in order to be simple, eliminate unnecessary detail, utilize new materials made with new processes, and produce results expressing the very essence of function that fit the living modes of today. Plate 58.

Some of the new products are light, gay, imaginative—full of charm. In terms of weight, however, from the standpoint of our classification, Modern on the whole runs a complete gamut of the

PLATE 58. *Modern chair by Robsjohn Gibbings. A fine example of the lighter phase of modern work.* COURTESY WIDDECOMB FURNITURE CO.

other groups, from Group 1 through Group 6. At present, therefore, that classification does not help to sum up the modern situation. The general tendency, as noted, is toward the medium and light. All Modern designers, however good, bad, or indifferent, stress simplicity, plainness of surface, elimination of moldings, and relationship of the essential planes to each other. These simplifications alone have brought a new note to the upholstery types. Fussiness, elaborate patterns with the older types of motion abetted by modeling with light and shade, whether large or small, have no place. Broad surfaces, textured surfaces, flatness of pattern planes, whether light, medium, or heavy in aspect, are absolutely necessary to accompany the simplicity of the furniture planes themselves.

17

Coverings That Were Used on Period Chairs

COVERINGS THAT BELONGED WITH THE PERIOD CHAIRS CAN TEACH US many lessons. For the most part, they re-expressed the chair characters. In some instances, of course, owners were as experimental and uncertain as we often are with results that are far from satisfactory except to the antiquarian. Few of these original coverings remain, and few of us have keen interest in the details of their appearance historically. We are more concerned with using the old chairs in our own modern homes. Yet thousands of us do have period furniture of some sort, originals or reproductions, and are genuinely interested in making sure that our upholstery selections at least harmonize with the inherent expression and character of the old pieces. We have no desire to outrage them with wholly inconsistent upholstery covers. To help in establishing the picture of these selections on a sound basis by understanding how the people who made them upholstered them, we shall analyze a few of these old coverings in this chapter, trying to keep the classification of "expression" as outlined in the preceding chapter.

GROUP 1

The sgabello of Italy, such as the one shown on Plate 49, had no covering. Dante and Savonarola chairs varied in upholstery treatment. When the frame was ornate, as in Plate 50, the chair upholstery was usually plain—in velvet or leather. The boldness of the frame was reinforced by the finishing trim—broad bands of galloon, cords, and sometimes tassels. When this same type of chair was of plain dark walnut, pattern was often used on the strap that formed the back, as well as on the seat cushion. Types of materials varied greatly, apparently according to the detail of the chair design. One of the

most common types was a small figured velvet similar to the pattern
type shown on Plate 30. The reason for its employment is apparent.
The areas to be covered were small. The best pattern for any chair
always gives the effect of being framed by the back or seat, i.e., the
form upon which it is placed. In this particular instance, on that
narrow strip across the back, any of the then current large patterns
would have looked as though they were "in transit," with only a
portion of them caught and remaining on the chair. This simple
point of harmonizing scale is fundamental. Another important point
appears in the type of pattern for this type of chair. As already
pointed out, the small patterns of this period had a sturdy blockiness
of effect. This aspect is in perfect harmony with the aspects of mass
and weight seen in the design of the chair itself. Many of these
small patterns were cut velvets, and this texture effect, due to the
lights and shadows in the fabric, was a material help in re-emphasizing
the aspect of the weight of the chairs.

The tall Italian Baroque chair, Plate 51, was covered commonly
with velvet in rich colors. Leather, both patterned and plain, was a
frequent variant. As we have seen, the chair itself often approached
the flamboyant in its exaggerated proportions. The plain velvet offset
this effect to some extent, providing much needed steadiness. The
contrast would have been too great, if the chair had not been trimmed
with sufficient boldness and strength to make the connecting link of
harmony between the plainness of the covering and the ornate exag-
gerations of the chair itself. Control of the degree of contrast accounts
for the fitness of the heavy cords, tassels, and galloon.

The patterned leather that was also commonly used gave solidity
of aspect but with enough variation because of its patterning to fit
well the movement of the proportions of the chair. Nail heads, its
customary finish, too, made emphatic accent with the patterning program set up by those proportions.

In the Baroque of the French, under Louis XIV, on the chairs
of the latter part of his reign, tapestry occupies an important place
as covering. Plate 53. The famous Gobelin looms were in full flower,
and France was justly proud of their product. They set a standard
for others. It is interesting to see how these patterns changed during
the last years of Louis' life. The earlier ones, along with the chairs
themselves, were formal, set, heavy. The later ones, like the chairs,
were freer. They showed the new occult balance with its use of

naturalistic forms of leaves and flowers. The set designs in frames
that were still in vogue, too, were often surrounded by a field of the
freer leaves and flowers, making a sort of matted background. Others,
like the one in Plate 53, show the use of the free balance in conjunction with the formal vase form. All are in accord with the development of the chair design in terms of lighter scale as well as freer
movement. However, many of the new meandering leaf-and-flower
designs failed to fit the shape of backs and seats. They wandered
off into space. Mastery of this particular phase of design was to come
later.

Across the Channel, the typical Charles II chairs, Plate 52a, did
not reach so far toward the new, freer type of expression as did the
French chairs of the latter part of Louis' reign. They still had the
marked rectangular quality of the Renaissance, though the arms show
the new French influence in their curvature. The rich carving is low
and flat, but the chairs as a whole still have the effect of static heaviness. The patterning of the cane used freely in back and seat echoes
that heaviness, too. Thus the soft thickness of the much used velvet
for the loose seat pads forms an excellent foil. It was the customary
upholstery. Finishing items, such as welt, cords, and tassels gave the
motion which, like the galloon on the Italian chairs, formed the connecting link between plainness of velvet and movement of the carved
decoration.

The new all-upholstered chairs of this period, with their high
raking backs and boldly curved arm supports, retained, too, the typical
Renaissance qualities of boldness and angularity. Their coverings
were mostly tapestry and, more frequently, needlework. We must
recall again the fact that Englishwomen had been famous for their
needlework for many years and that England had nothing really comparable to the Gobelin looms. Most of the needlework upholstery
of this period was of the coarser variety, either Turkey work, Plate
59, or Gros Point, with relatively few stitches to the inch. The result
in both kinds of work is a bold texture and a necessary boldness and
bigness in the drawing of the pattern which were not evident later
in the finer stitches of Petit Point. Fringe and gimp in blocky effects
of light and shade gave finish to these active needlework pictures. The
fitness of the type of upholstery for the chair is self-evident.

As with French chairs, the upholstery pictures of these new chairs
often got out of bounds, refusing to stay properly within the frames

made by back and seat. The patterns themselves were distinctly English in quality. Many had little scenes with figures, awkwardly drawn. Sometimes they were framed and surrounded by floral forms, freely

PLATE 59. *Side chair, Cromwellian type. Cover is seventeenth century—Turkey work.* COURTESY MUSEUM OF FINE ARTS, BOSTON.

done. But they were not spotted in the French fashion. They still retained the awkward casual spotting and placing of the typical English design. Sometimes the figures were large, not in a set frame, and less restrained. Then they were often surrounded by heavy scrolls, even with bits of classic ornament mixed indiscriminately with the free floral forms. All were admirably suited in design expression to the heavy scrolls of the arms and the awkward proportions of the furniture itself.

There were other coverings, too, materials that are now only names to us. As this book is not a history of upholstery materials, only one or two types that were in common use in each period are mentioned in order to keep clear the pattern expression of the fabrics in terms of fitness for the expression of the chairs as seen when both were being produced at the same period and were obvious products of the thinking and degree of skill of that time.

The William and Mary chairs of England also have been placed in this first expression group. Although the changes from the earlier Charles II forms were marked, these chairs, as a whole, never outgrew the heavy, massive, rectangular aspect, and their coverings followed suit. William reigned a brief stretch of time, only 13 years. Louis XIV was still alive and his Court at Versailles was still setting styles in all things for Western Europe. Again, velvet was a prime favorite for upholstery. The over-ornamented, clumsily rich carving of so many William and Mary side chair backs welcomed the rich plainness of the velvet on the seats. Trims were extravagant and strong in light and shade. They were used with a liberal hand—making balancing finish for the velvet as against the heavy ornamental chair backs. Plate 52*b*.

Both on the chairs with the carved backs and the all-upholstered ones of this time pattern, too, was used in the covering. It was mostly of the vigorous bold type, such as the Baroque Genoa velvets —cut and uncut against plain ground—or corresponding large patterns in velvets. Needlework also continued in high favor with designs similar to those of the preceding reign.

Wing chairs had appeared by this time and, although by no means plentiful, must have been a welcome addition. Plate 60. Their lines in this reign began to assume more of the shape that was to be fairly standard during the eighteenth century and continue into the present time. At this juncture, they partook strongly of some of the other unsettled aspects in chairs of the period—the sharp raking inclination of the back, the heavy scrolls of the arms, the ornamental curve at the top. The "flame-stitch" needlework seems to have been one of the favorite coverings for them, though by no means the only one. Its bold zigzag in sharply accented color fits well the marked movement of these chairs. Velvets likewise were popular; some of them were plain and were used with heavy trim; others were in the large formal Genoese-type patterns. Damasks apparently were not as common on these chairs. The more textured effects seem more fitting in view of the heavy lines of the chairs.

PLATE 60. *A late seventeenth century wing chair.* COURTESY MUSEUM OF FINE ARTS, BOSTON.

GROUP 2

With the Queen Anne product, we enter Group 2. As we have already seen, the design character of the furniture changed suddenly in England. France was still experimenting with the old idiom and the furniture stayed, predominantly, in Group 1. Perhaps it was the greater freedom of the Dutch and the English conditions that made faster progress possible. Thus we get those lovely free-curving forms of the Queen Anne period—still heavy, as we have seen, but with remarkable fineness in their curvature, proportion, and carved detail. Suddenly an idea flowered.

The upholstery changed too, although not to the same extent as the furniture. It changed faster in the realm of needlework to keep pace with the new furniture expression than in the realm of woven fabrics. For the most part, the velvets—cut and uncut, plain and patterned—and the damasks still followed the Baroque Italian and French types of patterns with leaves and flowers. The curves were bold and vigorous. Some of them looked extremely well on the sofas, now coming into more general use, with their pronounced backs, big scrolling arms and cabriole legs, and upon the upholstered chairs of the statelier sort. There was sufficient flowing motion in the furniture to echo these characteristics of the older type of fabric designs and harmonize with them. There were other patterns that seem to have been too stiff for the new furniture; they look ungainly to us today. But the newer type of fabric design, based on the newer brocades with their strong three-dimensional drawing in the new asymmetrical balance that re-emphasized the vigorous spotting and the rolling motion of the chairs, was perfectly tuned to the new chair designs, especially the forms that had moved farthest from the old William and Mary proportions. A great many of the chairs, and sofas, too, were covered with needlework quite unlike the type that had preceded it. Large flowers, turned at different angles, freely spotted and accompanied by naturalistic leaves—all in asymmetrical balance—became a peculiarly fitting type of covering, excellent in both scale and motion.

The needlework on the chair shown on Plate 54 is a fine example of this fitness of upholstery to chair. The amplitude of the cyma curves of this especially beautiful chair, the bold modeling of the legs, the generous curves of the seat, all call for the type of motion and the scale seen in the needlework of the covering for the seat. The pattern meanders boldly in perfect accord with the motion of the chair curves. But its meandering is quite unlike the cruder, untamed meandering of earlier needlework patterns. The flowers and leaves are placed with much greater skill. A new smoothness of movement is evident that goes well with the finished quality of the chair design. The scale of the flowers and leaves is still large. But it is not too large for the amplitude of the chair proportions. It is wholly suitable. There is happy accord between chair design and upholstery pattern. It is a fine example of adjustment with the pattern well contained within the frame of the new type of seat.

Both Groups 1 and 2 passed at the deaths of Anne and Louis XIV, in 1714 and 1715, respectively. In both countries a period of transition followed that has already been discussed in detail with reference to fabrics. The next major expression types come in the middle of the eighteenth century in both countries.

GROUP 3

This new type, Group 3, dominated the situation for a long time. As much of our furniture today of the traditional type is based on it, it is well worth while to be sure that we understand these basic upholstery combinations at their best.

Plate 61 is an excellent Chippendale-type chair. Some were more elaborate; some were simpler. This chair shows a mixture of several of the Chippendale ideas. The main body of the chair is one type; the central splat is another. The serpentine curve at the top is unusually rolling with exaggerated motion at the jointure with the side back rails. The arms retain the general shape of an earlier curve inherited from the Queen Anne types, although here reduced in curvature to suit the new expression of lighter weight and mass. The legs are standard type but have rather fine brackets for the whole style of the chair.

The upholstery material—not old—although theoretically it should be suitable in that it, too, is of the Group 3 expression type in terms of weight and general aspect, does not fit the chair very well. It is not bad; but neither is it very good. It lacks the same perfect accord that we saw in the case of the Queen Anne armchair.

Plate 62, on the other hand, is another Chippendale-type chair which does not give the decorator the same difficulties with which to contend. All the parts fit together easily, harmoniously, in one simple, over-all type of expression. And its upholstery repeats that mode of expression easily and pleasantly.

The difficulties presented by the first chair, Plate 61, typify a problem common to every owner of genuine old furniture and of period reproductions. Detailed analysis of the problem can help to determine a way of meeting it more adequately than was done in the case of the chair illustrated.

PLATE 61. *One of the Chippendale-type chairs with back showing the so-called Gothic motifs.* COURTESY METROPOLITAN MUSEUM OF ART.

Two leading points in design stand out sharply as we study the chair closely. First, the lower part seems lighter in aspect than the upper part. Second, the motion of the central splat feels quite different from the motion of the side rails and arms. The side rails and arms are heavier and bolder; the central splat closes up in smaller tighter movement. This movement, however, in turn seems rather heavy and stolid as compared with the quicker, finer movement of the little leg brackets, which are almost lace-like in comparison. The chair, on the whole, is excellent. We are considering it not as antiquarians but as students of design. And when we begin to study its upholstery possibilities it is necessary for us to consider all these divergent aspects.

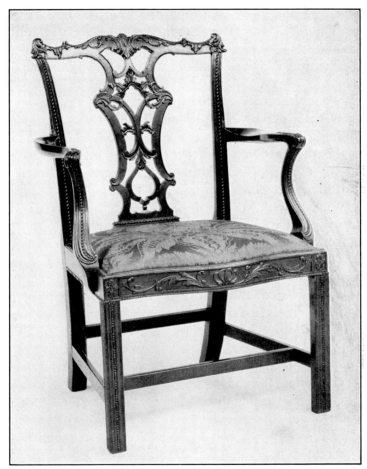

PLATE 62. *A Chippendale-type chair showing well-chosen upholstery.* COURTESY METROPOLITAN MUSEUM OF ART.

If we eliminate first the splat, for a moment, then the little brackets, the present seat cover seems excellent with the rest of the design. It follows the feeling of the weight and movement of the side rails, top, and arms. But, if we consider the splat, which is the controlling feature, the seat cover is too open, bold, and free. In relation to the brackets, it is even more so.   No likeness exists between the rolling scrolls which come over the front edge of the chair seat and those lace-like brackets.   Any pattern placed on that seat would have to be smaller in scale of its parts, more compact or closer in its repeat, less buoyantly flowing in movement in order to pull frame, splat, and brackets together.   A pattern that was right would be better than any plain material.   But, if the right pattern were not available, a plain material could be used.   At least, it would not introduce another, rather dominating, design idea at odds with one part or another of the chair design.

This example brings out the utter futility of trying to read the character of chair designs on the basis of what we think they should be, according to historic cataloguing.   The person who is most successful in solving these problems is not the one who acts on a set dogmatic basis but the one who sees sensitively and alertly just what he has in front of him with which to work.

The other chairs of this period, the wing, the so-called Georgian armchair with upholstered back and seat and small open padded arms —and its companion without arms—are a little less difficult because they were not made in such wide variety.   Damask was a common covering for the wings which had grown smaller, more compact, and with curves that flowed easily in both graceful and dignified fashion. Their proportions were now thoroughly mastered.   The very bold needlework of the preceding groups would look awkward and heavy on them.   When needlework was used, it was finer, with smaller figures, smaller details, and with the sizes changing more quickly from part to part of the design, thus adding to the accelerated motion that always tends to lighten the weight aspect.   Leather was much used, too.   Damask designs showed the same change as the needlework to smaller patterns with less bold curves and figures.   Velvets were used somewhat, but they were the plain velvets.   The big Genoese patterns were no longer suitable.

The so-called Georgian armchair in one of its many phases—when most like the French chairs—often was covered with brocade in typical French design.   But the simpler ones, of which there were a great many, were likely to be covered with needlework or damask in the lighter patterns just mentioned.   Some of these chair frames showed a great deal of motion; some were quieter, relatively severe.   The quieter ones were sometimes covered with plain goods or with leather.

The leathers themselves were plain, not stamped in pattern like the old Renaissance types.

It is impossible to give a simple, general idea for the chairs of Group 3. They were too diverse. Each one has to be studied for its own particular expression, as the side chair on Plate 61 was studied. Yet they are always full and rich in curve, robust without being coarse or awkward or exceedingly heavy. Their proportions are generous without being "big." Most of them have an aspect of richness, often of elegance, of amplitude, without excess weight. Fabrics for their coverings, at their best, followed suit. Plate 63 is an American example rather lighter in aspect than most of those of the middle of the century.

In France, diversity was present, yet it was not of the same sort. By this time, France had taken the leadership in silk production, and her brocades in bewildering variety led the world. Chairs, from the first part of the reign of Louis XV to its end, changed markedly in proportion but, on the whole, followed a few general types in contour. The earlier ones still retained some of the awkwardness of unmastered proportions that characterized the Régence. They were covered in the heavy bold patterns such as some of the cut velvets, damasks, and brocades, which had not entirely eliminated the static symmetry of the Renaissance, or, more occasionally, in the very new asymmetrical patterns. By the middle of Louis' reign, furniture designers had completely mastered the proportion problem. The best of their product was of the same general weight as the chairs of England of the same period. They still were ample, for the most part, generous in line and size, graceful and elegant. Their coverings reflected the same qualities. The brocades were a little lighter than earlier in the century, with much less modeling—and often not as well drawn. But they were full of charm and grace. By this time, some of the smaller chairs had appeared, and by the end of the reign the ample quality characteristic of the middle portion of the reign had practically disappeared. Chairs definitely were smaller, lighter, more dainty, and covered with very light fabric patterns. From this brief summary, it is easy to see that it is only the work of the middle of Louis' reign that is really comparable to Group 3 work as we have seen it in England.

Within this narrower range are the bergères, the larger open-armed chairs, and the smaller ones, with both open and closed arms.

As we are considering upholstery, the list does not include all sorts of chairs. Pads occur sometimes on the cane chairs—both side and arm—that also were common. All these shapes were diverse in detail.

PLATE 63. *Georgian armchair. Late eighteenth century. American type with high back.* COURTESY MUSEUM OF FINE ARTS, BOSTON.

The velvet or damask that was perfect in scale for the large bergères—nearest to a wing chair that the French had—could be entirely out of place on the gently curving back of a gondola-type chair. Plate 64. The damask that seemed made to fit that same graceful curve could be entirely out of place on the back of the large open-armed chair

with its wooden frame making the silhouette.   And the brocade that
fitted the large open-armed chair could be altogether too strong in
its motion and too large in its scale for the smaller chair that appeared
later with its quicker, more trivial motion.   The expression of each
chair and each covering must always be studied before they can be

PLATE 64.   *A Louis XV gondola-type chair.*   COURTESY METROPOLITAN MUSEUM
OF ART.

successfully combined.   Reference to Chapters 7–16 on the fabric
designs of the different periods will show clearly how the development
of the patterns synchronized with that of the chairs.

GROUP 4

Group 4 chairs cover the Adam, the Hepplewhite, and major
portions of the Sheraton types in England, those of the latter part of
the reign of Louis XV, and all those of the reign of Louis XVI in

France.   The change from the richness of the full motion of the Chippendale and the middle Louis XV type was marked—more so in English chairs than in those of France.   In England, the change was led by a designer with definite ideas—which meant the self-conscious introduction of a new style, the Adam style.   In France, the change was a gradual evolution, at least during the Louis XV reign; it is to be noted that the English designer himself was influenced in some degree by the French styles which still led the world in terms of furniture as well as clothes.   Between the chairs of Adam inspiration and the later ones of Sheraton inspiration, there is a great difference.   The Adam and the Sheraton represent the two extremes of weight expression of Group 4.   They must be considered separately because of the wide differences in fabrics usable on them.

On Adam furniture, needlework, as it had been known during the first part of the century, had about-faced.   Adam frequently covered his chairs with tapestry.   Much of this tapestry came from France; some of it was made in England.   From the design standpoint, two important facts stand out: (1) The patterns changed completely in character, the majority of them featuring handsome bouquets of flowers in stately urns; (2) The clusters of flowers were of size and shape (in mass) to fit the chair backs and seats perfectly.   They were obviously designed especially for them.   Furthermore, the fine tapestry work not only allowed fine detail, small and exquisite in its drawing and coloring, but also gave a texture that in its relative smoothness, as compared with the needlework on a Queen Anne chair, for example, was in perfect accord with the new smallness and lightness of aspect of the chairs themselves.

These tapestries were one of the dressier forms of covering.   It must be remembered that the 60–70 years since William and Mary had seen the gradual disappearance of forms, benches, stools, and tabourets as limited to the use of the master, the mistress, and their most important friends.   Now, everybody used chairs, and it is not surprising that, because of the great demand, there were cabinet-makers who made nothing else.   On these chairs now made for the simpler, less stately houses and rooms, simpler coverings were used.   Leather was a prime favorite, finished with nailheads.   The leather colors were inconspicuous, leaving plenty of opportunity for the delicacy of the design of the chair frame to be seen and appreciated.

Another favorite covering was horsehair, plain and patterned in small geometric designs. This, too, allowed the design of the chair frame to be seen to advantage. It also was a sturdy, long-wearing cover. The smoothness of both these types of upholstery, like the texture of the tapestries, was excellent with the low-relief ornamentation of the frame. Coarser textures, just as surely as large bold patterns or the smaller forceful patterns, would have overwhelmed the detail and spoiled the ensemble effect of the chair.

Satins, damasks, brocades, and small cut velvets were used on some of the dressier types but apparently were not the most favored for the ordinary types that were most commonly used. Most of the Adam chairs have a certain stogginess, a holding to the weight of the previous work while trying to emphasize the new ideas in the detail, changes of shape, and proportions. This quality made satins and brocades much less satisfactory than some of the more simple, less buoyantly active materials. Yet satins and brocades, especially the latter, were used. Adam designed some of them himself, using the same light forms that he emphasized in his wood detail and panel ornaments. Fine drawing of thin figures sparsely placed gave a delicacy that was the essence in general of the whole style. It is interesting that trims at this time had become much subordinated; they were merely finish where the material was turned under at its junction with the wood. Simple gimp or small nail heads in quiet patterning were the most common.

Hepplewhite chairs were still smaller and lighter in aspect. The wood parts seem to have been reduced to the least possible dimensions consistent with strength. Comparison of the silhouette of these chairs with the preceding ones shows a mastery of expression of the ensemble that the Adam chairs too often lacked. Now, form, mass, and detail were all telling the same story in the best of the work. There was no stogginess, no holding to the old ideas. The new idea of lightness and delicacy stood completely expressed. Many of the forms were developed from those that Adam evolved. The little chair with shaped, padded back in wooden frame was one example. Adam, in his turn, had borrowed from the French. Now Hepplewhite and his followers made it a truly English chair of delicate elegance and also most convenient. This Hepplewhite chair was the outstanding small upholstered chair of the group. The old big wing chair, except as it was made for someone who especially wanted it or in the provincial sections—including our own colonies—was out of fashion. It had been replaced by the tub chair, of which our modern barrel chair is a descendant, with low back rounding forward in a circle. The wing chairs that were made in the old style were lighter than formerly. The wings had more flare and usually were not continuous with the arms. The old Georgian armchair, of Chippendale period popularity, had maintained its own for a while under Adam, although it had been much modified. The nearest thing to it was the chair that persisted in our colonies; it is known now popularly as the Martha Washington chair.

The typical padded and shaped-back Hepplewhite chairs, based sometimes on Louis XV models and sometimes on those of Louis XVI, were covered variously. Some were very delicate and dressy in quite the French manner. Others were much less so. Some frames were of mahogany, others of satinwood, and still others were painted in the French manner. The detail, too, of back frame and legs varied greatly in its aspect of relative simplicity or dressiness. Some of the designs were exquisite in their curvature and balance; some were quite clumsy. Thus we find that material ranging from delicate brocades, small-figured cut velvets, satins, and, less often, damasks to the familiar leather and horsehair were common. Apparently, aside from the question of use, the scale of the detail and the finish of the chair largely dictated the choice. The satinwood and painted chairs gave a dressier, more delicate note than did most of the mahogany ones. It is easy to see that the detail of the back frame would count for much more in these finishes than in the darker mahogany where shadows, in the relief used, were partly lost. Thus the lively motion of the little velvet, the finely patterned small brocade, was a pleasing complement to the satinwood and painted chairs, whereas the quieter-motioned fabrics that were flatter in effect were better on the mahogany.

These same considerations guide us today. It is easy to overdo the motion on the seat of one of these side chairs in its covering, and thus spoil the unity of the design of the whole chair. It also is easy, with the daintier, lighter, dressier chairs, to underdo the motion and make the seat too plain and heavy. It is interesting that Hepplewhite himself wrote, "Mahogany chairs should have seats of horsehair, plain, striped, chequered." In these days when little horsehair is available and, in many rooms, is a complete misfit with the rest of the furnishings, we may perhaps translate that dictum into words such as these, "Mahogany chairs should have seats of some simple material that is quiet and unobtrusive, so that it will not detract from the effect of the frame of the chair."

Brocade patterns, as we already have seen, at this time were small and dainty for the most part. Stripes were rapidly becoming more numerous, sometimes plain, sometimes with little floral patterns intertwined with them. The silhouette of a Hepplewhite chair is so marked in its own characteristic scale and motion that the choice of a brocade or a stripe for one of them is a nice question. Plate 57 shows one of these chairs. It is a very beautiful chair—a masterly piece of exquisite grace and proportion. The upholstery is not so good. As a fabric it is mediocre in design. As upholstery for that particular chair it leaves much to be desired. The broad stripe interferes with the movement of the chair back, and the feeble little wreaths make irritating spots that interfere with the stripes and fail to support the lovely curves of the chair back. If a stripe were used, it should be (1) lovely in itself; (2) simple and flat enough to support the chair back—not to interfere with it. Too narrow a stripe, especially if in sharp color contrasts, would be cut up into too many parts—thus making motion too quick for the chair. Too broad a stripe would be too bold in motion. A stripe between the two, nearer the wider one than the narrower one, and quiet in color contrast would be better than the present one. But it is questionable if a stripe pattern could complement adequately that very smooth curve. A gentler motion in the repeat of a brocade might be much better. Plate 65 shows a very dressy American version of a Hepplewhite chair with a perfectly chosen flat stripe on it.

The Sheraton-type chairs at their best—in the type not strongly influenced by the changes of design in France or by the later ones after the French Empire was in full swing—showed a lightness similar to that of the Hepplewhite type but without the curves. Rectangular forms, horizontals, and verticals were handled with consummate skill. To apply the word grace to rectangular forms may seem odd. Yet the proportions in Sheraton chairs were so delicate, considered, and executed with such finesse that they really were graceful, easy, and elegant. As in Adam and Hepplewhite chairs, the upholstery varied according to the lightness, the openness, or the solidity of the chair itself. Some drew their inspiration from Louis XVI chairs, and these were for the most part more dainty, more dressy than the others.

PLATE 65. *An American Hepplewhite-type chair of unusual shape. The seat covering is a perfect foil for the chair back.* COURTESY MUSEUM OF FINE ARTS, BOSTON.

The chairs with very fine latticework backs—not the coarser ones—because of the thinness and lightness of their general effect also are usually grouped with the more dressy. Chairs with the solid vase forms and the key-shaped splats are likely to be much more solid in effect. Neither of these statements should be taken as wholly inclusive. We must always study the individual chair. The variations are too numerous to permit us to be sweepingly dogmatic about them. On the dressier ones, appeared the little brocades, the small light cut velvets, the plain velvets, these latter especially on the loose cushions for the cane-seated chairs. On the plainer chairs, were more likely to be found the leather or the very small-figured damask that called little

(a)   (b)

PLATE 66. *a. An American Sheraton-type chair with well-chosen seat covering that is wholly suitable for the chair back. b. The horsehair covering is perfect for this American Sheraton-type chair, more staid than* (a). COURTESY MUSEUM OF FINE ARTS, BOSTON.

attention to itself but, because of the vibratory effect of its small indistinct pattern, was more satisfactory than a wholly plain material. On the rather uncommon chairs that were upholstered on the framed back, a scarcely recognizable descendant of the Georgian armchair, large-patterned damasks were to be found too, in the light expression typical of general Louis XVI character. Stripes were commonly used, too, both figured and plain. They were gentle stripes, not very broad, not very strong in color contrast, so that they did not interfere with the over-all effect of the contour of the chair. Plates 66, 67.

With the change in heaviness due to the Empire influence, the gentleness and delicacy of the Louis XVI-type materials disappeared. Leather was used, and damasks showed the characteristic spottiness and blockiness of the French influence. Stripes were broader, bolder, stronger in color contrast, both in color and size, not always to the

PLATE 67. *An American-type Sheraton chair. The lightness and dressiness are well suited by the upholstery.* COURTESY MUSEUM OF FINE ARTS, BOSTON.

advantage of the chair ensemble. However, until the very end of the Sheraton influence, delicacy still was the major controlling aspect.

In France, brocades, satins, taffetas, damasks, and small cut velvets —also the new toiles—were the order of the day. The majority of the chairs belonging to this expression group were small, and their padded backs were framed in wood. There were a few larger ones, the bergères, on which the upholstery was continuous, as they were upholstered at the sides between arms and seat. The wooden-backed side chairs were very varied in detail, but all had the common attributes of straightness of lines and smallness of parts, and were light in aspect. Brocades, small in scale and daintily spotted, were common coverings for the little padded-back chairs whose wooden frame held their motion in check admirably. The small cut velvets were exquisite and, because

PLATE 68. *A Louis XVI side chair with characteristic stripe.* COURTESY MUSEUM OF FINE ARTS, BOSTON.

of their close-matted effect, made an excellent foil for the motion of the most active of these chairs. Stripes in satin, taffeta, damask, and brocade were numerous. Plate 68. For the most part, they were small stripes that fitted the quiet and simple lines of the chairs, even those that had the curving oval backs. They were chosen with exquisite taste, never having the effect of bursting rudely into the curved frames with their straight lines. Fascinating little plaid taffetas were in vogue, brought over from the preceding period. Tapestry, like that in England, was fine in texture and done mostly in formal, symmetrical floral effects, bouquets of flowers in vases and urns. It was woven to fit the forms on which it was to be placed and was admirably scaled. Damasks were used, both large and small. Always the parts into which they were divided, the sub-divisions of the patterns, were small and thus fitted the scale of the chairs. Plain satins, too, finished with lovely gimps, were common, especially on some of the dressier small bergères and as thick pads on some of the side chairs. The upholstery on these French chairs is seldom too prominent. They usually are fine examples of perfectly chosen coverings that keep their place in the ensemble of the chair design.

The next two groups may be passed over quickly. With the elimination of the best weavers of France and the evolution of the new type of furniture, a stage of experimentation was inevitable during which the results were relatively crude, as compared with the height of beauty that had been achieved previously through generations of growth and training.

The mannered curves of the Directoire chairs took stripes well, and many stripes appeared as coverings. But they were different stripes from those that had fitted the Louis XVI chairs so well. The contrasts were sharper, stronger—though the motion still was light—suiting the light motion that had been retained in the chairs themselves.

GROUP 5

The fuller expression of the new forms during the Empire changed this scale, and the stripes, again common, changed too. Boldness calls for boldness, and the new Empire stripes could hold their own against the heavy wood frames. They were simple and flat, not cut into small parts, with resulting quickness of motion as in the Louis XVI and Directoire stripes. Damasks were popular, with simple bold isolated repeats, heavy in contour and placed with little discrimination. But they were in perfect harmony with the chair expressions.

In England, the differences in upholstery characteristics in both the Regency furniture of the lighter sort—based on Sheraton forms—and the later Regency types based, like the French, on misappropriated and misapplied Egytian and classic motifs, were approximately the same.

GROUP 6

Much of the Victorian furniture, following in the wake of these influences, was bad also. So, too, was the upholstery. But there were bright spots in the picture. Some of the later Victorian forms took on the typical Louis XV curves and were really lovely. Usually these forms were very active, and the upholstery—damask, velvet (often plush or "velour"), and horsehair—were subdued and rich or sufficiently plain to accompany the active frames peacefully. The fat, heavy upholstered pieces were more likely to have the lush damasks —in scale of pattern about like those of Group 3—with heavy ornate fringe, as well as many buttons, for a finish. Rich plain satins with corresponding trim were also frequent.

GROUP 7

The last group, our own Modern, has already had great diversity of coverings. But the trend has always been away from the ornate, the merely pictorial, the modeled figures, toward coverings that would be simple and flat enough to fit the simplified flat surfaces and masses of the furniture and yet be interesting. Thus the emphasis has been on the textured materials rather than on the patterned ones, for furniture coverings. Decorators have had to learn that textures, too, have their own modes of expression and of character and that not every texture can be used safely on every chair in every place in the room. As a matter of fact, texture makes its own type of pattern, and the scale of the chair, its shape—straight or curved—its lightness or weight, all dictate what motion in the texture of the material for its covering can safely be used. Many patterns, flat and spreading for the most part, have been designed, but they have not yet been developed and used for upholstery purposes with the same skill as the textures. The need for a variety of textures has been and is still producing fascinating and stimulating results.

SECTION THREE

Choosing Coverings for Chairs of Today

18

A Summary of Elementary Principles Regarding Fabrics Used as Upholstery

FROM THE BRIEF HISTORICAL SUMMARY IN THE PRECEDING SECTION, WE can glean many facts to help us in everyday decorating. For the sake of simplifying the task, the following summary of this material is divided into three parts as viewed from the standpoint of design and expression: (1) pattern, (2) texture, and (3) color. Like all such divisions, this separation is very arbitrary. Actually, all these factors have to be considered simultaneously; they are but parts of the whole appearance, and it is with the whole appearance that we are concerned. It helps, however, to think about them separately at first, until we get to the point at which we are quickly sensitive to the whole unified impression and its own peculiar message.

PATTERN

SCALE IN PATTERN

Scale is used here in the sense of size. When looking at patterns with size in mind, we might be considering either the size of the whole unit of repeat or the sizes of the major spots. At the moment, only the sizes of the major spots are referred to. They are the determining factors for us in connection with the upholstery story for the most part. Sometimes very large units, even up to 60 inches, may give the impression of being small in scale because of the smallness of the parts of which they are composed and thus can be used in conjunction with delicate pieces of furniture. The chances are that, unless one is in the business of interior decoration, the actual measure of the unit repeat is not a matter of special consideration. But the sizes of the individual parts do give immediate impression of "large," "small," "medium" that either fits the character of the chair in question or does not. That is the scale to which reference is made at the moment.

How important this factor is can be seen easily from the following illustration. The needlework on the seat of the Queen Anne chair, Plate 54, has flowers and leaves that are large in scale. If that needlework were placed on the Hepplewhite chair, Plate 57, it would be ridiculous because of its large scale in contrast to the small over-all dimensions of the chair and the smallness of its parts. This fact seems obvious yet in everyday practice mistakes of this sort in scale are made constantly. One of the commonest examples of misunderstood scale is the use of the large Jacobean patterns with their huge awkward flowers and big meandering stems on wing chairs of the Queen Anne and Middle Georgian periods. The patterns are much too large, dwarfing the chair and calling far too much attention to themselves. Another common example is the use of the large-scale Italian-type damask on the seats of Hepplewhite and Chippendale chairs. The difficulty does not lie in the fact that the whole of the pattern cannot be contained within the area of the chair seat. Many excellent choices of damask patterns for this purpose are not so contained. The difficulty lies in the scale of the portions of the pattern that are seen upon that chair seat. They are so big that they seem to be bursting their bounds and refusing to stay peacefully on the chair seat. Both Plates 69 and 70 show excellent examples of damasks perfectly scaled to their respective chairs.

Still another phase of this misuse or this misunderstanding of scale is very common. It is the reverse of the two preceding examples —the use of scale that is too small upon the surface of sofas, chaises longues, and large chairs. It unfortunately is a very common practice to cover club chairs with patterns that would be right in scale for the seats of small pull-up chairs, and large sofas with little patterns that are adapted to side chairs. More leeway is allowable in the case of a chaise because of the fact that ordinarily all of its surfaces do not show as in sofas and large chairs. Piles of pillows and a throw at the base leave relatively little space where the original covering is seen. Thus one of the small-figured French velvets may be pleasantly usable. However, if much of the surface does show, that chaise is to be classed with the big chairs and the sofas in this respect. There is some excuse for this confusion because there are times when sofa, or chaise, because of its position in the room, should have neither an absolutely plain material nor a marked pattern. The plain material would make it too bare, thus calling attention to it by making it a hole in the rest of the room composition. A marked pattern would make it too prominent because of its activity. A small-scale pattern giving little motion may

PLATE 69. *A Colonial Chippendale-type chair attributed to Gillingham, Philadelphia.* COURTESY MUSEUM OF FINE ARTS, BOSTON.

seem to be the compromise. The problem lies in the fact that that small-scaled figure may be so definite in shape and obvious in size that it instantly becomes a matter of contrast to the size and expression of the sofa and is as unpleasant as the small brocade pattern would be on a Queen Anne chair. The answer lies in using a pattern that is so indistinct that it may not even be considered as a pattern; it is rather a matter of vibration that removes the feeling of excessive bareness and plainness, yet keeps the sofa, chair, or chaise in its place

PLATE 70. *A Colonial chair, Chippendale in type by Benjamin Randolph of Phila-delphia.* COURTESY MUSEUM OF FINE ARTS, BOSTON.

and not too conspicuous. It counts practically as texture. Then it can be highly satisfactory.

Briefly, pattern must be scaled to the size of the chair. It can show contrast but never so much contrast as to allow the upholstery to be overwhelming in its call upon the attention nor so small as to be a ridiculous comparison.

There is also the point to be considered that small-scale patterns can become exceedingly monotonous in their repetition over large surfaces. This statement is true in the case of upholstery; it also is true regarding obvious small patterns used as curtains and explains why some materials should always be used as short curtains.

MOVEMENT IN PATTERN

As we glance quickly at an upholstered chair, we are conscious immediately of the scale, discussed above, and also of the movement of the pattern. We may not realize immediately what gives this impression of activity nor why the pattern does not look right on that chair, even though it seems to pass the scale test perfectly. The answer may lie in this aspect of movement. Think for a moment of a large damask suitable for use with Group 1 furniture. The movement is slow, ponderous. Now think for a moment of the movement of a small French brocade suitable for use on a Louis XVI chair, Group 4, such as is shown on Plate 46. The movement is quick, vivacious. These are the two extremes. Between them lie many intermediate movement aspects. What makes these different expressions of movement? How does one learn to recognize them?

The major item that determines the quality of movement is the size relationship of spot to spot in any pattern. In a piece of typical Queen Anne needlework consisting of flowers and leaves, the changes in size from flower to flower are very moderate. The pattern does not have sharp size contrasts that are conspicuous. The same fact can be noted in the case of the leaves. Thus our attention moves slowly through those changes, in leisurely fashion. It can be further noted that these flowers do not show sharp changes in their variations of position from full view to three-quarter, to side, or to profile. Again, our attention moves slowly through these changes in direction. We thus have slowness of movement, due both to sizes of parts and to positions of parts with reference to the directions in which they turn. If we look again at the little French brocade, we find that the changes from size to size are much greater than in the needlework, and thus they give accelerated motion. The positions of the parts, the directions in which they turn or point, also show much greater variety, again making accelerated motion.

We also find that the manner in which the pattern is placed upon the background plays a part in this motion. Properly considered, the size and shape of the background are always integral parts of a fine pattern—a fact that is sharply focused for us in the story of upholstery. Those small-scale spots with their quick interrelation of sizes certainly are giving an effect of lightness and theoretically may seem to be suitable for any one of a dozen chairs of Group 4. Actually, they may not work out that way in practice. One pattern may be spaced rather sparsely over the background; another may be spaced much more closely. Both are connected with the usual little airy stems and tendrils. The difficulty for practical and successful use here lies in the fact that the first pattern shows much more movement than does the second one. The second one, although not what would be called a closely matted design, does not range over the surface but is quiet in its compactness. Thus, if the chair itself happens to be quite active in line, this last pattern is likely to look better on it than the first one. The first one has so much motion that it will conflict with the motion of the chair contour with resulting restlessness and loss of the unity of impression of the chair ensemble. This is a mistake often made in choosing brocade patterns for late eighteenth century chairs, both French and English. In Plate 61, we saw a similar mistake made with the covering of a Chippendale-type chair.

The movement aspect is very marked in stripes. Aside from considerations of the weight aspect, such as light, intermediate, and heavy, their movement may be the determining factor in their successful use. Assume two light-weight stripes at hand. One, because of its contrasts in size and color, gives a feeling of a good deal of motion. The other, with less contrast in size and color, gives a feeling of less motion; in fact, it may give very little. Still another, so small that it could never be regarded as heavy, with stripes of exactly the same size but sharply contrasting in color, could have much more motion than the last one. Number 1 would require a chair that was steady enough in its own motion and strong enough in contour interest to hold the stripe in place. Number 2 would be used on a chair with much more motion of its own. The choice between Number 2 and Number 3 would depend upon the detail of the chair—a point for later discussion.

SHAPES IN PATTERN

The character of the shapes in the pattern also is a determining factor in choosing upholstery, as are also the inseparable factors of the type and quality of their rendering. As these items have already been discussed to some extent in the preceding pages, it seems unnecessary to repeat the details. The roundness or the flatness of the units, considered in conjunction with the scale and the movement, are of paramount importance when seen with the shapes and the lines of the chair itself. The skillfully drawn, rounded forms of the Régence types are obvious companions for the curving robust forms of the early eighteenth century chairs. The flatter, as well as smaller, flower forms of the middle eighteenth century still are more modeled than the majority of the later ones of the latter part of the eighteenth century. This flatness, combined with the small scale and type of movement, suits well that later period. The rather bold, coarse contours and flat drawing of the early nineteenth century tell the same story as the forms on which they are placed. It is not surprising to see roundness and increased sizes, with great variety of shape, reappearing with the Victorian, especially that which savors strongly of Louis XV types in proportion, curvature, and detail of ornament. It is logical, too, that, with the elimination of detail and increased emphasis on the importance of plane against plane in modern work, pattern should again go flat, running in general to the larger shapes which in turn are much conventionalized and simplified in accordance with many phases of the non-objective dictum.

TEXTURE IN PATTERN

The texture aspect of upholstery, as already noted, plays an exceedingly important part today. It has always been important, although accepted for the most part as an adjunct of pattern. Today, however, relatively few of the plain-surfaced chairs and sofas of strictly modern style carry pattern as we have thought of it in the past. It is difficult to find many really fine modern patterns for upholstery, and most of the old types look quite ridiculous on modern furniture. They are usually entirely out of harmony with it. Sometimes in thinking of textured fabrics we forget that the variations are just as marked and distinctive within their structural ranges as the variations in pattern. The dictionary defines texture as "the arrangement or character of the threads of a woven fabric." The arrangement may result in a fabric that is smooth, medium smooth, or rough. In any practical consideration of texture from the upholstery standpoint, the whole gamut should be included.

The arrangement of the threads also gives a distinct motion aspect, which, although not pattern in the usually accepted sense of definite figures arranged upon background, does have form. Thus the effect of a basket weave gives a problem in upholstery quite different from that of a herringbone weave as in plain twill. These are but two very obvious examples. Careful observation of a dozen modern "texture" weaves will disclose the fact that in addition to being smooth, less smooth, or rough, they also control the attention and move it in various directions by means of their texture patterning. How important this can be may be illustrated by the fact that one material, even though it is not too rough, may seem to be too active for a small modern chair of a size that would correspond to the older type 4 pull-up chair. Or, a texture, seemingly right as far as degree of roughness-smoothness is concerned, may have the effect of making the wood of a big modern sofa too prominent; the upholstery "pattern" of texture is not strong enough in attention value. Not rougher texture necessarily, but more active texture patterning may be the answer.

The disposition of the threads, aside from their composition, large, small, knotted, smooth, etc., breaks the flow of light over the surface of the material. Sometimes, without having the material rougher, we need more vibration to avoid excess plainness against solid, plain pieces of wood. Actually rough texture would be too strong—like a heavy pattern of the old type on a light small chair. But the right degree of roughness-smoothness, interpreted in terms of right degree of vibration or motion, by means of this texture patterning, can give wholly satisfactory results. These variations in texture patterning as they are used in really fine modern rooms account for the fact that the upholstered surfaces do not feel monotonously plain with merely rough-smooth contrasts. Unfortunately much decorative thinking of the modern type stops with the rough-smooth idiom, especially in the lower-price brackets.

In the traditional field, velvets give us one of the best examples of the texture story. Confining ourselves for the moment to the so-

PLATE 71. *A handsome large-scale design that in the detail of its patterning scale is in accord with middle eighteenth century furniture.* COURTESY SCALAMANDRÉ MUSEUM OF TEXTILES.

called silk velvets that are silk pile and cotton back, the most used sort, we can get striking illustration of this point. Velvets were used liberally on Queen Anne chair seats. They were also used for some

PLATE 72. *A distinguished contemporary design whose bold flatness is in sharp contrast to the small-scale modeling and effect of the lampas on Plate 71. Although not a large repeat, it needs furnishings of equally bold definition to accompany it.*
COURTESY SCALAMANDRÉ MUSEUM OF TEXTILES.

of the pads that were placed on the cane seats of the very late eighteenth century chairs of Sheraton inspiration. To interchange two of these velvets, each one suitable for its own chair, would provide results as ridiculous as the interchange of the needlework and brocade patterns discussed under pattern. The velvet suitable for the Sheraton chair would look trivial on the Queen Anne chair. The velvet suitable for the Queen Anne chair would look heavy, soggy—a weight upon a delicate form—on the Sheraton chair. The question is not primarily one of color, although that is an important secondary element. It is primarily a question of texture—arrangement of threads—which con-

PLATE 73. *A handblocked linen from the house of Caesar Rodney of Delaware, one of the signers of the Declaration of Independence.* COURTESY SCALAMANDRÉ MUSEUM OF TEXTILES.

trols the manner in which the light breaks as it falls across the surface. The Queen Anne chair needs a feeling of depth, of strength, which can come from bigger threads and deeper pile. The Sheraton-type chair needs a feeling of lightness, of thinness, which can come from smaller threads, possibly more lustrous or closer together, so as not to break up the light with so much motion. Again, the problem should not be confused with mere smoothness-roughness. The Queen Anne velvet can be very smooth yet give the required effect. There is not as much leeway in the Sheraton type. Smoothness and the particular quality of lightness that is essential seem to be close partners.

PLATE 74. *A fine contemporary texture in intaglio effect, perfect for one of the sofas or chairs where vibratory aspect is needed without too much definition of shape.* COURTESY SCALAMANDRÉ MUSEUM OF TEXTILES.

The horsehair that looks well on the Hepplewhite and Sheraton chairs has both smoothness and depth. It is a peculiar combination of qualities that makes an excellent foil for the majority of these chairs —except the dressy ones—regardless of the variations in the details of their designs. Satin, on the other hand, lacks the depth of the

PLATE 75. *Another not too definite pattern that can be used when vibratory effect and a gentle all-over movement are desirable.* COURTESY J. H. THORP & CO.

fine-grade horsehair and is usable, unpatterned, on relatively few of these chairs; those that follow the French tradition and have a wooden frame to hold the fabric down are an exception.

Leather has been a favorite covering for centuries and still is. Modern furniture is often covered with it. Yet not every leather can be used on every type of chair, either traditional or modern. Practical

(a)

(b)   (c)

PLATE 76. *Three fine examples of modern textures giving different movement types.* a. COURTESY KNOLL ASSOCIATES. b. COURTESY ARUNDELL CLARKE. c. COURTESY ARUNDELL CLARKE.

considerations determine its use, for example, whether this or that leather is too heavy to be fitted over the rather thin arms with their knife edges of a given chair. But the texture of the leather does have to be considered in relation to appearance. Some leathers absorb

PLATE 77. *A handsome Georgian damask.* COURTESY J. H. THORP & CO.

a good deal of light; some reflect it. Some seem to have a motion that calls for sturdy frames or shapes to hold it on the chair. Others have a smoothness and slickness that can remain peacefully only on light forms. Still others are between these two in effect. Fine-grained dark leather of medium weight was in common use on the chairs of the late eighteenth century. These seats were not smooth and shiny. They were about the same in feeling as those that were coverd with horse-hair. Leather was used also on chairs of the early eighteenth century. It was no longer the heavy stamped leather of the preceding century, although it was firm and heavy enough to suit the furniture.   On a late eighteenth century chair it would have been much too heavy and solid.   Modern furniture in its present unsettled condition due to

PLATE 78.   *A traditional material treated in the modern idiom.*   COURTESY JOFA, INC.

constant changes from experiments runs the gamut from the heavier leathers to the very light ones, depending on the needs of the individual items of furniture.   There is no settled type or style yet.   The situation is fluid, a healthy condition.   Plates 71, 72, 73, 74, 75, 76*a, b, c,* 77, and 78.

COLOR

Color follows the pattern and the texture stories and has already been discussed historically in Section 2. Briefly, the bolder patterns that suit the chairs of bolder design need the same quality in the color. The stronger textures like the velvets that suit the Queen Anne furniture need the color that corresponds. The color suitable for the Sheraton chair would be anemic on the Queen Anne chair. This statement should not be interpreted to mean that all the stronger colors have to be dark, and all the lighter-weight, gentler colors, pastels. A close study of historic fabrics quickly disproves that idea. There are many light colors among the earlier, heavy fabrics, both Renaissance and Queen Anne. Many dark colors are found among the thin fabrics of the late eighteenth century. But the earlier ones have force, power, due partly to their inherent chroma and partly to their effect in juxtaposition with other colors. The late ones are flatter, thinner, less chromatic, and, as in brocades, in their relationships with other colors, give movement that is easy and dainty. The red velvet of the Queen Anne type is a full-bodied red; that of the late eighteenth century is apt to be a little lighter, less chromatic; thus it appears thinner, lighter in aspect of weight.

19

Some Important Design Qualities
of Chairs as Basis
for Fabric Choices

ONE MORE POINT OF GENERAL CHARACTER NEEDS TO BE CONSIDERED BEFORE we go shopping among the myriad tantalizing fabrics of all periods that are available as well as the current designs that cannot be classified as of any specific period, and the strictly modern ones.

Enthusiasm about antiques sometimes blunts our common sense to such a degree that we forget that our ancestors, too, varied in the quality of their productions. Some were fine; some were poor. Some were dressy and elegant; some were as good in decorative quality as others but did not have that extra touch which would have made them dressy. Some were still simpler, yet excellent in design. Dressiness and fine design are not necessarily synonymous. Still others were coarse and rough, frankly cottage types of the simplest kind. Over here in the colonies, the very best work seldom had that extra touch that spelled elegance. There were many fine chairs excellent in design, and they were perfect for the dignified and comfortable homes in which they were placed. There were others also that were good in design which belonged in the simpler houses where rooms were smaller and the other furniture, too, was simpler. Such houses were not the poorer homes in the sense of real want, but, as the owners were not affluent, there was less money to spend and the furnishings and buildings had to be much simpler. Below this grade, there were the really crude cottage-type homes that had the very simplest of furnishings. The reproductions and adaptations that the majority of people are still using are based on all these major types of our ancestors.

The importance of this to us lies in the fact that the fabrics followed suit and today, to keep within character, should continue to do so. Too often they do not because we either overestimate or underestimate these important aspects from elegance to simplicity. Consequently, the very simple chair is given a covering that should be on the elegant chair, and the medium chair receives a covering that should have been reserved—possibly a fine brocade—for the elegant chair in the best room of one of the more elegant homes. It is by no means easy to read these upholstery materials correctly and place them on the right and suitable types of chairs. In a way, upholstery fabrics are roughly comparable to dress fabrics, which, however, present a much simpler problem. Some silks are dressy; some wools have a fine finish but are not dressy like fine silks; tweeds and cottons are not at all dressy but are excellent within their scope.

A glance at a few old chairs will help in solving the problems of today. For example, the Queen Anne chair with the needlework with which we are already familiar is definitely an elegant one which probably graced a luxurious, dignified room. Plate 54. On Plates 69 and 70 are two fine products from our own colonies, made by two of the best chairmakers, Randolph and Gillingham. They are of the next period, the Middle Georgian, and are in the Chippendale style. They are handsome chairs, excellent in proportion, excellent in detail, yet they do not have that little extra quality which gives the elegance of the Queen Anne chair. The question is not one of inferiority; it is a difference in expression. They are simpler, a little less suave and subtle in their lines and proportion, yet beautiful in their quiet simplicity.

To sum up these new aspects that are so important for consideration when we are choosing upholstery, we can establish a classification for the furniture like the one below. Like all classifications so arbitrarily made it cannot be set up with rigid boundaries.

Group 1. Dressy	Group 2. Less dressy	Group 3. Simple
1. Fine design.	1. Fine design.	1. Fine design.
2. Fair to good design.	2. Fair to good design.	2. Fair to good design.
3. Poor design.	3. Poor design.	3. Poor design.

It will be noted that, in addition to the separation into three major groups, there are sub-divisions based on design values necessary to keep these products in some sort of proper perspective from the practical standpoint of finding modern upholstery for them. Whether we are considering antiques or reproductions, we shall always find that there are dressy, elegant chairs, for example, that are handsome in design and others that, although equally dressy, are quite horible in design, anathema to anyone with good taste. In each group there are these two extremes, good and poor, and the intermediate values. It is of utmost importance to learn to distinguish these differences. Many people are deceived by mere dressiness and think that dressiness and fineness are synonymous in terms of chair design; others are deceived by mere crudity and too often think they have a "find" in one of the simpler chairs and mistakenly elevate it to a place where it never should be used. The same distinctions appear in fabrics. We must learn to avoid the poor dressy ones, the poor medium ones, and the poor simple ones. There are plenty of good products in all three classifications.

Careful observation of the upholstery on some of the chairs we have been discussing and others will show how satisfactory coverings can be when well chosen. From this standpoint, as well as those that have already been discussed, the needlework is perfect on the Queen Anne chair. Even if it were the right scale for the two Chippndale-type chairs, Plates 69 and 70, it would not fit them. It has the little extra touch that goes too far for their simpler, sturdy, and straight-forward expression. The damasks, however, that already are on them are excellent. They are not simple chairs by any means, but they are not so dressy as the Queen Anne chair. It is notable also that each damask looks better upon the chair on which it is placed than it would upon the other one. Why? Because one chair is a bit more solid in effect, has less action in the back interlaced splat than the other. Thus the quicker motion of the damask on Plate 70, excellent in its present place, might be a little too quick for the slower motion of the splat of the one on Plate 69. Its damask has more solidity.

The chair on Plate 79 actually is not so fine in design as many another of its general type made in the colonies. In spite of some very awkward proportions, it somehow succeeds in telling us that it is on the whole dressy and can be used with other very nice furniture. The flare of the back and the top curve, the shaping of the seat, the detail of the legs, all indicate that it belongs with Group 1 rather than Group 2. Possibly, if the covering were different, we might be tempted to drop it back into Group 2. As it is, the damask with which it is upholstered is in itself dressy, perfect in scale and motion for the chair. From the academic design standpoint, if we wish to be

PLATE 79. *A dignified and elegant Middle Georgian chair, showing some traces of the earlier feeling.* COURTESY MUSEUM OF FINE ARTS, BOSTON.

very particular, we might say that the damask really is better in design than the chair and has much to do with giving the very interesting effect of the chair. This brings up two more points for practical consideration. Many small upholstered chairs are good in design and invaluable in all kinds of rooms. Few of them are what would be called outstanding in design, either definitely dressy and elegant or fine in design in one of the other classifications. Yet they can be used satisfactorily in all three kinds of settings, provided that they are covered with upholstery that fits the conditions. On the other hand, far too often, we see an ordinary chair of stupid design, or worse, covered with a fine material. If the chair is really commonplace, probably the fine material—supposedly of excellent design—will make it look worse because it offers too great a contrast and shows up all the faults of the poor design of the chair itself. It would have been better to have chosen a fabric of less finesse that would not have been too great a contrast for the chair design, yet would have been enough better to have improved the effect of the ensemble. To determine how far one can go safely in lifting a mediocre chair to better appearance by means of its upholstery is a nice question of decorative judgment. In the case of this old Chippendale-type chair with Queen Anne characteristics, the upholstery is not overdone in terms of fine and dressy because so much about the chair, too, is fine. The upholstery supports these aspects, thus building up a characterful, decorative, and elegant effect.

The reverse side of the story is illustrated clearly by the Queen Anne-type chair on Plate 80. This chair is in Group 2, even less dressy than the Randolph or the Gillingham chair but still excellent in design within the scope of its expression. The type was common in colonial days in the medium sort of home. The brocade on the seat is a very beautiful one and in color is perfect with the chair finish—a mellow, very soft yellow that tones pleasantly into the light, soft brown of the chair frame. The scale is excellent; the motion is excellent; it is perfectly placed on the seat. It is one of the large-scale patterns mentioned earlier that is adjusted here to a small space —perfectly. But with all these good points in its favor, it is still a misfit. It is far too dressy for the rather simple colonial expression of the Queen Anne chair form. The brocade is the type that would look well on a fine French Régence chair of Court type—one of the smaller ones. It is of the late Louis XIV lace-design type, rather smaller than ordinary, and very beautiful. Perhaps the owner was dressing up a bit! Even the colonial owner sometimes indulged in overdressing his furniture as witness the damask used on some of the very early chairs placed in those crude early rooms.

In the later, lighter range, the two chairs on Plates 81 and 82 illustrate clearly the point under discussion. Chair 81 is a particularly

PLATE 80. *A favorite simple form of the Queen Anne-type chair in the Colonies, 1725–1750, New England.* COURTESY MUSEUM OF FINE ARTS, BOSTON.

fine example of the Phyfe type with subtly shaped back and arms and fine general proportions. It shows the thinking of a very skillful worker. Much fine detailed thought and consideration are evident

throughout the whole design.   The chair definitely belongs in Group
1.   The quiet stripe with which it is covered sets the chair frame off

PLATE 81.   *A fine example of Phyfe armchair.*   COURTESY MUSEUM OF FINE ARTS,
BOSTON.

to advantage.   It is an excellent example of upholstery that is perfectly chosen.   Because it is quiet does not imply that it is crude or
simple.   It, too, is a piece of finished thinking in terms of design.

The mahogany side chair on Plate 82 is much simpler in its effect, although it is excellent in design. It seems to belong in Group 2 rather than in Group 1. It is a fine chair, simply not as dressy and

PLATE 82. *An excellent Phyfe side chair of less dressy character than the one shown on the preceding plate.* COURTESY MUSEUM OF FINE ARTS, BOSTON.

subtle in form and detail as the chair shown on Plate 81. The plain dark leather makes a perfect covering for it. The modest stripe that was on the preceding chair would be incongruous. It would assume undue importance against this frame, detracting from the chair itself. But the plain leather is excellent.

20

Upholstering Large Lounge Chairs

IN THE NEXT FEW CHAPTERS, WE SHALL SEE THE APPLICATION OF THE points discussed in the two preceding ones. In order to make our work as practical as possible, furniture pictures have been taken from stock that either is current or has been so within a reasonable time, so that they show in general the chair types we meet everywhere both in homes and stores. They cover most of the variations, large, medium, and small, of easy chairs, fine reproductions and good reproductions or adaptations, from dressy to simpler types but without any effort to catalogue them completely.

CHAIR 1. PLATE 83. LOW FIRESIDE CHAIR

This chair almost defies classification of dressy to simple. It can be combined with furniture of various styles and weights. It also can be used under a great variety of conditions from the dressier to the simpler effects. Its air of complete self-possession and fitness is due to the work of a succession of designers who have modified a little here, a little there, until all oddities that might call undue attention to themselves have been eliminated, and consequently there is no straining for effect. This careful consideration is one of the reasons that the chair has an air of elegance and could be used in a room with the finest of antiques. Yet it is so simple in its lines that, properly covered, it could be used under much less dressy conditions, provided that the other furniture was good in design, either antiques or reproductions. It would never be right, of course, under one of the very simple cottage conditions.

On the whole, as the aspect of this chair in other respects tends toward the rather heavy expression, it is easy to see it in a room where there is some early eighteenth century walnut perhaps with some Chippendale, the whole key of the room being between these two in terms

of weight.   It could be used, however, in a room keyed to the intermediate Chippendale weights, too, with perhaps a few lighter accents,
a few Hepplewhite or Sheraton pieces, for example.   And in a room

PLATE 83.   *A luxurious low fireside chair.*   COURTESY WOOD & HOGAN.

styled to the Mid-Victorian period, it could be at home.   These statements are based solely on the chair itself, not on the effect with the
covering.

UPHOLSTERY

The type of covering chosen would make marked changes in
aspect.   The slightly rough but still dressy texture shown on it in
the illustration is an excellent choice for one of the finer effects.   It

gives full value to the heavier aspects of the chair. The heavy fringe at the base is well chosen as to weight, with good light-and-shade motion to go with the surface of the material and the aspect of weight set up by the buttoned planes and the roll of the chair surface. Note

PLATE 84. *Chair similar to Plate 83 but showing marked change of expression due to the difference in type of covering.* COURTESY WOOD & HOGAN.

that the texture motion is perfectly adapted to the chair; it stays within the chair frame, giving only moderate activity.

If the chair were covered with a handblocked linen of medium-sized pattern, the effect would be surprisingly different. It would lose much dressiness, although never its dignity and its excellent design. The particular type of the linen pattern, in turn, would determine in large measure the suitability of the chair, as a whole, for different

Plate 85.   Large Lounge Chair   263

settings.   A matted pattern of medium scale with all-over effect in rather subdued contrasts, for example, would be likely to keep the chair closer to the dressier effect than one with large flower-and-leaf bunches.   A large flower-and-leaf design would fit the chair into a more informal living room, a morning room, or a library.

The matted pattern described, partly because of its closer following of the chair form itself and more conservative movement, would give a considered trimness of quality and be less free and easy.   Plate 84.

PLATE 85.   LARGE LOUNGE CHAIR

The chair of Plate 85, also excellent in design, is a little less dressy than the preceding one.   Even if it were covered with a dressier ma-

PLATE 85.   *A finely proportioned large lounge chair with excellent modeling of the upholstery.*   COURTESY WOOD & HOGAN.

terial, its own lines and proportions would still express ease and comfort in a more informal room. But, like the first chair shown, it is very versatile. It is large, but it makes no awkward or cumbersome movements. The modeling of its arms and its general proportions are excellent, finished design of this type. In weight aspect it will combine easily with early eighteenth century, middle eighteenth century, and even with some of the late eighteenth century furniture, provided that the key of the room is a little heavier.

UPHOLSTERY

The upholstery shown on it fits it admirably in about the lightest expression that could be used satisfactorily. From this light aspect we could go toward somewhat bolder, heavier patterns with larger flower bunches, less open active space, and slower scale of movement.

If the chair were to be used under dressier conditions, linen or chintz—the latter usually not preferable for a chair of these proportions—might be too informal. But the chair would still look its best if given some pattern or a texture effect that was not too strong. A very rough texture would destroy the niceness of the shape, the fine modeling of the arms, for example. A very simple, lustrous texture with inherent formality would be entirely out of keeping. There is no slickness or hardness, no marked firmness in the chair itself; thus these qualities in the covering would scarcely be in complete harmony with the chair's own character. Hence we find ourselves turning toward not too lustrous damasks and the gentler-textured novelties that have a feeling of "finish," that are not too tweedy, in order to get the most effective combination.

One word of caution may not be amiss here. This general type of chair is often covered with a small-figure damask or velvet. Decoratively, these are mistakes. Both give monotonous repetition over the large surfaces as well as the feeling of being small and set, a feeling wholly alien to that of the chair which is definitely large, free, and easy. Often these misused types are employed because someone has a desire to make the chair very dressy. The chair should not have been bought for that purpose. It is essentially a lounge chair belonging to an informal room. The room may be richly furnished with the finest antiques, and yet not be formal, necessarily.

PLATE 86. LAWSON EASY CHAIR

Plate 86 is a fine example of the popular Lawson club chair, well modeled and of excellent proportions. When well done, as is this one, this chair is a useful item in almost any kind of living room. When poorly proportioned with clumsily shaped detail, it is very

PLATE 86. *The familiar Lawson club chair in especially trim proportions, modeling, and finish.* COURTESY FURNITURE SPECIALTIES CO.

awkward. It never is a dressy chair; it never spells elegance. But it is one of the best all-round-use chairs in the field, fitting into many types of settings from heavy to light—when the latter is of the simpler type.

UPHOLSTERY

The material shown on it in the picture is well suited to it. The medium bold flowers held together by the closely matted leaf design give the all-over effect that keeps the simple motion of the chair planes intact. If a more open pattern with open spaces and meandering lines, such as we saw on the preceding chair, had been used, the simple flow of line, the trim plainness of surfaces characteristic of the Lawson would have been broken and the result would have been less pleasing. There is variety, interest, in the covering, but it is held down to the amount of action in the chair itself.

There are some damasks—not too dressy—and some textured materials that would look well on this type of chair. In both, the flatness and simplicity of the chair itself, its planes and lines, dictate the choice. Very large flowing damasks would be misfits. The lines of the chair are not flowing; they are neat and tidy. Very small damask patterns also would be misfits for the most part. They would look smug and tend to be monotonous on the broad plain surfaces. Something of moderate scale and motion would provide the answer and fit the trimness of the chair lines and proportions. Similarly, in the textured effects, something not too slick, yet not so rough as to destroy those trim contour lines, should be selected.

PLATE 87.   TUXEDO TYPE CHAIR

Plate 87 is another much-used chair type of versatile character. When well designed, as it is here, it is a fine chair. When poorly designed without understanding of the interrelation of line and proportion, of shaping of the modeled surfaces, it can be very awkward and clumsy. A fine one, like the model shown, can fit a great variety of conditions. Its definiteness of form gives it a quality of firmness not found in many of the larger lounge chairs. It can be used in range from fairly heavy settings to lighter ones, provided that the latter are not too formal and delicate.

UPHOLSTERY

The chair is not in the elegant and dressy group. It belongs at the top of the second group. Again, it seems wise to mention the fact that all such classifications are very arbitrary. There might be places where this chair would be in the dressy and elegant classification. But on the whole, that is not its native element. It lacks the kind of style that would make it a usual choice for such a room.

For the same reason, highly styled, lustrous damasks are out of place for its upholstery. Yet there are many damasks of less dressy character that would be admirable for it if they were properly selected also for scale and motion. There are some of the small-figured damasks

PLATE 87. *An interesting up-to-date interpretation of the favorite Tuxedo chair in well-fitting contemporary covering.* COURTESY CHARAK FURNITURE CO.

also that would be suitable. They should be neither too small nor too set. Some of the slightly textured materials also could be excellent. These could be slightly lustrous, if that quality were needed for the room, but not smooth and slippery like regular satin. If the chair were to be used under simpler conditions, the texture of the upholstery should express those conditions, too. Care should be taken to make sure that it was thin enough to retain the clean-cut edges and smooth rolls of the chair frame. A thick or a bunchy material would ruin the chair design, making it bungling and clumsy. Sometimes a velvet that was not too soft nor too lustrous might be satisfactory. On the other hand, most cotton velvets are too thick for these shapes and edges, and a velveteen is too thin and flat—too light for the chair aspect. Some of the moderately textured silks might give the desired dressiness better because they would fit the chair shapes better.

PLATE 88.   A BIG EASY CHAIR WITH STYLE

The large lounge chair of Plate 88 differs from the others in that it is large, yet has that intangible quality called style. Like the others

PLATE 88. *A really big chair that has both style and elegance.* COURTESY WOOD & HOGAN.

we have discussed, it is a finished piece of design with carefully modulated curves and shapes that flow together easily without any clumsiness. This is a real achievement in a chair of this size. It can be used in some of the dressier rooms; it also can be used advantageously in the best of the less dressy ones. Of course, circumstances dictate the use of furniture sometimes—at least temporarily—in places where they do not really fit. Skillful decorators, however, can usually succeed in pulling such rooms together and achieve a reasonably good result. The result is always a compromise, and, until one understands and appreciates the fundamental conditions—the basic assets—compromises of this sort are apt to be sadly lacking as far as the best choice of materials is concerned. It is for that reason that stress is being laid on the inherent qualities of these pieces of furniture. Where can they be used normally? The understanding that is needed as the basis for good work even when compromise is the order of the day is contained in the answer to that question.

UPHOLSTERY

The plain material with its slight texture effect with which the chair is covered is excellent. The real interest of the chair design lies largely in the shaping of its surfaces, and the lack of definite pattern allows those surfaces to be seen without interruption. The slight texture gives a bit of vibration that is pleasant without being intrusive. Many of these smoother-textured materials would work in similar fashion.

This statement should not be interpreted as barring pattern. The chair may be in a room where pattern seems necessary. A plain material, even with a strié effect, would allow the chair to make a hole in the room composition because of its very plainness. Probably a texture could be found somewhere that would still be the best solution, something with more vibration, but, if it were not available, a self-colored pattern in damask, not too large, could be used. The buttoning of the back does not lend itself to much pattern, but it by no means precludes the use of a well-chosen figure. A rather small, indefinite repeat, not too small or too trivial for the scale of the chair, would be one good choice under these conditions. All-over effect, with as little disturbance as possible of the movement of the modeled planes of the chair, is the goal for the best results, as far as the chair itself is concerned.

Chintz or, better, linen, could be used but the result would be likely to have much less style.   Other lounge chairs, without this inherent style, would take the informality of the linen better.   If it were used, the all-over effect with rather rounded motion and matted pattern—not open and scrawly—would give the best results.

PLATE 89.   SMALL CLUB CHAIR

A club chair of medium size yet light enough to look well with the light furniture of the late eighteenth century is hard to find.   The

PLATE 89.   *A small club chair of exceptionally neat and trim aspect.*   COURTESY
WOOD & HOGAN.

one shown in Plate 89 is an excellent example. Although so rectangular, its lines give the effect of trimness and ease.

UPHOLSTERY

The simple surfaces allow wide variation in coverings, from damasks with not too flowing patterns to velvets—not too lush—and thence to the linens of lighter aspect and the chintzes.

21

Upholstering Wing Chairs

WING CHAIRS REALLY FORM A SEPARATE GROUP BY THEMSELVES EVEN though they may be considered lounge chairs. Until the advent of the Victorian easy chairs, the wing was the only really comfortable chair that could be said to approximate our present-day lounge chairs. Both the old ones and the present-day versions vary widely in type, and so, too, do the types of materials that can be used successfully on them. Unfortunately, a wing chair is a wing chair to too many people, and the results in terms of upholstery are sometimes startling.

Wing chairs appeared in the latter part of the seventeenth century. On Plate 60 is a fine example of one of these early ones. It is tall and ungainly and is seldom copied nowadays because of the fact that few rooms are decorated today with the heavy furniture of that period. The rich velvet with which it is covered fits its static dignity perfectly.

In all these early wing chairs, the back has an awkward rake, the wings are rather clumsily shaped and are continuous with the arms. Usually there is a heavy whorl or scroll where the arm joins the seat frame. At this period, chairmakers did not understand upholstery and were quite incapable of shaping those forms any better. The awkwardness is not the type of awkwardness that comes from slovenly workmanship but the type that comes from experimenting with new forms and methods before they are mastered.

PLATE 90. EARLY EIGHTEENTH CENTURY WING CHAIR—ENGLISH

Plate 90 shows the type that has been the basis of most of our reproductions of today and was the basic form of the English designers of the eighteenth century. The wings have a little more motion and freedom than was often the case but otherwise the chair is very char-

acteristic. It is easy to see it as a companion of the finest of the Queen
Anne chairs already shown.

PLATE 90. *Wing chair, English—early eighteenth century.* COURTESY MUSEUM OF
FINE ARTS, BOSTON.

UPHOLSTERY

The upholstery shown on it—needlework—is thoroughly characteristic of the period—rich, handsome, and as full and rolling in expression as is the chair form.

PLATE 91.   REPRODUCTION OF EARLY EIGHTEENTH CENTURY WING
CHAIR—ENGLISH

This is a fine example of the wing chair of the same period reproduced from one that is a little less rolling in form than the preceding

PLATE 91.   *Wing chair—a reproduction with the full flavor of the Queen Anne
period.*   COURTESY WOOD & HOGAN.

one and consequently much more usable under present-day conditions.
It has the full flavor of the period. The heavy curves are ample and
easy. We need only place it beside the chair on Plate 54 to see the

Plate 92. Wing Chair of Middle 18th Century 275

similarity in expression of the major lines. The modeling of the upholstery follows closely the historic lines which, as already pointed out, still were awkward due to the fact that the furniture makers were novices, relatively, in the upholstery field. The shaping of the wings continuous with the arms follows the more common type of Queen Anne wing than does the roll in the chair on Plate 90. Yet the arms are not clumsy. The chair is dressy and has much genuine style, a native of Group 1 but usable under many conditions in Group 2 also.

UPHOLSTERY

The upholstery shown on it is perfect in type and scale. However, few people today can afford material of this type, even assuming that it can be found. The present-day alternative probably would be either a handsome damask or a velvet. If the chair were used with Group 2 conditions, these two fabrics could be translated into simpler, less dressy terms—as a less distinguished damask, less lustrous, or possibly a fine wool damask. The chair seems to need pattern to complete it and diplay it to its best advantage. However, if pattern were impracticable in view of the place the chair would occupy in the room composition, some textured material that would not be too bumpy or clumsy to roll over the full curves of arms and wings might be found. It should be smooth enough to allow the planes of the upholstery shapes to flow easily into each other.

Leather could be used but it would not be so attractive as the other textures on those rolling forms. It is better suited to thinner, more-shaped wings and arms. Chintz would be too light in effect as a general rule for a permanent cover, but handblocked linen could provide a good answer if the chair were not to be used in a very formal room. In that event, the pattern should not be open and sprawling to set up opposing motion to the lines of the upholstered surfaces. It would be much more effective if it were in rather close repeat and of rather large-scale pattern to fit the chair scale of movement and sizes of parts.

PLATE 92. WING CHAIR TYPICAL OF MIDDLE EIGHTEENTH CENTURY

Plate 92, a present-day interpretation, is a particularly happy illustration of the modern chair of medium weight based on the old wings of the middle eighteenth century. Comparison of these shapes with those of the three preceding ones shows quickly how far chairmakers had gone in mastering the shaping of surfaces in upholstery.

PLATE 92. *Wing chair in the style of the middle of the eighteenth century.* COURTESY THE PAINE FURNITURE CO., BOSTON.

Many of the forms were much more rounded than this one and had cabriole instead of straight legs, but close observation will show their similarity of expression.

UPHOLSTERY

Upholstering these modified forms of today requires careful thinking. In this case, the leather that has been used could not have been bettered. It is soft enough and thin enough to keep the very nice chair curves and the modeling of both wings and arms. Many other materials could have been used—damask, textured material of medium aspect, not too rough, and handblocked linen.

PLATE 93. *Wing chair in the style of the late eighteenth century. American.* COURTESY THE PAINE FURNITURE CO., BOSTON.

PLATE 93. WING CHAIR LATER IN THE EIGHTEENTH CENTURY

Plate 93 is another present-day interpretation showing the next stage in weight, lighter than the preceding one. It also is a little less finished in line than the preceding one which could be used under dressy conditions if upholstered in something other than leather. It is interesting that these wing chairs actually grew larger during the century—the eighteenth—but, at the same time, grew lighter in aspect. The distance is long from the weight aspect of the first three chairs in this chapter to this one. Another fact should be clearly noted with regard to this chair. It is a very characterful one, thoroughly interesting but not dressy. This difference is seen in the slightly less skillful shaping of the upholstery of the wings and the proportion relationships. It is one of the types from our own American background that looks as though it might be in a setting where there were some pieces of old furniture, although the room as a whole would not be classed as either elegant or formal.

UPHOLSTERY

The upholstery on it, a slightly textured damask, presents just this aspect and suits it perfectly. The chair could have been formalized a little more with a different type of damask pattern and been very nice. It could take either a handblocked linen or a chintz that was not too light. It seems to need pattern to complement the shaping of the back and the wings.

PLATE 94. A VERY TYPICAL MODERN WING CHAIR

The chair of Plate 94 is a little lighter than a typical Middle Georgian one and has the squarish base and flaring arms that prevailed later. The legs are of the early eighteenth century type. The employment of these varied elements is very characteristic of the majority of the wing chairs of today. Few of them are strictly period in type. Few of them are dressy enough for very formal rooms, and few of them have the elegance of the first plates shown in this chapter. They fit our present-day living rooms which for the most part are comfortable and nice if not luxurious. Another respect in which the modern version of the wing chairs differs radically from the old ones is in

Plate 94. A Very Typical Modern Wing Chair 279

having springs in the back. The old chairs were shaped and balanced so that in the best of them one is wholly comfortable. Most of the new ones, however, have the springs in the back. Unfortunately some

PLATE 94. *Wing chair typical in proportion and shape, as of today.* COURTESY FURNITURE SPECIALITIES CO.

of the poorer grades of manufacturers trust too much to the softness given by the springs and too little to the proportions and rakes of the chair as related to the balancing of the human body. Thus many of them are uncomfortable even though soft and springy. It is interesting that the modernists are placing so much emphasis now upon the actual balance in the posture of the body in a chair. In the picture, the flaring wings, separate from the arms, the flat front of the arm supports, and the T cushion all indicate production of today. It is an excellent chair and should be judged with due consideration of the foreshortening of the photograph which makes the back look lower than it really is.

UPHOLSTERY

Although the chair is definitely light as compared with all but the last chair shown, the upholstery shown on it is a little too light for it. The squarish effect of the frame needs a little more support than the rather sparse bunches of flowers give to it. Further, the nice sweep of the wings gets no support from the irregular light flower bunches. A more closely matted pattern, a chintz or a linen, with motion sufficiently subdued so as not to interfere with the motion of the curves of the top and the wings but to remain subordinate to them, would be much better. Many of the not-too-heavily textured materials, too, would be excellent. If the chair were being used in a very nice living room with some fine furniture, it could be covered to advantage possibly with a good damask of medium weight. Leather could be used, as the arms and wings are well modeled so that the leather would shape well over them, but the chair form would not be so well displayed as with a covering that was a little more active, yet not active enough to disturb the motion of the wings and top.

PLATE 95.   TUB CHAIR

Plate 95 is a modern reproduction of the late eighteenth century tub chair which followed the heyday of the wing chair in the middle eighteenth century. In fashionable circles this new style replaced the old tall chair with its flowing lines. The low back with its continuous curve into the small wings is very characteristic of the general change toward lightness that took place at the time. Sometimes the backs of this type of chair were fluted; sometimes the backs were much higher, either fluted or unfluted; but the old rolling wings were outmoded. Plates 96 and 97. All give the impression of lightness. The degree of lightness, elegance, and finish varies greatly according to the skill of the designer and the type of market for which the chair is planned. A manufacturer has to provide designs to fit all kinds of taste, and a great deal of it is very bad. But the designer cannot change that. This chair, Plate 95, is a particularly lovely one of its type. It is nice in proportion, in the consistent, controlled movement of the curves and in the shaping of the arms. It is likewise

PLATE 95. *A fine reproduction of an eighteenth century tub chair of the English type.* COURTESY CHARAK FURNITURE CO.

very comfortable. It also has the virtue of being usable with both the dressy and the moderate groups.

UPHOLSTERY

The motion of the chair is light; the motion of the fabric must follow suit. The unbroken curve cannot have a fabric that tends to stop the eye anywhere except at the terminals.   Thus we find that a small-figured material, a plain material—not too lustrous so that the high lights will break the movement—or a leather of the thinner, finer kind are the best coverings for it.   Others can be used, but the chair is likely to lose some of its pleasing quality.   For example, not-too-pronounced damask patterns of medium scale are by no means impossible.   But the easy, graceful flow of the lines of the chair are likely to be checked to some degree.   Many textured materials, too, are in the same category—usable with caution.

PLATE 96.   BARREL CHAIR, FLUTED

The fluted version of this type of the barrel chair comes in three sizes.   One is about the height of an ordinary wing chair; one is the size of a small pull-up chair; and another is between these two.   The

PLATE 96.   *An excellent model of the late eighteenth century type of fluted barrel chair.*   COURTESY FURNITURE SPECIALTIES CO.

Plate 97. Barrel Chair, Unfluted   *283*

one shown on Plate 96 is the small one.   None of them gives quite the feeling of finish, has quite the style aspect, of the regular tub chair of the period, such as is shown on the last plate.   They belong rather in the Group 2 classification of medium dressy and fit into medium-styled rooms rather than in very elegant and luxurious ones.   In terms of weight aspect, all of them are in the light group.

UPHOLSTERY

The fluting adds to the difficulties of upholstering in terms of selection of materials.   The inward curve still has to be considered. Added to that is the fact that it is split into parts that round out to catch high lights and go back into deep shadow lines.   The latter make vertical ridges, up and down across the curve.   Accentuation of these vertical lines can have the effect of almost breaking the curve of the back.   Thus the best material to use is one that avoids over-accentuation of the vertical and re-emphasizes the roundness of the flutes as they follow the roundness of the curving back.   A plain material usually is excellent.   It may be slightly textured; it should not be too lustrous.   Some damasks the patterns of which are not sharply defined can be used successfully.   There also are some of the small-patterned damasks with closely placed figures, not in sharp contrast to their backgrounds, that are good.   Among the chintzes and linens, the choice lies with those that will give a steadiness of tone.   They will have few sharp contrasts of light and dark or bright and dull with figures of moderate size or less.   Any contrasts that would force the eye to jump from flute to flute would destroy the continuity of line that is an inherent quality of the chair design.   Smoothness of effect, without high luster, which would make sharp vertical ridges of high lights, whether the material were patterned or plain, would be the right answer.

PLATE 97.   BARREL CHAIR, UNFLUTED

The tall unfluted version of the barrel chair has been a prime favorite for some time.   It can be dressed up to suit handsome, rather formal interiors; it can be covered simply and fitted into interiors just short of very simple ones.   It always gives the effect of lightness in terms of weight.

PLATE 97. *An unfluted version of the barrel chair, late eighteenth century type.*
COURTESY CHARAK FURNITURE CO.

UPHOLSTERY

Notwithstanding all their versatility with respect to use, these are difficult chairs to upholster satisfactorily. The sweeping curve running back into the depths of the chair, combined with the height, makes a hard problem. A pattern that is bold enough to be consistent with the scale of the chair back can easily be too strong and too bold for that sweeping movement inward toward the back. The figure may tend to pull the back forward, thus spoiling the outstanding aspect of the curving design. A pattern that successfully keeps the curve intact, on the other hand, may have the fault of looking picayune in relation to the size of the chair. Somewhere between these two obstacles lies the best choice. Usually, it is found in slightly textured materials, not heavy, not rough, but with characterful "tooth," or in small-figured materials that tend toward the indefinite in quality so that they keep the curve of the chair back receding as it really does. Leather, too, sometimes is a good answer, and so also is the closely matted pattern similar to the one shown in the plate. It could be of that scale and motion, generally speaking, in chintz, linen, or even damask.

22

Upholstering Various Types
of Chairs in Use Today

IN THIS CHAPTER, WE SHALL CONSIDER A FEW OF THE MISCELLANEOUS types of chairs that are in common use.

The first of these is the chair developed from the so-called Georgian armchair. During the middle of the eighteenth century, this model was a great favorite and shared honors with the wing chairs in terms of comfort. Chippendale was responsible for many variations of the design, some based on French chairs, some with straight legs, some with cabriole legs, some fairly simple, others very ornate. Some reproductions of the fine ones are always on the market, but most of those seen in ordinary homes are simplifications built in general aspect on the older theme.

It is from this type of chair that the so-called Martha Washington chair developed. Its early form—before the Revolution—followed the English Middle Georgian feeling. It differed radically from the originals in that the back was very much higher. It has been reproduced widely in this country and is familiar to most people. Its later version—late eighteenth century—is of the same shape but lighter and thinner and the front arm supports often follow the Sheraton type, delicately turned.

The more dignified and elegant of the old chairs were covered with silk damask—sometimes with plain cover in matching color on the back. They were also covered with needlework, the patterns being much smaller than those of the early eighteenth century. The American chairs likewise, at their best, were covered with damask. The tall Martha Washington chairs were often covered with smaller-figured damasks, such as the one shown on the American chair on Plate 79. The larger repeat on many of the typical chairs of the sort would have

Plate 98.   A Modern Chair Based on Georgian Design   287

been too big and flowing, calling too much attenion to the bold tall back in proportion to the rest of the chair.

It is easy to see why, in the simpler versions of today, some of the wool, cotton and wool, or cotton tapestries are so commonly used. Some of them work out well; some of them are very bad because too spotty.

PLATE 98.   A MODERN CHAIR BASED ON GEORGIAN ARMCHAIR DESIGN

Plate 98 is a comfortable, good-looking version that has been widely used. Its effect really is a little different from that shown in the picture

PLATE 98.   *A present-day version of the Georgian armchair.*   COURTESY FURNITURE SPECIALTIES CO.

where the back appears lower than it is because of the foreshortening. Both the sturdy base and the ample proportions bespeak their Middle Georgian origin and are moderately heavy. If one places two side chairs, one Chippendale, the other Hepplewhite, beside this one, the likeness to the Chippendale form and expression is apparent immediately.

UPHOLSTERY

This chair could be upholstered in damask, needlework, tapestry or, as shown, brought very much up to date with its delightful not-too-rough textured material. If damask were used, the pattern should be of medium size, avoiding both the small, set, picayune effect and the too large, too-much-motion aspects. Leather also can be an excellent answer in this case. A material that is too plain, other than leather, is unsatisfactory on this chair form in any of its variations. The upholstered portion seems to need the re-emphasis that pattern gives to make the solidity of the back count against the wooden frame and the open spaces. It is easy to have the upholstery so plain that the plain back seems either to stare emptily into space or to be lost in comparison with the framework. Which one of these effects would appear would depend on the color or the texture of the chosen fabric. This statement holds true particularly in the two versions of the Martha Washington type— both the earlier and the later ones.

On the other hand, some of the plain materials may look better on the smaller and much simplified forms under most living conditions of today than the majority of the flowing damask patterns. Smaller patterns occasionally are usable, but great caution should be exercised to avoid a spotty effect, thus attracting too much attention to the chair for the emphasis that it should provide, normally, in the room composition, as well as overdoing the upholstery at the expense of the effect of the chair ensemble. Usually, in these much simplified versions of the Georgian chair that are likely to be smaller and have less action in the frame and in the proportions, as well as being plainer in both line and form than the full-period type, only a little action on seat and back covering is safe. Leather or one of the new slightly textured fabrics often supplies the best answer.

PLATE 99.   A SIMPLIFIED VERSION OF THE GEORGIAN ARMCHAIR

Plate 99 is an unusually well-designed simple version of this type of chair, consistent in both line and proportion. It fits into many rooms

PLATE 99. *A much simpler version of the Georgian armchair, as of today.* COURTESY CHARAK FURNITURE CO.

where the heavier version would be out of place with the rest of the furniture.

UPHOLSTERY

The little figured damask probably looks quite different in reality than in the picture. Here, there are very sharp light and dark contrasts which have a tendency to overemphasize the figures—in themselves well-scaled to the chair. Visualize them in softer aspect, and the effect is quite different.

There are many of these small-scale damasks available which have much satin ground showing; they are excellent on the dressier chairs of this scale. They are better than the small, over-all, closely matted, repeat damask of the older type, as they give the marked spotting that the chair size and shape seem to need.   However, the right one may easily be overlooked in favor of one that is too set, too spotty, that will

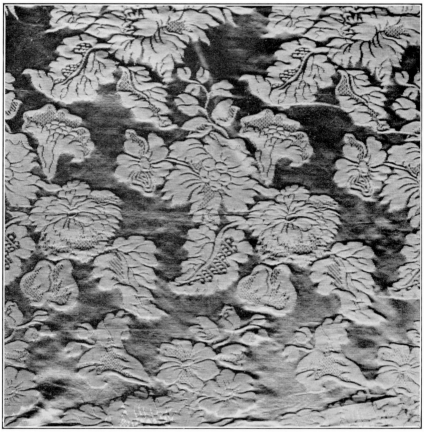

PLATE 100.   *Asymmetrical balance of the early eighteenth century in modern damask.*   COURTESY H. B. LEHMAN-CONNOR CO.

always be a too noticeable element to the detriment both of the chair form as a whole and the part the chair plays or should play in the entire room composition.

Small-figured—not coarse, not rough—tapestries also are usable. Leather is often excellent, although it is apt to look hard on one of these smaller-scale chairs.   A few of the textured materials also are suitable.

Plate 101. A Very Useful Queen Anne Chair   *291*

PLATE 101. A VERY USEFUL QUEEN ANNE CHAIR

The Queen Anne-type chair of Plate 101 is a most useful one, especially where a measure of comfort is desired but the space or the effect in the room composition limits the chair type to something with a relatively straight back. A chair with wood back may be too stiff. On the other hand, a heavy lounge chair may be too ponderous, and a

PLATE 101. *An unusual and very useful Queen Anne-type chair of dignity and character.* COURTESY CHARAK FURNITURE CO.

smaller easy chair too low or too square.   The need for this type of chair occurs often where a comfortable chair is to be placed flat against a wall beside a table.   A much-padded chair, whether large or small,

PLATE 102.   *A small-figured damask with well-covered surface and of easy move-ment.*   COURTESY J. H. THORP & CO.

is too rolling in front of the straight vertical plane of the wall.   But a chair with high vertical back, such as the one shown—with the virtue also of being comfortable—is an admirable answer.   Often, too, a chair is needed that by a table or in a group is high enough to be a connecting link to hold groups on opposite or neighboring walls together. Too low a chair leaves a hole in the space composition. This chair could be an excellent answer—because of its interesting contour; it is not too stiff.

The weight of the chair is somewhere between the full flavor of the Queen Anne and the lighter but still robust Middle Georgian.

UPHOLSTERY

This chair takes well a number of coverings from dressy to medium dressy. Damasks, properly tuned in scale and weight aspect can be used in great variety from luxurious ones to very simple ones in wool, cotton, or the not-dressy silks. Any small-figured pattern should be

PLATE 103. *A simple but fine Directoire chair with striped upholstery that is in perfect accord with it.* COURTESY JACQUES BODART CO.

chosen with careful avoidance of tight, smug, or spotty effects. The lines of the chair are quite daring, very free. Similar freedom of pattern movement held to the right scale can do more for the chair than a very set pattern. There are many moderately textured materials that can be used, especially those that are thin and flexible in their structure. Leather is a possible covering, but it lacks the softness that best fits the gentle shaping of the curves of the chair back.

PLATE 103.   DIRECTOIRE CHAIR

The handsome Directoire chair of Plate 103 can be placed in the finest setting within the range of its lightness.

PLATE 104.   *A large-scale damask of much beauty.*   COURTESY JOFA, INC.

UPHOLSTERY

The stripe shown on this chair is excellent. It complements the chair with its simple flat planes and emphasis on straight lines. It also has the virtue, seldom seen in the much-abused stripes, of staying within the chair frame as a subordinate interest in the whole effect of the chair. One does not see the stripe first and eventually find the chair. The chair itself is the dominating item with the stripe subordinate, thus complementing and completing it.

Other coverings could be successful. Plain satins, satins with a slight texture effect but light in aspect, and very thin fine velvets or thin velveteen, all are usable. Occasionally, a brocade might be found that would be sufficiently simple and flat for the chair design. Some of the small-figured damasks also would be suitable. However, the

PLATE 105. *One of the usable small chairs that changes its aspect with its upholstery and thus fits in many places.* COURTESY FURNITURE SPECIALTIES CO.

smoothness of not-too-lustrous satin with not-overemphatic stripes is one of the best choices.

PLATE 105.   SMALL UPHOLSTERED CHAIR

A small upholstered chair of versatile character, excellent in rooms as widely different as living rooms and bedrooms, is shown in Plate 105. It is light in aspect, but it can be used as accent in many rooms of heavier expression.

UPHOLSTERY

This chair is best covered in medium-type upholstery, small damasks that are not too lustrous and are rather light in weight aspect, some of the textured effects and the light-aspect cotton tapestries when

PLATE 106.   *Another of the very usable small chairs, excellent under widely varied conditions.* COURTESY FURNITURE SPECIALTIES CO.

they are of good design. Many chintzes also and a few linens of the light type would be excellent.

PLATE 106. SMALL UPHOLSTERED CHAIR

Another small upholstered chair of versatile character (Plate 106) is usable under a wide variety of conditions. The trimness and smartness of its shapes lend themselves to somewhat dressier conditions than the preceding one. Like the other, it is light in aspect but can nevertheless be used as accent in many rooms of heavier expression.

UPHOLSTERY

The greater smartness of this chair as compared with the preceding one permits the use, advantageously, of some of the dressier materials, such as velvets, velveteen, possibly silk under some conditions, as well as all those recommended for the other chair.

23

Textured Fabrics
for Modern Furniture

THE MODERN GROUP BRINGS US TO THE CONSIDERATION OF MANY TEXTURED materials and the relatively new problem of adjusting them in roughness and texture-pattern movement to the shapes and sizes of the chair frames. Texture has been considered throughout all the periods but never with the same emphasis that it now receives in the newer expressions of form.

PLATE 107. MEDIUM-SIZED MODERN CHAIR

Upholstery should never outdo the chair frame in attention value. When it does, the effect of the chair as a unit is ruined. Yet we often see a chair on which the upholstery stands out so boldly that for an instant we are scarcely conscious of the chair frame and shape. At the other extreme, there is the chair on which the upholstery is so underdone that it does not hold its own, with consequent overemphasis of the frame. Between the two extremes lies the best answer from the design standpoint—the upholstery that is active enough to keep the chair frame and the planes upon which it lies doing their share of the work without overdoing or underdoing.

The chair on Plate 107 is an excellent example of texture perfectly suited to the chair shape and proportions. The texture stays within the frame; it has a certain amount of ruggedness that echoes the similar quality of the frame; it has enough texture pattern to hold its own yet seems complete within the boundaries of the chair planes. It stops where they stop. It does not call undue attention to itself.

Some modern chairs show no wood frame above the seat or even at the seat level. The upholstered seat and back rest upon the wooden legs with no transitional assistance. It is as though the upholstered section were made separately and dropped down on the leg section.

Plate 107. Medium-Sized Modern Chair   *299*

This entails a difficult problem in terms of upholstery. The material so successful on the chair of Plate 107 would be a sad mistake on this type, because the slightly striped effect in the Plate 107 material would

PLATE 107. *Medium armchair of modern type. Well-considered texture scale and movement in the upholstery for this forthright design.* COURTESY KNOLL ASSOCIATES.

not be quite rugged and sturdy enough to make the upper portion complete in itself. The planes of such a chair, i.e., of the upper part, depend on the upholstery for their final definition. A too suave material would allow the upholstered portion to float off into space. A too strongly textured material or one with too marked patterning would destroy the solidity. Under conditions of this sort, the upholstery should have sufficient ruggedness to make the upper portion an entity resting upon its base. It has to seem complete within itself, stop within its own edges.

PLATE 108.   LOUNGE CHAIR WITH BASKET-WEAVE UPHOLSTERY

The bold planes of the chair seat and back in Plate 108 with the consistent broad flatness of the supports give an interesting effect of balanced weight and force.

PLATE 108. *Lounge chair. A daring design that stresses comfort, due directly to perfect shape and balance.* COURTESY KNOLL ASSOCIATES.

UPHOLSTERY

The bold, flat basket weave is one excellent solution of the upholstery problem. The scale of the squares that form the pattern is perfect for the chair. In the more usual cloth textures, the same bold flatness should be emphasized. For example, the material shown

PLATE 109. *A modeled form instead of the conventional modeled padding establishes the comfort quickly in this chair.* COURTESY KNOLL ASSOCIATES.

on Plate 76*a* would be impossible. It would be too busy and small in feeling in conjunction with the chair frames. The material shown on the chair on Plate 110, on the other hand, would be too flat, characterless with this bold chair design. The texture should be bold but flat.

PLATE 109. LARGE LOUNGE CHAIR

In sharp contrast to the preceding chairs is this new lounge chair shown on Plate 109. Here curve flows into curve without sharp delineation, and the edge itself is curved to contain the larger surfaces. All is smooth, edgeless.

UPHOLSTERY

Again, we have an example of perfectly chosen upholstery. It is a modern texture the small movement and relative softness of which give fitting play to the gently curving planes and allow the material to move easily, inconspicuously, over the edge. Any other material would need the same qualities to be wholly successful.

PLATE 110. MEDIUM LOUNGE CHAIR

Plate 110 is another striking and interesting illustration of the newer type of lounge chair. Close comparison of these shapes with those of the chair on the preceding plate will disclose the marked difference in design expression. The heavy, bulging planes of the back in contrast with the flatter seat give the aspect of strength and mass without excess emphasis. They are positive in shape even though large and rolling—quite unlike the thin planes of the preceding chair.

UPHOLSTERY

If this chair did not have upholstery of very firm texture, those back rolls would lack somewhat in expression of the essential qualities of their shape. Too much softness would tend to make them pudgy because they would feel incompletely finished in shape. This rather hard-textured material firms them, defines them, as they should be defined, to carry out the full effect of the chair design.

Plate 111. Four Modern Fabrics—Striped   *303*

PLATE 110. *Padded lounge chair. The firmly textured material is excellent for the heavy padded, modeled shape.* COURTESY KNOLL ASSOCIATES.

PLATE 111. FOUR MODERN FABRICS—STRIPED

These four textured stripes of Plate 111 illustrate clearly the same story as that told by the textures used on the chairs in the preceding plates. *a* is a fairly bold texture contrast; but, on a large modern easy chair, of the type in common use where the forms are based for

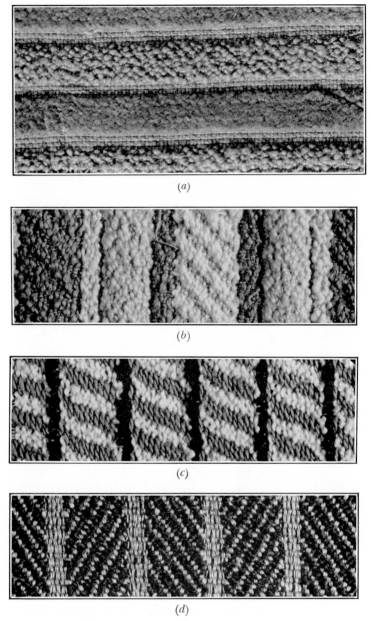

(a)

(b)

(c)

(d)

PLATE 111.   *Four modern texture stripes.*   *a.* COURTESY STROHEIM & ROMANN.
b. COURTESY J. H. THORP & CO.   *c.* COURTESY H. B. LEHMAN-CONNOR CO.   *d.* COUR-
TESY HILDRETH & DUNLOP.

Plate 112.   A Lighter Lounge Chair   305

the most part on the older forms but with sharp simplification and elimination of curves and all complicated modeling of surfaces, it would be excellent.   These bold, simple forms are often based on rectangles that would carry this type of tetxure contrast very well. The self-hued color maintains an all-over solidity suitable for these chairs.   For most of the newer types of chairs based either upon the lighter Swedish modern or developed as a result of daring experiment with new materials and processes, this material would be too solid, too massive.   It would be especially good on some of the larger chairs and sofas of the type cited above.   *b* is a much bolder effect in design than *a,* due in part to the looser, more open texture, to the contrast given by the diagonal movement, and to the clear, direct reinforcement of these texture movements by the color.   It is a handsome stripe that needs vigorous bold form to hold it in place when used as upholstery.   *c* and *d* offer interesting contrast in terms of use.   If we go back to the statements made earlier in this chapter regarding the unity of effect of any chair obtained by proper balance of attention due to the attractions established by frame and upholstery, it is easy to see that *d* is widely usable on many types of modern chairs and sofas—as well as some of the simpler old ones.   It is bold; it is direct; but the alternation of movement through both texture and color is subordinated sufficiently so that the material would not be likely to interfere with the frame.   It would also give an easy run-along-the-surface effect that would follow the upholstery planes and stop where they stopped.   Fabric *c,* on the other hand, is much more marked in its movement.   Its effect is also that of running along the surface, even though it is so sharply accented.   Compared with *b,* it would require a less forceful frame.   Compared with *d,* it would require more marked vigor in the frame to hold it within its proper confines and maintain a balanced chair ensemble.

PLATE 112.   A LIGHTER LOUNGE CHAIR

This lighter modern easy chair of Plate 112 has a trim cleanness of line and proportion that is most satisfying and gives interesting style and character.   It also has a finesse of line and proportion that makes it usable under luxurious conditions as well as simpler ones.

PLATE 112. *The light frame of this chair with its rounded forms demands texture that is not too marked. Designer, Robsjohn Gibbings.* COURTESY WIDDICOMB FURNITURE CO.

UPHOLSTERY

These qualities of finesse of line and proportion dictate in large measure the type of upholstery. The one shown in the picture is perfect. It is somewhat textured, but, like the chair, with finesse that gives exactly the right amount of contrast to the smoothness of the shapes, proportions, and finish of the chair itself.

PLATE 113.   THREE MODERN TEXTURED FABRICS OF PLAID TYPE

The same points that have been emphasized regarding the striped textures of Plate 111 need similar emphasis for these plaids of Plate

Plate 113. Three Modern Textured Fabrics   *307*

113. By now, one should read them easily and place them properly. Of the three, *b* is the one that "runs along easily" and requires the

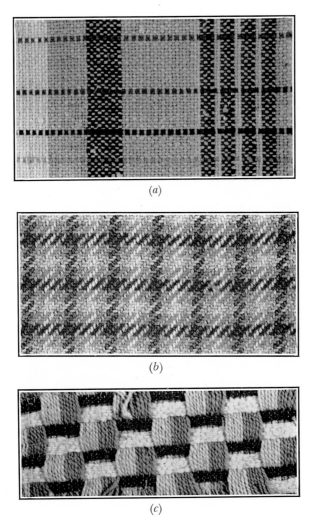

(a)

(b)

(c)

PLATE 113. *Three modern plaids. a.* COURTESY STROHEIM & ROMANN. *b.* COURTESY PETER SCHNEIDER'S SONS. *c.* COURTESY F. SCHUMACHER & CO.

least boldness in the supporting frame—either chair or sofa. Fabric *c* is compact and self-contained but, because of its boldness and color contrast, requires more ruggedness and boldness of the frame than *b*. The big plaid *a* is a type often misused because what the movement established by the scale of its pattern and accentuated by the color does to our attention is underestimated. It needs large plain surfaces and bold form to hold it in proper subjection to the chair and sofa ensemble.

PLATE 72. A HANDSOME MODERN FIGURED PATTERN

Plate 72 is a fine example of contemporary design with bold flatness that is finely characteristic. As curtains, it would be stunning, provided that the furnishings were of equally bold character and as fine. As upholstery, it would be most effective with furniture of distinguished design in the rather luxurious ranges. The furniture should be boldly designed—but suave, not rugged. This material has the virtues of boldness, the directness of Modern, as well as elegance.

24

Reading Present-Day Fabrics
for Their Inherent Expression
and Character

IN THIS CHAPTER WE HAVE THE FINAL TEST OF OUR ABILITY TO READ
fabrics. As we have learned in the foregoing chapters, there are four
major phases to be considered.

1. To recognize the natural, inherent expression or character
   of the fabric and thus place it in its normal category from the
   standpoint of use, not history. Heavy, medium, light, etc.
2. To perceive its range of possibilities so that we shall avoid making either of the following mistakes: (*a*) limiting its use to
   the period when it was produced or from which it was adapted;
   (*b*) stretching it beyond the reasonable bounds of its native
   expression.
3. To know when the fabric can be used under dressy conditions,
   simple conditions, or conditions between these two extremes.
4. To recognize when the movement and the scale of the pattern
   suit the shapes and sizes of the parts of the individual chair
   that is under consideration.

Beyond these factors, of course, lies the whole problem of combining
fabrics that is a part of the study of room composition, with which we
are not concerned in this book.

For our final tests, a number of fabrics, the majority of which are
current market materials, are shown in this chapter. One of them
has been analyzed on the basis of the outline given above. For the
remainder only a few suggestions have been made, in order to allow
for individual problems. The author makes no pretense of being
able to answer Point 2 completely in any analysis. It would be
absurd for any one person to assume the possession of so much ability.

The limits that are suggested are the rather obvious ones that all can see because they are based on the principles already explained. Beyond these, special conditions, special needs, acute sensitiveness, and keen discrimination can carry the user of these materials into additional fields of decoration where they may be used with perfect propriety from the standpoint of design. The uses given are "safety-first" examples.

PLATE 71. A BEAUTIFUL LAMPAS BASED ON MIDDLE EIGHTEENTH
    CENTURY MOTIFS

1. Plate 71 is a handsome design in the middle range of expression, very French in quality. It is beautifully drawn, skillfully balanced—altogether an outstanding example.
2. Although its motifs and detail are unquestionably rococo—Louis XV—in type, there is sufficient range of expression to allow it to be used with both earlier and later styles in combination with other types of furniture if the key expression of the whole room retains this medium-weight quality. In a room with Queen Anne furniture exclusively or its French contemporary, Régence, it would be too light. In a room with only late eighteenth century furniture it would be too active. But in a room keyed between the two with accents perhaps running in either or both directions, it would be all right.
3. It is dressy, elegant, luxurious.
4. The pattern, although large, is so well drawn that it can be used on many types of fine chairs and sofas—large or medium. Although curtains are not our subject at the moment, it seems wise to mention that this material could be used for them in still wider range than upholstery because of the partial obscuring of the scale by the folds of the curtains. The pattern is too large for small chairs. It is best for sofas and large chairs. Care also should be exercised in the placing of the unit on both seat and back.

PLATE 73. HANDBLOCKED LINEN—OLD—OF THE LATE EIGHTEENTH
    CENTURY, A DOCUMENT

The linen of Plate 73 is an old one from the home of Caesar Rodney of Delaware, one of the signers of the Declaration of Inde-

Plate 74. Modern Texture Based on Intaglio Effect   311

pendence. It was produced in Alsace during the latter part of the eighteenth century.

The design is a type that was popular during the early portion of the eighteenth century, but, as sometimes happened both in Europe and in the American Colonies, it was also being used some 60–70 years later, even though the style trend was then in another direction. Comparison of this one with one of the earlier ones (Plate 137) shows immediately a difference in expression character. If the material were being used as curtains, in folds, the difference would be immaterial. But if it were stretched out flat as upholstery, the difference would have to be considered. For example, it is one of the handblocked-linen types that lends itself particularly well to wing chairs on which the long line of the tree trunk and the flower spots have a fair chance for full or nearly full display. If this particular linen or a reproduction of it, handsome and interesting as it is, were placed on a real Queen Anne wing chair, the chances are that it would not feel quite right. It would be a little too light. If it were placed on a reproduction Queen Anne wing chair that lacked some of the full flavor because of less robust proportions, less full curvature, less awkwardness in the detailed shaping of the wings and their modeling, it might fit very well. To view the question the other way around, if placed on a typical light-scale late eighteenth century wing chair with light flaring wings (a wing chair, not a tub chair), rectangular base, and smoothness of both proportion and shapes, it could look quite clumsy, too heavy. But on a fine Colonial wing, original or good reproduction, of the type made in the middle of the century with some degree of heaviness and some slight awkwardness—not too suave—it could be excellent. We find, in comparing the older linen and this one, that the late eighteenth century version of the motifs runs quite a bit lighter with the shapes a little smaller, the curves a little quicker, the movement a little smoother—all accounting for the tendency to lightness as compared with the one of the early part of the century. Its most satisfactory placing as upholstery would require keen perception and sensitiveness.

PLATE 74. MODERN TEXTURE BASED ON INTAGLIO EFFECT

Plate 74 is a fine example of finished thinking in modern texture design; it is the type of thinking that always underlies elegance in expression. It has a wide range of uses. On large or medium-sized surfaces where vibratory aspect without too much definition of shape in the pattern is needed, it is especially valuable.

PLATE 75.   MODERN TEXTURE WITH SLIGHT PATTERN EFFECT

The texture effect of Plate 75 is quite different from the intaglio pattern of the preceding plate. The surface is flatter, the shapes give a more confined effect—smoother and more like the older pattern forms. This material too has a wide range of uses.

PLATE 77.   GEORGIAN DAMASK

The dignified large-scale damask of Plate 77 requires corresponding bold and vigorous chair forms. On some of the heavier, fuller types of the Middle Georgian wing chairs—and sofas—it would be very handsome. The rich roll of the curves and detail is identical in expression with that of the curving forms of wings, arms, and, in the case of the sofas, with the tops of the backs.

It is interesting, too, that this heavy, full pattern can be cut nicely to fit over the cushions and chair backs of some of the dressier present-day easy chairs and looks well on those that are sufficiently formal to harmonize with its richness. On some of the larger, dressier side and armchairs it could also be used.

PLATE 78.   MODERNIZED DAMASK, HIGH-STYLE TYPE

Plate 78 is neither a period damask pattern nor a strictly modern one in the sense of typical modern effects. It shows modern thinking based upon use of an older type of material. It is a very handsome version of this so-called high-style type of design—usable with traditional furniture when the room is keyed to the newer ways of handling color and form, although it still retains fundamentally the integrity of the basic traditional forms.

The bold and direct handling of the flower forms with their many parts against the simplified leaf forms—both in sharp silhouette against the background—give the design theme an expression entirely different from the traditional. However, enough of the older type of size movements and motion in the drawing of both petals and leaves remain to keep the fabric harmonious with period types of

Plate 104. *Large Pattern, 18th Century Damask* 313

form expression—traditional furniture. Thus it is useful for high styling.

It is both elegant and handsome and can be combined easily with the broad, flat-textured surfaces of other fabrics to keep the high-style flavor. It expresses modern directness of thinking in conjunction with older subtleties and nuances.

PLATE 100. EARLY EIGHTEENTH-CENTURY-TYPE DAMASK WITH ASYMMETRICAL PATTERN

The early eighteenth century type of pattern of Plate 100 has been skillfully styled for use today under many conditions. The modernizing shows in the flatness of the figures and their accompanying lightness of scale and openness. There is none of the naturalistic roundness of modeling of the Régence. It is usable on our many interpretations of period items as well as on those of today but not those that are strictly modern. It is moderate in weight, dressy with moderation.

PLATE 102. DAMASK WITH SMALL FIGURES

Several times in this book, reference has been made to small-figured damasks with quiet all-over effect. The one shown in Plate 102 is an excellent example. It is easy to see how well this would fit many of the small pull-up chairs, upholstered, or even those of medium size with the difficult curving backs that demand consistent unobtrusive motion. It is too light in aspect for very large chairs.

PLATE 104. LARGE SYMMETRICAL PATTERN, EIGHTEENTH CENTURY DAMASK

Plate 104 is one of the types of damask patterns so often misused. It is handsome and elegant. On a wing chair of the early eighteenth century the full curves and boldly accented figures could form excellent counterpart and finish. But when people use a damask of this character on chairs as light as those on Plates 92 and 93, the result is rather bad. The curves in the fabric are shaped to suit bold contours. As a seat covering on a Chippendale chair for which it cannot be cut satisfactorily, the result is even worse. Yet this type of mistake is constantly made.

A word may well be said here about the difference between using some of these patterns on chairs as compared with sofas. It is often possible to put a heavier, more expansive pattern on a sofa than on a chair of the same period. "Period" here is used only in order to draw the description to a little sharper focus. The same is true of non-period items. For example, this particular fabric could be used to advantage on innumerable sofas from Queen Anne through Chippendale, early eighteenth century through Middle Georgian. But on the back of a Middle Georgian armchair, even a heavy one of generous scale, it probably would be too broad and heavy, whereas the pattern of Plate 123 could be excellent. Plate 104 pattern is unthinkable also on a late eighteenth century sofa of any kind, whereas the Plate 123 damask could be very lovely. On the other hand, Plate 123 probably would be much too light and active, too quick motioned for most of the early eighteenth century sofas. The rolling curves of Chippendale sofas would make perfect frames for it and, in the field of non-period sofas, it would be at its best on sofas whose frames had a good deal, i.e., a fair measure, of motion. The contrary is true of the damask of Plate 104. The frontispiece shows a late eighteenth century sofa with damask covering perfectly scaled.

The fact that the pattern is repeated along the length of the sofa often makes a great difference as far as usableness of patterns is concerned. On a chair, the damask of Plate 123 would look heavier than when it was repeated over the sofa surface. Hence sufficient motion in the sofa form is needed to frame it and make a proper finish. Repeated over the sofa surface, the damask of Plate 104 would appear flatter, be quieter, than on a chair back, and, up to the point of too sharp contrast of weight aspect—as between sofa form and damask—it could work well on many a sofa, whereas it would be too heavy for a chair of the same general type.

PLATE 114. AN OLD ENGLISH PRINT

Plate 114 is a delightful design in a printed fabric in the lighter expression. Note the very nice balance of parts and the fine drawing —by no means always found in prints of this type. It has inherent style.

Although unquestionably light, as of the late eighteenth century, there is enough feeling of body and mass in the flower groups so that

Plate 115.   Old English Print   *315*

the design could be used easily in rooms with some heavier furniture, provided that the key expression of the rooms retained the medium-light quality.

The pattern is fairly open but is not a sprawling one.   It has enough solidity, compactness, to make it usable on many all-uphol-

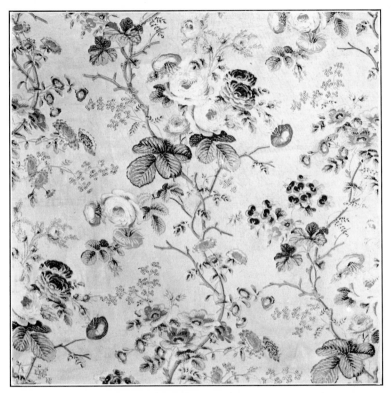

PLATE 114.   *A late eighteenth century print, light and graceful.*   COURTESY THE GREEF CO.

stered chairs.   In detail, these two statements can be translated as follows: (*a*) the material would stay within the frame properly and well on many chairs of ordinary size; (*b*) it is too light for a very big chair but excellent for medium and smaller ones.

PLATE 115.   OLD ENGLISH PRINT

Plate 115 is a handsome print with both dignity and verve.   It is neither very heavy nor very light, although it tends toward the lighter phases rather than the heavier ones. It is finely drawn and designed. Short of the elegance expressed only by much display of silks and velvets, it could hold its own in rooms of definitely fine and dressy

PLATE 115. *A fine print with beautifully drawn detail.* COURTESY THE GREEF CO.

character. With ordinary furniture, not cottage, care should be exercised that it is not so much better in design than the furniture as to make the faults of the furniture conspicuous in contrast. Furniture that could be described as nondescript in design quality would come within this category.

Plate 116. Handblocked Linen   *317*

The design has a stripe, a well-integrated one. Care should be taken to make sure that this vertical motion fits the seat, back, and arms of the chair. Patterns such as this are misused constantly on chairs with much curvature—at complete variance with the verticality of the stripe patterning. The result is most unpleasant. The fabric pattern is warped out of its natural movement and distorted. Furthermore, the chair design is usually lost completely. Comparison of this stripe with the equally interesting and lovely one on Plate 136, in terms of upholstery, gives interesting illustration of how widely two similar patterns can differ in details of their satisfactory use. The one on Plate 117 also has variations and "fill-in" portions in its design which make it much less dominantly vertical in effect.

PLATE 116.   HANDBLOCKED LINEN

This very unusual linen design of Plate 116, so Chinese in feeling, is handsomely drawn and designed and can be used under the finest furnishing conditions. It illustrates very clearly a point that is often misunderstood by novices in the decorating field. A common saying regarding both chintzes and linens limits their use to rooms where only cottons and non-luxurious fabrics are used. The statement is very misleading and quite untrue. Many linens such as this one and the one on Plate 137, for example, because of the fine drawing and design and the quality of the movement in the modeling of the figures almost demand silks and velvets. They go down into rich shadows; they come up through richly modulated lights, giving great variety in their action. Only velvets and silks will echo and act as counterparts to that richness. If only the flatter, less luxurious materials are used, the room is apt to have a sort of dryness of aspect that is far from the inherent expression of the linen. The same fact holds true, usually in lighter vein, in the case of the finely drawn chintzes. Both the chintzes on the preceding plates, as well as those on Plates 117 and 136, for example, would be excellent—probably at their best —with silks such as taffetas and some of the lighter velvets. Careful observation of the very lovely nuances of movement in their patterning tells the story.

The linen of Plate 116 also illustrates admirably the point regarding chairs versus sofas in terms of scale of upholstery pattern. As a covering for a really fine Chippendale sofa, it would be difficult to find anything better. In repetition over the surface it stays flat enough

PLATE 116.   *An unusual and handsome design of great dignity.*   COURTESY J. H.
THORP & CO.

Plate 116.   Handblocked Linen   319

to be a perfect foil for the rounding curves of the back and arms of
the sofa.   Yet the shape, sizes, and motions in the lesser parts of the
pattern give sufficient activity to harmonize exceedingly well with
those rolling curves of the sofa form.   It would be equally fine on
many of our present-day sofas, where the curves are sufficiently full
and even on some of the simpler ones that in their bulk and shape
express the same general weight character.   It is a little more difficult
to use on chairs, but on some of the more generously proportioned
wings, as well as some of the larger easy chairs, it could be very handsome.

PLATE 117.   *A lovely striped floral print.*   COURTESY H. B. LEHMAN-CONNOR CO.

PLATE 117.   STRIPED FLORAL PRINT

Plate 117 is a very lovely pattern of its type with innumerable uses. The adroit manner in which the stripe has been broken to avoid a too strong vertical effect has already been pointed out. It is a beautiful little pattern of the late eighteenth century weight.

PLATE 118.   DOCUMENT PRINT, CHINTZ

Plate 118 is a very small pattern, a six-inch repeat, with very lively and interesting movement. It is of the closely matted type referred

PLATE 118.   *Reproduction of a document print showing marked movement.*
COURTESY THE GREEF CO.

to earlier in the book, but, because of the freedom and vigor of its motion, it has a wide range of usefulness. It is fine in its decorative quality.

Plate 119. A Stately and Formal Lampas 321

PLATE 119. *A handsome lampas used in the Supper Room of the Governor's Palace, Williamsburg, Va.* COURTESY SCALAMANDRÉ MUSEUM OF TEXTILES.

PLATE 119.   A STATELY AND FORMAL LAMPAS

The beautiful large-scale pattern of Plate 119 is the one that is used for curtains in the supper room of the Governor's palace in the Williamsburg Restoration.

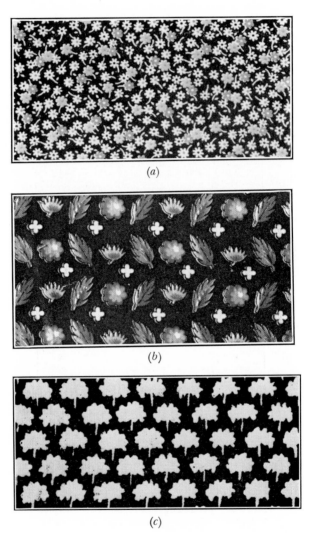

(a)

(b)

(c)

PLATE 120. *Five small prints suitable for widely varying chair types. a.* COURTESY F. SCHUMACHER & CO. *b.* COURTESY F. SCHUMACHER & CO. *c.* COURTESY F. SCHU-MACHER & CO. *d.* COURTESY STROHEIM & ROMANN. *e.* COURTESY F. SCHUMACHER & CO.

Plate 120.   Five Prints of Widely Varying Character   323

PLATE 120.   FIVE PRINTS OF WIDELY VARYING CHARACTER

All the designs of Plate 120 are small.   The little flower spots of
a are not more than an eighth of an inch in diameter.   Those of *b* are
a quarter to a half inch; those of *c* about a half inch.   The repeat of
d is about two and one-half inches, the flower groups themselves being
about an inch in height.   The linen *e* has flowers that are about an
inch and a half in size.

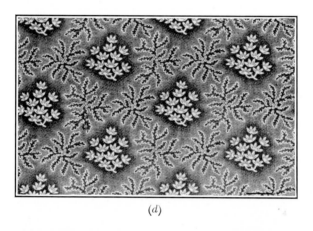

(*d*)

(*e*)

PLATE 120—*continued.*

PLATES 121 AND 122.   TWO BROCADES OF FRENCH TYPE

In Plates 121 and 122 we have two brocades, both of them excellent.   At first glance, they seem quite similar, but a little study of

PLATE 121. *French brocade with slightly heavier movement than the one on the following plate.* COURTESY J. H. THORP & CO.

scale and motion shows quickly that they would be likely to be used under very different conditions.   Both are typically French in expression. Both belong to the general medium weight of the Louis XV period, the Plate 121 pattern being suitable for some of the heavier

PLATE 122. *Brocade with fine late eighteenth century design.* COURTESY J. H. THORP & CO.

chairs of the middle of the reign and the Plate 122 pattern being lighter in aspect and probably better for some of the lighter, smaller chairs of the latter part of the reign. Again, it should be remembered, that these are the very obvious uses that are being cited, and that during the period there was great diversity of expression with less clearly marked intervals than may seem to be suggested by the above statements. But the general statement regarding obvious uses must be made first before we can study exceptions intelligently.

The motion of Plate 121 is free and flowing. The motion of Plate 122 is much more compact, rather self-contained. Plate 121 would be best on a chair that was large enough and definite enough in shape to accept and absorb that flowing motion. Although free, it does not sprawl, leaving large open spaces in the background. The eye travels easily from spot to spot. On some English, as well as French, chairs it would be excellent, chairs that in their own designs have enough feeling of scale, motion, and sufficient shape definition for the pattern to be a fitting complement. For example, on some of the dressier Chippendale-type chairs it would be excellent. The material on Plate 122, on the other hand, could scarcely be used under the same conditions. Lovely as it is, on a Chippendale chair dressy enough to take this type of patterning, it would probably look smug. The swinging lines of those chair frames are too free for the character of this movement. On the broad bold backs of the middle Louis XV chairs with their generous curves, the same would be true. But, within the wooden frames and the smaller, less rambling shapes of the later chairs of the period, it would be a perfect fit. It could be excellent also on some of the chairs of the Louis XVI period if the floral forms of this scale were not too big. A quick glance at the sizes of the subdivisions of the two brocades immediately tells us that the Plate 122 pattern has much of the quickness of motion that was a marked characteristic of that last great period of fabric design in the eighteenth century in France.

PLATE 123. GEORGIAN DAMASK

Plate 123 is a dignified and lovely damask of the Middle Georgian type with flowing pattern and of medium weight. It can be easily used on both wing chairs and good easy chairs as already noted under Plate 104. Care should be taken in placing it to have the leaf group as center of interest rather than the stem group as shown in the cut. As previously noted, too, it is especially good for many sofas.

Plate 124. Brocade, Chinese-Type Pattern 327

PLATE 123. *A fine damask of medium weight, usable under many conditions.*
COURTESY H. B. LEHMAN-CONNOR CO.

PLATE 124. BROCADE, CHINESE-TYPE PATTERN

The interesting brocade of Plate 124 belongs obviously to the middle of the eighteenth century in weight and character. One of the likely uses for it would be, of course, the seat of a Chippendale chair. From Section 2 should have been gleaned the fact that all fabrics suitable in general character for chairs of a given period are not necessarily suitable for specific chairs of that period. There was great diversity of expression in the fabric designs as well as in the chair designs.   To fit fabric to chair—of specific character—is not always easy.   Analysis, from the standpoint of the design of the fabric, may not

PLATE 124.   *Brocade of Middle Georgian character.*   COURTESY J. H. THORP & CO.

be amiss in this case.   For example, the pattern is not large, but it is very active.   There are quite marked open spaces in the background due to the shapes in the patterning and to light and dark color contrasts rather than to size.   The silhouettes of the figures are thrown into sharp relief.   The brocade has a nice scale of motion from the

Plate 125. Empire Brocade   329

groups of the larger masses through the intermediate details to the smallest parts. All these items help to explain the activity of the pattern. For example, the rather static quality usually prevalent in one of the so-called Gothic-type Chippendale chairs would not accept the freer motion of this fabric. The quiet motion of the typical ladder-back chair with its long sweep would never look right with this material below it on the seat. Some of the interlaced splats run toward solidity and quietness; others are quite active. On one of the more active ones, this might be usable. On the other hand, a typical ribbon-back Chippendale chair back is full of quick changes of direction that make motion, and this pattern could be too slow, too open for them. In comparison with these quick changes, it would almost sprawl, even though it is far from being a sprawling pattern. It would complement some of the chairs of the Chinese lattice type perfectly; for others it could be too quick, or too slow, in movement. The space divisions of these Chinese lattice-type chairs vary widely in their expression of motion. Those with the sparser openings would find this fabric too fast and active. Those with the finer divisions would be likely to be good choices if they were not too compact and close so that the contrast between seating material and back of the chair would be too great.

The fact that both the chair and the fabric are Chinese-type design is insufficient alone as basis for satisfactory selection.

PLATE 125. EMPIRE BROCADE

The brocade of Plate 125 has been included because it is a good example of the static Empire type and illustrates clearly the points previously made about the fitness of shapes in the fabrics for the shapes of the chair form. Entirely aside from its period aspects, one glance at this patterning tells us that it must go on a chair or a sofa which stresses the rectangular in its character and that has clean-cut style. Any curves that vary from the obvious and geometric ones would cause the pattern to stand out in resistance. It is symmetrical, geometric, obvious in its method of repetition over the surface, thoroughly of the period. On either the rectangular padded chair backs and seats of the period or the curving forms that seem like rectangles bent into that form, it fits.

The fabrics shown on the following pages should be studied in detail for their characteristics—in the manner already indicated.   From

PLATE 125.   *A clear example of the static quality of Empire design in traditional period pattern.*   COURTESY J. H. THORP & CO.

Plates 126 to 135 only brief comments are made in most cases; these may serve either as general guides or as indicating new points that need consideration.

PLATE 126*a, b, c*

Plate 126*a, b, c* shows three easily used, interesting materials.

Plate 126 331

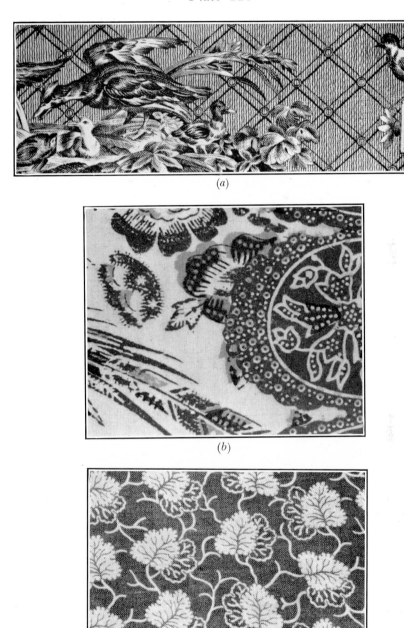

(a)

(b)

(c)

PLATE 126. *Three prints of widely diverse character. a is a small Toile. Both a and b are unglazed. c is glazed.* a. COURTESY JOFA, INC. b. COURTESY F. SCHU-MACHER & CO. c. COURTESY BAILEY & GRIFFIN.

PLATE 127*a, b, c, d*.   THREE DAMASKS AND A BROCATELLE

Fabric *a* is a damask, excellent for light-weight furniture where some vibratory effect is needed but without distinctly marked pattern. Fabric *b* is a brocatelle, a heavy, small pattern which because of its quite marked pattern and feeling of force is best on small surfaces. Fabric *c* is a small, heavy damask, usable like *b* on small surfaces. Fabric *d* is a light, small pattern, excellent where some motion is needed but the fabric cannot afford to call any attention to itself.

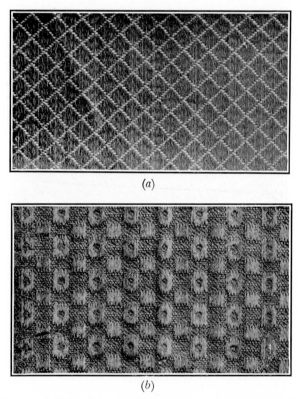

(*a*)

(*b*)

PLATE 127.   *Four materials giving marked contrasts from use standpoint.*   COURTESY J. H. THORP & CO., CHENEY BROS., and F. SCHUMACHER & CO.

Plate 127　　　　　　　　*333*

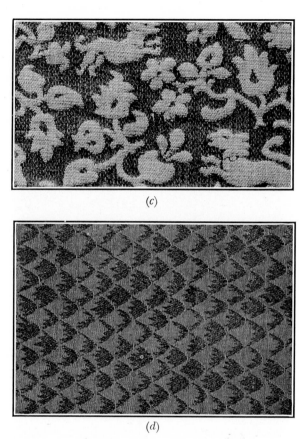

(c)

(d)

PLATE 127—*continued.*

PLATE 128*a, b*.   TWO SMALL VELVETS

Plate 128 is two small cut velvets, late eighteenth century, French, with widely varying possibilities in terms of shapes of pieces of furniture and amount of area over which they could be seen advantageously.

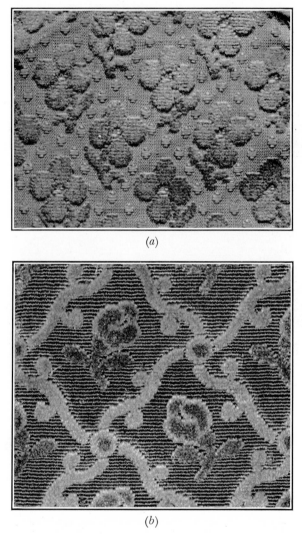

(*a*)

(*b*)

PLATE 128.   *Two small-figured cut velvets.*   COURTESY F. SCHUMACHER & CO.

Plate 130.   Antique Satins   335

PLATE 129.   A SILK REPP SHOWING PATTERN VARIATION

Plate 129 is a finely styled material for surfaces where flatness is essential but some slight motion can give interesting variation.

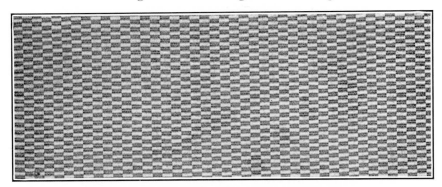

PLATE 129.   *A small-textured repp of silk.*   COURTESY F. SCHUMACHER & CO.

PLATE 130.   ANTIQUE SATINS

The two antique satins of Plate 130 show wide range of texture expression.   Between these are many intermediate degrees of roughness-smoothness.

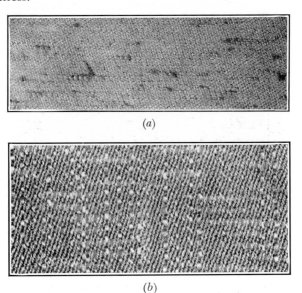

(a)

(b)

PLATE 130.   *Two antique satins showing wide diversity of texture.*   a. COURTESY F. SCHUMACHER & CO.   b. COURTESY JOFA, INC.

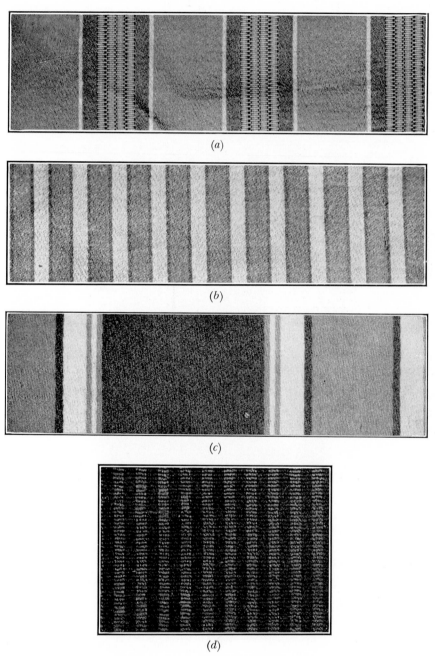

(a)

(b)

(c)

(d)

PLATE 131.   *Four stripes.   a, b, and c are satin stripes.   d is an uncut silk velvet.*
a. COURTESY SCALAMANDRÉ SILKS.   *b.* COURTESY STROHEIM & ROMANN.   *c.* COURTESY
STROHEIM & ROMANN.   *d.* COURTESY former PROCTOR CO.

Plate 132.   Cotton Tapestry   *337*

PLATE 131*a, b, c, d*.   FOUR STRIPES

The four stripes of Plate 131 are suitable for different types of chairs.   Stripe *d* is an uncut velvet with low pile, thin and fine.   The remainder are satin stripes of varying expression.

PLATE 132.   COTTON TAPESTRY

A well-designed small-scale cotton tapestry shown in Plate 132 is for small upholstered chairs.   It is useful on a great variety of shapes. It is small in scale and light in expression—an excellent material.

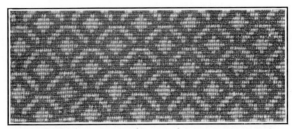

PLATE 132.   *One of the excellent designs in cotton tapestry.*   COURTESY JOFA, INC.

PLATE 133*a, b, c*.   THREE TEXTURED MATERIALS

The three moderately textured materials of Plate 133 show sharp differences in movement patterning.

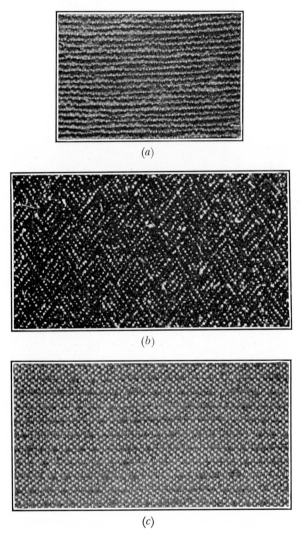

(a)

(b)

(c)

PLATE 133. *Three textured fabrics moderate in movement. a.* COURTESY HILDRETH & DUNLOP. *b.* COURTESY J. H. THORP & CO. *c.* COURTESY HILDRETH & DUNLOP.

Plate 134 339

PLATE 134*a, b, c, d.* FOUR TEXTURED MATERIALS SHOWING SHARP DIFFERENCES IN TEXTURE PATTERNING

Material *a* gives a moderately squared-off effect. Material *b* is much bolder in the same square effect. Material *c* is still heavier and bolder. Material *d* is very vigorous and bold.

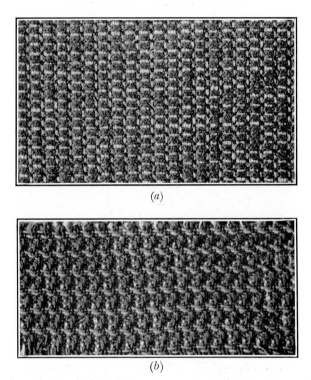

(*a*)

(*b*)

PLATE 134. *Four textured fabrics showing marked variations in scale and movement.* a. COURTESY HILDRETH & DUNLOP. b. COURTESY JOFA, INC. c. COURTESY JOFA, INC. d. COURTESY H. B. LEHMAN-CONNOR CO.

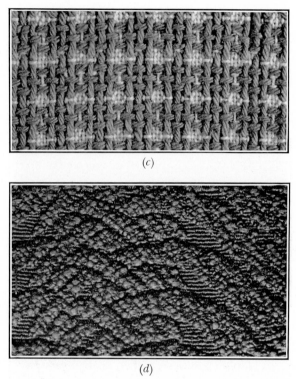

(c)

(d)

PLATE 134—*continued.*

PLATE 135.   LINEN IN FLAT-STYLED PATTERN, MODERN

The very adaptable pattern of Plate 135 is modern in one of its quieter aspects. Because of its flatness and relatively quiet motion over the surface—corresponding roughly to the matted, all-over effects that have been emphasized in the traditional—it can be used under a great variety of conditions. It will slip into the composition scheme more easily than many of the more sharply accented, more open ones. Attention is carried smoothly over the whole surface by the pattern; thus the enclosing form of the chair would not have to be markedly bold to contain the pattern of the upholstery. It is moderate in weight and scale—two additional assets from the standpoint of easy use.

Plate 135. Linen in Flat-Styled Pattern, Modern   *341*

PLATE 135. *A modern design of the quieter type.* COURTESY H. B. LEHMAN-
CONNOR CO.

PLATE 136.   LATE EIGHTEENTH CENTURY CHINTZ

The fabric of Plate 136 and that of Plate 137 give the limits of the whole gamut of weight and motion from the early eighteenth century to its end, before the advent of the mannerisms of the Directoire.   Many a light, delicate, beautifully designed wing chair of the late eighteenth century would look well in this thoroughly characteristic period material (Plate 136), as would also many of the lighter easy chairs that could be used with this type of furniture.   It has the full flavor of the delicate refinement of the period.

PLATE 136.   *A fine late eighteenth century print.*   COURTESY H. B. LEHMAN-CONNOR CO.

Plate 137. Early Eighteenth Century Linen 343

PLATE 137. EARLY EIGHTEENTH CENTURY LINEN

The vigorous early eighteenth century linen of Plate 137 with characteristic interpretation of the Tree of Life idea of an earlier period is a handsomely drawn and designed fabric that belongs with the heavier aspects of early eighteenth century furniture. Its fullness and robust strength are wholly characteristic of the period, and it can be used with the finest furniture of appropriate weight.

Comparison of this pattern with that of the similar type of design of Plate 73, the Caesar Rodney curtain material, gives illuminating illustration of how deep seated were the changes in weight aspect over periods of time, even when the same or similar motifs were used.

The next nine plates are modern, showing in the newer idioms the range of expression that, roughly, approximates the similar range from heavy to light, forceful to mild, large to small, that we have seen in the traditional field. Their uses are as diverse and individual as were those of the traditional, and we should be careful not to make broad generalizations without considering the possibilities of particular circumstances and conditions.

PLATE 137.   *A handsome early eighteenth century handblocked linen.*   COURTESY JOFA, INC.

PLATES 138, 139, 140, AND 141. SMALL MODERN PATTERNS

Plate 138 is a very skillful design that displays ease within the limits of a small set design—a technical achievement of note. It probably would be at its best on small, not very heavy surfaces. Notwith-

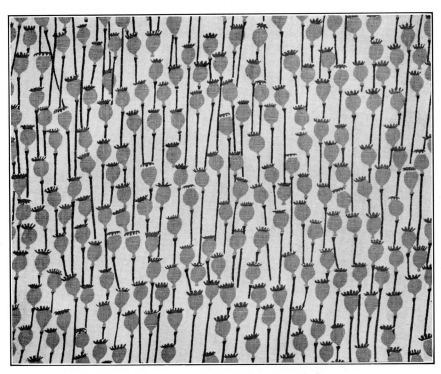

PLATE 138. *A modern linen. Skillfully handled movement in piquant effect.* COURTESY HAMBRO HOUSE OF DESIGN.

standing its fascinating pertness and piquancy, it could be monotonous over a very large surface because of its definiteness.

Plate 139 is likewise a small pattern in which, although all the forms are in the new flat mode, totally devoid of modeling, the movement is easy and flowing. It is light in feeling and because of the easy meandering motion could be used over fairly large surfaces, if they were not too heavy in effect.

Plate 140 is small and compact. It is as forceful and vigorous as the sturdy strong designs of the small velvets of the Renaissance

ever were. It is a characterful little pattern, and it calls for corresponding strength in the chair or sofa form that it covers.   The movement

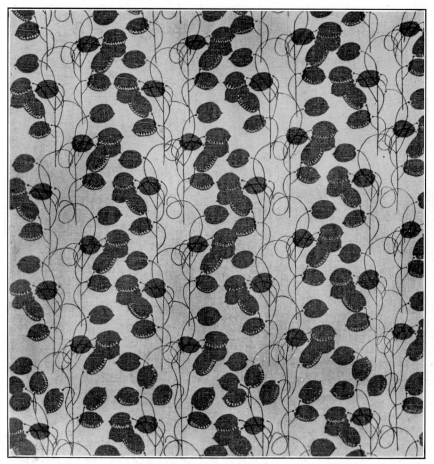

PLATE 139.   *A modern linen in all-over effect, graceful and easy.*   COURTESY
HAMBRO HOUSE OF DESIGN.

is self-contained, and so it can be used over either large or small
forms. The patterning is handled so skillfully in conjunction with
the texture that there would be no question of monotony. The fabric
has vibration and continuous movement even though the units are
small and blocky.

Plate 141 expresses a totally different idea, light and easy because of its skillfully handled spacing and spotting, in perfect and delight-

PLATE 140. *The amusing name of this characterful and vigorous modern texture effect is "10,000 B.C."* COURTESY ARUNDELL CLARKE.

ful balance. The placing of the dots with the oblongs and the carefully modulated irregularities of the oblongs avoid all stiffness. The pattern would "run along" easily over a surface and would stop with equal ease within the given frame spaces of small chairs. The texture shown is for curtains only, as it is very thin.

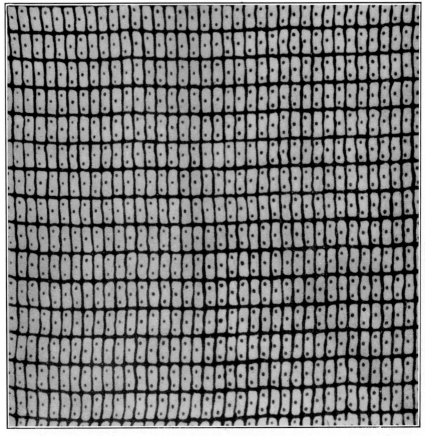

PLATE 141. *Pure design. Modern. Curtain material only as shown here.* COURTESY ARUNDELL CLARKE.

PLATES 142 AND 143. TWO MODERN PATTERNS OF MEDIUM SCALE

Plates 142 and 143 show two very characteristic patterns of fine type in moderate scale in the modern idiom. Both are all-over effects that, in the traditional field, would be matted patterns. The figures are close, thus making a fairly solid all-over movement. Both are very usable and keenly interesting.

Plate 142 is the simpler of the two, also the heavier and, because of the shapes of the forms against the background, would require more strength in the chair form to frame it adequately. The attention slips easily from part to part, and the curves are so fluid that it would be very easy to use.

Plate 143, on the other hand, with greater diversity of form adroitly combined, exquisitely balanced, gives a much lighter effect. The balances, to the last small details, are handled in masterly fashion. The whole fabric gives such compact easy movement that it would fit chairs of any of the moderate weights, even some of the lighter ones.

PLATE 142. *Modern with a primitive flavor.* COURTESY ARUNDELL CLARKE.

PLATE 143. *Masterly handling of very varied, massed forms. Appropriately named,* "My Garden." COURTESY HAMBRO HOUSE OF DESIGN.

Plate 144.   A Bold Modern Design   351

PLATE 144.   A BOLD MODERN DESIGN

Plate 144 is a bolder, heavier effect than the last two, splendid where flatness of large surfaces needs to be maintained. Its quality would be lost in a measure on small surfaces. It is a fine example of modern skill in one of its simple phases; if it had not been done with great care in the handling of the variations of shape that lead to its smooth all-over movement, it could have been very uncomfortable. As it is, the effect is a handsome one and the material has much dignity.

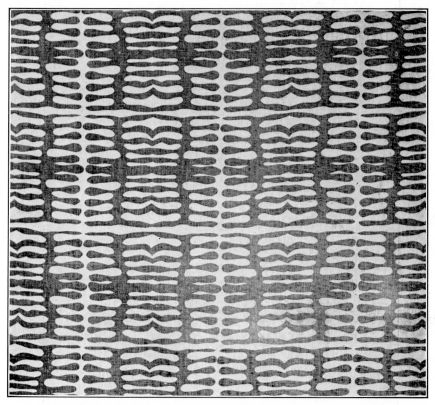

PLATE 144. *Dignity achieved through great sensitiveness in the handling of these shapes.* COURTESY ARUNDELL CLARKE.

PLATE 145.   A BOLD MODERN DESIGN

Whatever these spots represent, they form a stunning design whose directions, sizes, and shapes could not be moved an iota without destroy-

PLATE 145.   *A stunning example of bold modern thinking in terms of forms and balances.*   COURTESY ARUNDELL CLARKE.

Plate 146   *353*

ing the fine challenging sweep and balance of its parts. Their boldness calls for clean-cut definition of form in the furniture on which
the material is placed. It is of vital importance that the unit of this
pattern, as in the case of many traditional damask patterns, be set in
proper position on chair or sofa forms.

PLATE 146. A MODERN INTERPRETATION OF AN OLDER TYPE OF
       PATTERN

The simplification of form in the material of Plate 146 gives very
different effect than the one set by the forms in the material of Plate

PLATE 146. *Modern with an Oriental flavor.* COURTESY HAMBRO HOUSE OF DESIGN.

142.   Whereas those of Plate 142 gave the flavor of primitive drawing, these give the flavor of Oriental drawing and spacing as adapted
by modern thinking and the flat mode of modern design.   The design
has easy movement, is of medium weight aspect, and is easy to use.

Index

Fabrics, Régence, relation to Louis XV
types, 158–160, 163
summary of expression character, 163
Fabrics, Spanish, color types, 150, 187, 188
development of designs: early, 145–147;
height and decline, 148–150
fabric types: Cordovan, 105; under
Christian rule, 147; under Moslem
rule, 145, 146
influences: Italy, 144–147, 150; Egypt,
146; Asia Minor, 146; Persia, 146, 147;
China, 147; pure Islamic, 147
Faille, definition, 46
for bedspreads, 47
for curtains, overdraperies, 47
for dressing tables, 47
for upholstery, 47
hanging modes, 48
types, 46, 47
Fasces in design, 186
Ferdinand and Isabella, 148, 149
Feudal subjects in design, 104, 113, 147
Fiberglas fabrics, 94–96
Filet, color, 26
effect with overdraperies, 26
for curtains, glass, 26, 27
types, 26, 27
Fireside chairs, 260–263
Fleury, Cardinal, Regent, 158, 159, 164
Floral forms in design, 59, 62, 82, 91, 92,
104, 105, 118, 124, 131, 133, 146, 154,
160, 161, 165–167, 169, 170, 172, 174,
210, 211, 214, 215, 222, 225, 230, 236,
239, 240, 263, 280, 312
Florence, benevolent tyrants of, 15th century, 107
decadent rules after Lorenzo, 125
decline after Lorenzo, 123, 124
design types, 114
great men working, 126
growth of arts in 15th century, 108
Medici, main branch, 108
prosperity under Cosimo I, lesser branch,
125
silk weaving begun, 107
Fluting, ornament, 195
Francis I, France, real beginning of weaving, 140
French doors, materials for, 25, 26
French Revolution, 176, 182, 183

Frieze, 76
Fringe, 210, 231, 262
Frisé, 75, 76, 78
Fundamental weaves: plain, 7, 8; satin,
31; twill, 49, 50
Furniture, decorative expression of; classification of relative weight aspects, 192–
207; heavy, 192–198, 210, 212; medium, 198–201; lighter medium, 201–
203; light and delicate, 203–205;
clumsy heaviness, 205; medium heavy
Victorian, 206; Modern, heavy to
light, 206, 207
Furniture, decorative expression of, dressy
to simple, 252–254
Furniture, period types, decorative expression of: Adam, 203; Carolean, 196;
Charles II, 196; Chippendale, 201–
203, 206; Cromwellian, 196; Directoire, 205; Empire, 205, 206; Georgian,
Late 18th century, 203; Georgian,
Middle 18th century, *see* Chippendale; Hepplewhite, 195, 203; Jacobean, 196; James II, 196; Louis XIV,
201; Louis XV, 203, 204, 206; Louis
XVI, 203–205; Modern, 206, 207;
Queen Anne, 198, 200–202; Régence,
201, 202; Regency, 205, 206, 230; Renaissance—Dutch, English, French, Italian, Spanish, 192–196; Sheraton, 204,
205; Tudor, 196; Victorian, 206; William and Mary, 196
Furniture, period upholstery for: Adam,
221–225; Charles II, 210–212; Chippendale, 215–219, 222; Cromwellian,
210; Directoire, 230, 294; Empire, 225,
228, 230; Georgian, Middle, 218, 219,
224, 227; Hepplewhite, 221, 223–225;
Louis XIV, 209, 210, 215; Louis XV,
210, 219–222, 224, 231; Louis XVI,
221, 222, 226–230; Modern, 192, 231;
Queen Anne, 213–215, 222, 291–293;
Régence, 219; Regency, 230; Renaissance, Italian, 208, 209, 219; Sheraton, 221, 222, 225–228, 230, 244–246;
Victorian, 231; William and Mary,
212–214, 222
Furniture trims, period: buttons, 231; cord,
208, 210; fringe, 210, 231, 262; galloon, 208, 210; gimp, 210, 223; nail-